Bulbs for Garden Habitats

Bulbs for Garden Habitats

by Judy Glattstein

Timber Press
Portland • Cambridge

Frontispiece: *Tulipa aucherina*. Photo by author.

Mention of trademark, proprietary product, or vendor does not constitute
a guarantee or warranty of the product by the publisher or author and does not
imply its approval to the exclusion of other products or vendors.

Published in 2005 by
Timber Press, Inc.
The Haseltine Building
133 S.W. Second Avenue, Suite 450
Portland, Oregon 97204-3527, U.S.A.

Timber Press
2 Station Road
Swavesey
Cambridge CB4 5QJ, U.K.

www.timberpress.com

Printed through Colorcraft Ltd., Hong Kong

Library of Congress Cataloging-in-Publication Data

Glattstein, Judy, 1942–
    Bulbs for garden habitats / by Judy Glattstein.
       p. cm.
    Includes index.
    ISBN 0-88192-693-0 (hardcover)
  1. Bulbs—United States. 2. Bulbs—Habitat—United States. I. Title.
    SB425.34.U6G59 2004
    635.9'4—dc22

2004012746

A catalog record for this book is also available from the British Library.

Contents

Acknowledgments

Gardening is a never-ending story, with another page to turn and endlessly more to read and learn. Many gardening books have been written, and I am grateful for those who authored other printed texts. However, I am especially appreciative and indebted to those who wrote in their gardens the text left by trowel and spade and the gardener's footsteps, embellished with the illustrations of leaf and branch, flower and seed.

My own garden continues to instruct me. I also learned from the gardeners you'll meet in these pages, and special thanks go to them. Several nursery proprietors (distinct from garden center operators, who merely buy in and sell out) discussed their experiences in growing and propagating bulbs for commercial purposes.

Three other individuals were instrumental in making this book what it is. Lew Tucci of Kew Professional Photo Labs in Norwalk, Connecticut, once again used his expertise, this time to see that the beauty of bulbs add their color to the printed page. Neal Maillet at Timber Press was a keystone in my efforts, coaxing, cajoling, and patiently urging me along the way so that the end result of my efforts was the book we both envisioned at the start. The bedrock and foundation of support comes, as always, from my husband, Paul, not a gardener but ever ready to see me grow and flower.

To everyone—those back through the centuries who were the first to grow some new introduction and share the information, to today's gardeners, who experience the pleasures of cultivating a garden—I dedicate this book.

CHAPTER 1

An Introduction to Geophytes: Observations and Definitions

I like all kinds of plants, from conifers and deciduous trees to shrubs and vines, annuals, and perennials. But something about *geophytes* (a catchall term for bulbous, cormous, tuberous, and rhizomatous plants) is especially appealing to me. Their often lumpy brown packaging holds a rainbow's worth of flowers. Like good houseguests, the spring-flowering sorts appear, bloom, and depart in a timely manner. Every fall, nurseries, garden centers, and even home-improvement stores sport bright banners announcing "Holland bulbs are here!" And in one of the immutable autumn rituals, gardeners and yarderners alike stuff geophytes in the ground. Tulips get lined up in soldierly rows along the front walk, while daffodils resemble a line of lollipops stuck in front of a fence. But there should be a caveat, a warning, that not every bulb grows satisfactorily from east to west and north to south. Unlike the homogenous uniformity of American malls, plants still insist on growing where conditions suit them. Most anywhere (except perhaps Colorado and regions with similar climatic conditions), flamboyant hybrid tulips are a one-shot, maybe two-time deal. Worse, gardeners in southern California pay extra for precooled tulip and daffodil bulbs that have been deceived into thinking they've experienced winter. That works only the first time around, however: the first spring after planting. By their second spring, such bulbs, no longer deceived by a refrigerated stay, are unable to form embryo flowers and are thus incapable of a flowering display.

But why pretend to live in New England? Gardeners in southern California can grow geophytes. They should consider those wonderful bulbs, corms, rhizomes, and tubers naturally adapted to the local growing conditions, Mediterranean in its weather pattern with dry summers and winter rains, where winter is the growing season and summer is a time of rest. Although it doesn't freeze during the coldest portion of their mild, moist winters, temperatures will drop to the 40° to 45°F (4° to 7°C) range. Compare this with Florida, where the frost-free Zone 11 locations might drop down into the 50°F (10°C) range at night and rain arrives year-round. Gardeners should learn to choose geophytes appropriate for their regions, and the gardens that they make will be more successful.

Gardeners can learn about plants in three ways. The first and perhaps best way is to learn from the plants themselves, studying how they grow in the garden. Of course, that leads to a certain amount of dismay and disappointment as plants fail to thrive despite our best efforts. Next is to go garden hopping, visiting other gardens, both public and private, to see how plants grow there. Perhaps a conversation with the gardener in charge will provide more information, conceivably leading to a friendship and further discussions. And then there are always books. In this one, all about choosing and using bulbs to enhance your garden, I've tried to share what I know from personal experience. When discussing regions outside my own, we'll take a garden tour to discover what can be learned from other skillful gardeners. And then, since we are just the current link in the chain of discovery about plants and gardens, we'll get information from those who have wandered down the garden path in bygone days.

Most novice gardeners are convinced that when autumn arrives it means that, along with raking leaves, it is time to plant bulbs, and bulb planting means daffodils and tulips. That's true, but it can be so much more. A huge diversity of bulbs, corms, tubers, and rhizomes exists. Everything does not grow everywhere. Different geophytes are appropriate for different regions. Some geophytes perform in seasons other than spring.

Hyacinth bulbs with their reddish purple tunics, chestnut-brown tulip bulbs, and onionlike daffodil bulbs, together with small, tan-skinned crocus corms, offer little hint of the variety of colorful flowers they'll offer in the spring—if they're planted in autumn. Photo courtesy of the Netherlands Flower Bulb Information Center.

I must confess that originally this book was going to focus on naturalistic design—the informal use of native and exotic plants in a casual, plant-community–based design. However, my books seem to have the habit of grabbing the topic in their teeth and running off with it; so it is with this one. Part way into the process it told me that it wanted to be more than what I first envisioned, with information on different regions, their climates, and the geophytes that grow there, as well as various garden habitats, such as a rock gardens and sites with damp to wet soil. So I found myself expanding, opening up, and discussing the diversity of geophytes that are out there for curious gardeners to explore. Welcome, and I hope that as well as new plants to pique your curiosity and add to that wish list every gardener maintains, you'll find some old favorites, perhaps presented in a new light.

Mad About Bulbs

Bulbs are good-natured. Hold them for a week, a month, or even longer after purchase, and most often they won't mind. Plant them upside down and they'll still manage to send roots down and flowers up into the light of day. When you consider what you get for what you pay, bulbs offer more bang for your buck. Bulbs are available for every season: some flower before winter has released its grip on the landscape, some bloom in autumn when the landscape falls to rest, and others wait for spring and summer. The most familiar—daffodils, tulips, and hyacinths—need a garden with at least moderately cold winters and middle-of-the-road summers; if that is not available, the gardener either provides shenanigans to fool Mother Nature or, more wisely, chooses to grow bulbs appropriate to the climate.

The seasons will dictate what grows where. The first few days are enjoyable, when winter comes and dumps its load of snow as temperatures fall. When week follows week and I have not seen the ground in all that time, I think how nice it must be to live where winter is a minor rather than a major change of seasons. Then summer comes with its heat and humidity, and I realize it is not the intensity of either season, but the duration. Spring and autumn pass immoderately quickly, while the dog days of summer and winter's icy grip seem excessively long. All too often, though, nostalgia takes hold and snowbird gardeners in Florida pine for the daffodils of New England, where each fall gardeners must dig and store their cannas (and dahlias, gladiolus, and other tender geophytes) if they are to avoid freezing to death. Ignore attempts to homogenize the country. Celebrate regional differences: major differences as you travel north to south, east to west, from sea level up the mountain, and local variations where the sunny side of the street (or even your house) offers a different microclimate than the shady one.

The bulbs I've grown in the three gardens we have owned, all on the East Coast of the United States, have created enduring memories. Currently I garden on almost nine acres of sloping, wooded ground in western New Jersey, not far from the Delaware River. Plants that I grow must be able to care for themselves. The soil is heavy clay laced with rocks. We're on a well, and hoses can stretch only so far. Bambi and his relatives come to dine, and woodchucks (groundhogs) and rabbits, voles, and mice are also considerations. Knowing that I must do something if there would be flowers to welcome my first spring in the Garden State, I planted 8000 bulbs the same fall that we moved. In the next five years I planted over 30,000 more. They have consistently been a joy and a pleasure.

Each of our gardens has taught me more about plants and gardening. We first had a small house on an eighth of an acre in Norwalk, Connecticut. A sheltered nook next to the foundation provided an ideal site for winter-flowering crocus such as *Crocus laevigatus* 'Fontenayi', with its lavender flowers, in December. With flowers outdoors in the open garden 12 months of the year, I claimed we never had winter. After several years we moved about 10 miles away to a larger house on just over an acre in Wilton, Connecticut. Now we were that much farther from Long Island Sound and on the far side of a ridge that intervened, imposing its bulk between the water's moderating influence. My garden no longer had flowers in December and January. We lived in Wilton for 25 years. I settled in and made a garden. Snowdrops nestled against the roots of 100-year-old white oaks, *Quercus alba. Arisaema*—both our native Jack-in-the-pulpit, *A. triphyllum*, and several Japanese and Chinese species—did well. And cyclamen would self sow, both the spring-blooming *Cyclamen coum* and the autumn-flowering *C. hederifolium*. In September 1995 we moved to western New Jersey. Our property is wooded with tulip poplar, *Liriodendron tulipifera;* northern red oak, *Quercus rubra*; and overshadowed old-field cedar, *Juniperus virginiana*, which are dying out. The land slopes to the north-northeast, with an intermittently flowing drainage channel (mostly dry in summer) more or less along the eastern property line. The soil is clay laced with red shale, in all sizes from gravel to one-woman, woman-and-man, to too big to budge. Weeds abound—everything from multiflora rose (*Rosa multiflora*) and Japanese honeysuckle (*Lonicera japonica*), to garlic mustard (*Alliaria petiolata*) and Japanese stilt grass (*Microstegium* species). Weather is variable. In the less than a decade we have lived here, two winters were notable for low temperatures and quantity of snow and another was quite mild. Some summers we have rain, while others are drought-dry.

I did my best to move my Wilton garden, digging and potting and traveling with my plants. I planted communities. A 15 gallon (57 liter) or larger nursery pot would receive a cherished shrub such as enkianthus or *Rhododendron yakushimanum*, together with some woodland perennials such as trillium, bloodroot, and ferns. Then I'd tuck in dormant bulbs, such as snowdrops (*Galanthus* species and cultivars), some cyclamen, and winter aconite (*Eranthis hyemalis*) that I managed to unearth. I'd top things off with a nice ground cover such as evergreen woodland phlox (*Phlox stolonifera*). Some perennials went into 1 and 2 gallon (4 and 8 liter) pots. Every carload I drove west included two or three, 5 gallon (19 liter) sheet rock buckets filled with compost. Unintentionally, by the end of summer I had emptied out the entire compost heap. It was interesting and instructive to discover how accurate, or not, was my mental map of where dormant bulbs were hiding in the garden. Those under ground cover might cause more disruption to dig but were easier to find than those under mulch. The New Jersey place is a larger garden, nearly an order of magnitude larger than the old spot. As many plants and bulbs as I moved, they are just a drop in the bucket here; this is a garden for large sweeps and drifts of plants. And so, that fall as we settled into the house, I also settled into the garden, planting bulbs—everything from hundreds of daffodils to thousands of little ones such as chionodoxa, galanthus, scilla, muscari, and more.

I've kept it up, more or less, and now about 40,000 bulbs are planted here at Belle-Wood Garden. Beyond their beauty, my criteria for bulbs are as follows: they need to be self-sufficient, deer-resistant, and preferably capable of naturalizing, by which I mean increasing through seeds or offsets. The little guinea hen flower, *Fritillaria meleagris*, does quite well, as do the camassia I moved from Connecticut and other camassia that I've added. Wood hyacinth, *Hyacinthoides hispanica*, is welcome to spread itself around the woodland, for there is room enough here for it to multiply without becoming a hindrance; in the Wilton garden I had to deadhead old flowers rigorously to prevent it from seeding about. Spring snowflake, *Leucojum vernum*, was moved here from Connecticut and is settling in quite happily. Summer snowflake, *L. aestivum*, a new addition, appears to be making itself at home.

Daffodils also perform well under the conditions my garden has to offer, though they prefer the lighter shade near the edges of the woods or in glade openings that were created from tree removals, either by weather-related incidents or selected tree cutting. I find that Division 6, the cyclamineus cultivars (of which *Narcissus* 'Dove Wings' is perhaps my favorite), and Division 9, the poeticus cultivars, are good, reliable performers. Over the course of three planting seasons, I put in about 1400 poeticus daffodils, everything from the reliable old stand-bys such as *N. poeticus* var. *recurvus* (pheasant's eye) to more contemporary cultivars like 'Felindre' and 'Cantabile'. Some Division 1 trumpet daffodils are also dependable. 'Rijnveld's Early Sensation' welcomes the spring, untroubled when, perforce, it needs must nod under a coating of snow. 'Dutch Master' thrives at the bottom of our driveway near the mailbox, interplanted with the orange ditch lily, *Hemerocallis fulva*.

Many more bulbs, corms, and tubers galore grace my garden in spring, summer, and fall, and a couple even manage to take winters in their stride. You see, this is not just a book written from research; it is written about a subject near and dear to me.

Holland and Bulbs

Consider the bulb fields of Holland. Each spring, the *bollenvelden* region, located between Leiden and Haarlem, is transformed into a multicolored checkerboard as red tulips, yellow daffodils, and lavender hyacinths burst into bloom. Thousands of tourists drive by—even the Dutch. (I saw a family sit their two young children down between the rows of red tulips, little red stocking caps on their heads. A Kodak moment, the picture taken, and next December's Christmas card was in the camera.) These artful rectangular Mondrian blocks of color are just as much production agriculture, or farming—like the cornfields of the U.S. Midwest—as ornamental horticulture. Their beauty is incidental, rather than the goal, the end product of all the work of planting and tending.

Bulbs that bloom in the spring: tulips, daffodils, and hyacinths, plus crocus, are even more distinctive in bloom than they are below ground. Drawing courtesy of the Netherlands Flower Bulb Information Center.

Across the globe, each fall the signs go up, the bulbs arrive, and nurseries and garden centers are filled with bags, boxes, and bins of bulbs. They are often produced in Holland: grown, dug, cleaned, packed, and shipped around the world. But these bulbs are not native to Holland; they have been introduced from abroad—selected, developed, and bred for bright, showy flowers. Triumph and Darwin tulips no longer resemble the species that grew in Turkey when Olgier Ghislain deBusbeque first sent their

More attractive than a cornfield, thousands of brilliant red tulips grace this growing field. Photo by author.

seed to his friend, Carolus Clusius, in the 16th century. Today the bulbs arrive packaged by fives and tens in perforated plastic bags and are planted as one of autumn's rituals, along with leaf raking and sweet cider drinking.

Geophytes are patient and forgiving. Most of the time they'll manage some sort of performance even after abuse, and many of them are willing to accept a week or two, or even longer, delay between purchase and planting. After all, geophytes are tough plants that developed a method of storing food and/or moisture reserves to get them through hard times, whether winter cold or summer drought. And, unlike many other plants, they're not so fussy about planting depth. They have the power of vegetative locomotion; were it not for contractile roots that adjust their depth, how could their seeds fall to the surface of the ground yet the bulb, corm, or tuber end up down in the dirt? Many geophytes are good doers. Daffodils persist, continue to flower, and even multiply in the dooryards of abandoned, burned-out houses. The problems come after their blooms fade. "Ugly foliage!" exclaims the gardener. "I [choose one] braid, fold, bundle, cut it off." Then they wonder what should be done about the bare spots and why their bulbs don't come back next year.

I remember clearly my first visit to Keukenhof, the fabulous display garden of bulbs in Holland. It was late April 1973, and the day was overcast, with occasional rain, and then fleecy clouds and blue sky before the spattering rain returned, which is typical spring weather for the Netherlands. The gray day seemed only to intensify the colors of the flowering display—rivers of smoky blue grape hyacinths, *Muscari armeniacum*, pooling between sweeps of vivid red tulips and yellow daffodils. Fragrant hyacinths were carefully partnered, underplanted with Grecian windflowers, *Anemone blanda*, so that the colors of the small, daisylike flowers accented those of their taller, fragrant companions. Precise, looping bands of hyacinths bi-

In 1594, Carolus Clusius was the first European to grow tulips, at the Hortus Botanicus in Leiden, The Netherlands. The original tulips he raised from seed were nothing like the large hybrids we now grow in our gardens. Photo of reenactment courtesy of the Netherlands Flower Bulb Information Center.

sected the intensely green grass lawn with their arching ribbons of soft pink, white, and soft blue. All of the bulbs were magnificently in bloom. Each bed of tulips, for example, was flowering in regimented precision, uniform in height and perfection of display. Along with other visitors from around the world (coach tours from adjacent and not-so-nearby European countries, Great Britain, America, and Japan), we strolled the paths beneath the ancient beech trees leafing out in tender spring green and admired the display. Sixty-nine gently hilly acres were laced with small canals and little lakes, serene white swans floated on the dark reflective surface of the water, and everywhere the lavish colorful display of flowers.

I've been back to Holland many times and in several seasons—spring, summer, and early autumn. And, of course, I've returned to Keukenhof, but only in the springtime. This display garden of the more than 90 members in the associated Dutch bulb growers' organization is open only when the bulbs are in bloom and closed at other times of

Stiffly formal, the upright spikes of hyacinths lend themselves to precise design—as elegant an image today as it was when the photo was taken in 1973. Photo by author.

year. Every year the member bulb growers submit their design proposals for approval. Fresh, top-size bulbs—6 million of them—are planted in the fall. New bulbs provide the best, most magnificent display the following spring, after which time they are removed. The ground sits fallow over the summer, and then in fall the cycle repeats again.

Public parks and gardens operate under standards different from those of individual gardeners. When visiting, we, the public, are there to experience the passing moment and expect to see lush and lavish displays. Consider The New York Botanical Garden's tulip walk display. Two hundred feet (61 m) long, double-bordered, in spring it is a rainbow display of 13,000 tulips. In late May or early June, when the tulips are a fading memory, the bulbs are removed, discarded, and replaced with an equally wonderful display of annuals and tender perennials. Few home gardeners have the budget to purchase 13,000 tulip bulbs for a one-time display, or the staff to plant them. This style of intensive gardening is expensive. It provides a sound bite of display but lacks endurance. This is not necessarily the result of any inherent flaws in the bulbs. The congenital defect of mass planting and carpet bedding is one of design, not material; it ignores the "what comes next" factor. For the home gardener, bulbs are better utilized in combination with perennials, annuals, trees, and shrubs to create a balanced garden design, a community of plants rather than a lopsided display. And planting the right bulbs in the correct place will yield flowers year after year.

The tulip walk at The New York Botanical Garden is a tapestry of color. Once through flowering, the bulbs are dug and discarded, to be replaced by annuals and perennials for the summer season. Photo by author.

Geophyte—Some Definitions

The common point that all bulbs, corms, tubers, and rhizomes share is the ability to store food and moisture during adverse conditions. This enables spring-flowering bulbs such as daffodils and snowdrops to get a jump-start on the growing season when nutrients are still in short supply while the ground is cold, if, indeed, it is not still frozen. Nutrients are not available to plants until microorganisms in the soil become active, usually during the spring in temperate systems. Equally, wild tulips in their arid homeland regions such as Turkey and Iran initiate growth of their root primordia in late summer before the autumn rains begin, using reserves of moisture stored in the bulb. Many of these little wildings, such as *Tulipa bakeri*, have a fuzzy lining to their tight brown tunic that even plugs the hole left by last year's withered stem to reduce evaporative losses over the arid summer.

Bulb

Gardeners tend to use *bulb* as a generic term for all of these lumpy underground structures, insouciantly applying the term to true bulbs, corms, tubers, and rhizomes alike. There are, however, structural botanical differences between these. The fact is, horti-

A handful of little species tulip bulbs show just how distinctive they can be. From the left: *Tulipa turkestanica*, *T. bakeri*, *T. tarda*, and *T. clusiana* var. *chrysantha*. These little wildings often have a sturdier tunic than the large hybrids, sometimes lined with a slight fuzz that plugs the neck opening and protects the bulb from drying out in the arid summers on the steppes of Central Asia. Photo by author.

cultural implications prescribe how bulbs should be handled in storage and planting. They differ for corms, tubers, and the rest, and these are important for gardeners to know. You could explore some of these details in the kitchen: onions are an example of a well-developed true bulb, while leeks are an example of a primitive, poorly developed bulb. Kohlrabi and celeriac are corms, Jerusalem artichokes and potatoes are rhizomatous tubers, and carrots and parsnips are unspecialized root tubers.

Let's begin at the beginning: What is a bulb? How does it differ from a corm? Where does a tuber fit in? And why should a gardener even care about these botanical details?

A true *bulb* is composed of modified leaves called *scales*. That kitchen lily, the onion, is an example with which everyone is familiar. Slice an onion apart and all the tightly nested rings are revealed. In bulbs, the scales may be tight and compact, as in onions and narcissus, or loose and open, as in lilies. Some bulbs, such as tulips, have a thin papery covering called a *tunic*. Others, such as fritillaria, do not. Roots grow from a basal plate located at the bottom of the bulb. Slice a hyacinth bulb from top to bottom in the autumn, and you will see the embryo plant complete with flower buds. True bulbs form offsets from lateral buds on the basal plate.

Since true bulbs have a vertical orientation, it is a good idea to plant them right side up. (Though I did know someone who once planted 35 tulips upside down, assuming the pointy end was where the roots would emerge. The tulips knew up from down bet-

In addition to the large wholesale vendors who ship bulbs around the world, smaller specialty growers also operate in Holland. At Rita van der Zalm's nursery, wicker baskets hold neatly bagged bulbs that have been pulled for a domestic order. Photo by author.

ter than he did, and all of them flowered in the spring, though somewhat later than might be expected of that cultivar.) You may read useful-sounding yet invalid suggestions concerning bulbs such as crown imperial, *Fritillaria imperialis*: "Plant these sizable bulbs somewhat tilted or sideways so that water is able to drain away from the hollow at the top and not collect between the scales." Hmm, sounds good, except that roots pull downward, the shoot pushes upward, and over time the bulb will right itself. If the site is so wet that moisture could prove fatal, your choice is either to improve the drainage or select a different site.

The apparently simple theme of "bulb" has a lot of variation. *Hippeastrum* has the simplest type; its bulb scales are formed from the base of old leaves, and flowers appear from one side of the centrally produced leaves, from between old leaf scales. The scales are closely wrapped around one another and attached to a basal plate. New leaves form in the center. Compare this habit of growth with that of the daffodil, in which the

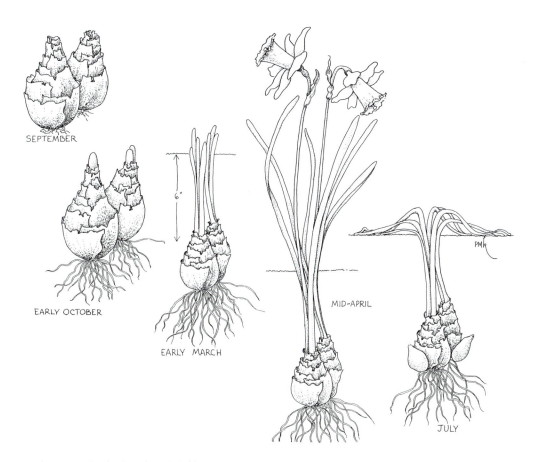

Growth cycle of a *Narcissus* hybrid. Copyright Patricia M. Kay, 1993.

flower appears between the current year's youngest leaves (like an onion that sprouts in the cupboard). Hyacinth is similar. The outermost scales become papery and dry, forming a tunic. Tulips have a few-scaled bulb. Mature tulips have no basal leaves, so all the scales are formed inside the bulb around the stem. Old scales form the tunic when they dry, and in many species they are covered inside with silky hairs that help protect the scales from desiccation in the arid summers on the steppes of central Asia. In lilies, the bulb scales are separate and do not encircle the bulb. Also, no tunic is formed. Most lilies have only stem leaves unless they are immature. Bulb scales are formed separately, around the base of the stem. Young, immature lilies have basal leaves, and the bases of these leaves swell to form the first scales. Most lily bulbs have a short vertical orientation. Bulbs of some American species, *Lilium canadense* for example, have creeping horizontal orientations. And the Madonna lily, *L. candidum*, is intermediate between other lilies and *Cardiocrinum* in that basal leaves form bulb scales

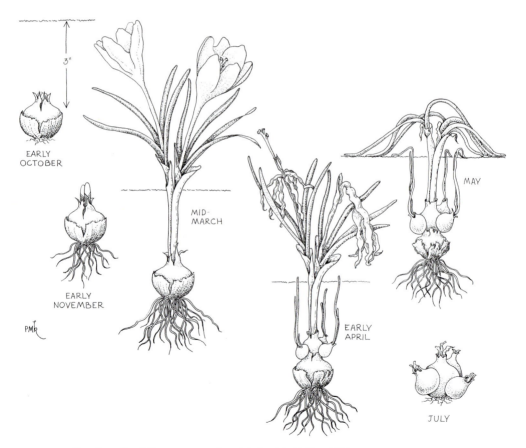

Growth cycle of *Crocus vernus*. Copyright Patricia M. Kay, 1993.

at the same time that the flowering stem forms. *Fritillaria* are closely related to lilies. Most species of *Fritillaria* have a few-scaled bulb without a tunic. In the crown imperial, *F. imperialis*, the scales are wrapped around each other on a large, almost spherical bulb. *Allium*, *Fritillaria*, *Galanthus*, *Lilium*, *Narcissus*, *Tulipa*, and *Scilla* are all examples of true bulbs.

Corm

A *corm* is a mass of undifferentiated storage tissue derived from modified stem growth. All corms always have a tunic or covering formed by dry leaf bases. These coverings may be *reticulated* (netted) or *annulate* (ringed). Roots grow from a basal plate. The growing points on the corm's top may be single or multiple. Like bulbs, corms have vertical orientation. From a gardener's viewpoint, an important aspect of any corm's growth cycle is that the old corm is used up in leaf and flower growth, and a new corm

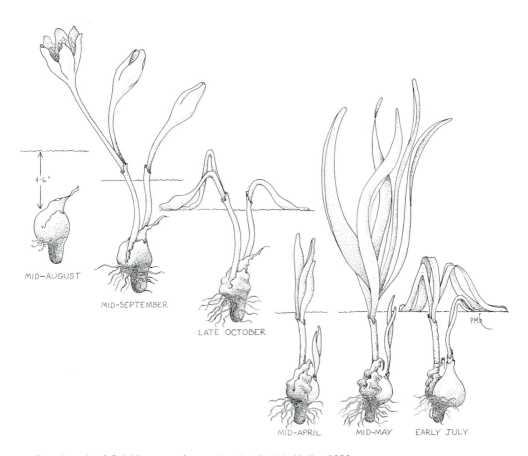

Growth cycle of *Colchicum speciosum*. Copyright Patricia M. Kay, 1993.

is formed each year. Remember that gladiolus you bought at the garden center, with a plump corm surmounting a wizened, wrinkled, flat, and dry corm? The hard, dry corm was the remains of last season's growth, while the plump one was waiting for the next growing season. *Colchicum*, *Crocus*, *Erythronium*, *Freesia*, and *Gladiolus* are all corms.

Tuber, tuberous root, and rhizome

A *tuber* is a solid mass of modified stem tissue, like a corm, but it lacks a tunic or covering and has no basal plate. Roots and shoots arise from growing points, or eyes, scattered over the tuber. Some, such as arisaema, have a more pronounced vertical orientation than do others, such as Grecian windflower, *Anemone blanda*. *Arisaema*, *Caladium*, *Cyclamen*, and *Eranthis* are tuberous geophytes. *Tuberous roots* are often similar in appearance to tubers, but they are composed of root tissue, not stem tissue. Fibrous roots are produced during the growing season, and new growth buds arise at the base

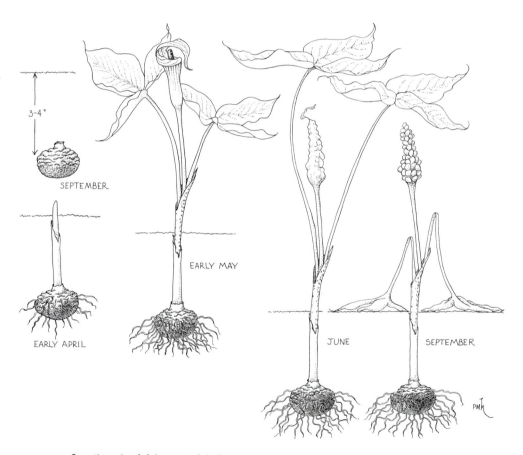

Growth cycle of *Arisaema triphyllum*. Copyright Patricia M. Kay, 1993.

of the old stem. Examples are *Begonia ×tuberhybrida*, *Dahlia*, and *Polygonatum*. Lastly, *rhizomes* are composed of swollen stem tissue growing laterally at or just below the surface and generally freely branching. Roots develop from the lower surface, shoots on the upper part. *Canna* and *Convallaria majalis* grow from rhizomes.

The diversity of bulbs, corms, tubers, and rhizomes is a clear indication of how useful plants find this means of surviving winter cold or summer drought, though not all species in a genus necessarily take this route. Grecian windflower, *Anemone blanda*, is a tuber; Japanese anemone, *A. hupehensis*, has fibrous roots. *Iris danfordiae*, *I. histrioides*, and *I. reticulata* are dainty little spring bulbous iris, while *I. sibirica* is fibrous rooted. Of the familiar geophytes and uncommon ones, many are readily grown and others are very finicky in their requirements. What I can assure you is that there are geophytes for the novice gardener and others for those who love a challenge, geophytes for gardens anywhere, and flowers to grow in the garden, in the house, and for bouquets.

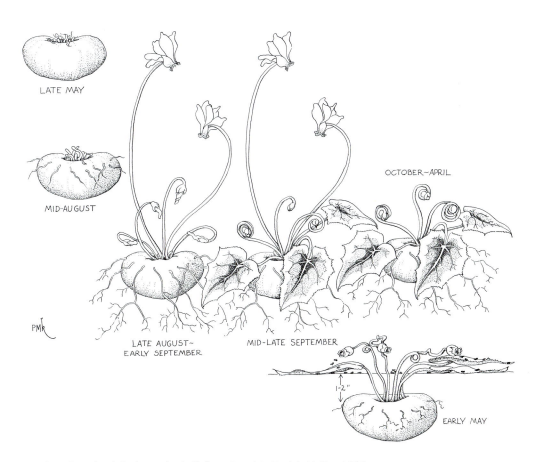

Growth cycle of *Cyclamen hederifolium*. Copyright Patricia M. Kay, 1993.

Geophyte Families

Just as it is helpful and important to know what makes a geophyte a bulb, corm, rhizome, or tuber, equally compelling reasons exist for knowing geophytes' family connections. Taxonomically, the majority of geophytes are found in three plant families: Liliaceae, Amaryllidaceae, and Iridaceae. In addition, a diversity of plant families include one, two, or a few geophytes.

Liliaceae, the lily family

With approximately 3600 species contained in 240 genera, the lily family, among the most popular with gardeners, including such genera as *Hyacinthus*, *Lilium*, *Trillium*, and *Tulipa*. Other popular geophytes such as quamash or camass (*Camassia*), glory of the snow (*Chionodoxa*), autumn crocus or naked ladies (*Colchicum*), lily of the valley (*Convallaria*), dog's tooth violet (*Erythronium*), crown imperial (*Fritillaria*), wood hyacinth (*Hyacinthoides*), grape hyacinth (*Muscari*), *Ornithogalum*, *Puschkinia*, and *Scilla* are also liliaceous. All plants found in the Liliaceae are monocots, which means that they germinate with a single leaf. They are found around the world, most abundantly in temperate and subtropical areas. Many geophytes in the lily family are bulbs; some, such as tulips, have a tunic; and others, such as lily and fritillaria, do not. While bulbs are most common, some genera have tubers and others, such as colchicum, have a corm, but these are less common.

Amaryllidaceae, the amaryllis family

The amaryllis family, Amaryllidaceae, includes approximately 1200 species contained in about 90 genera. Favorite geophytes in this family include the naked ladies, *Amaryllis belladonna*, which are popular in California, as well as the *Hippeastrum* cultivars, so well-liked for holiday flowers in the wintertime. Ornamental onions (*Allium*), snowdrops (*Galanthus*), snowflakes (*Leucojum*), yet another naked lady or surprise lily (*Lycoris*), and ever-popular daffodils (*Narcissus*) are also Amaryllidaceae. This is important information, so pay attention: geophytes in this plant family are generally ignored by deer, rabbits, voles, mice, and other gnawing, nibbling, chewing, devouring garden pests. Coming as they do from South America, South Africa, and the Mediterranean region, the amaryllis family includes many geophytes that are useful in mild winter regions such as southern California: *Amaryllis belladonna*, *Lycoris*, and *Nerine*. Geophytes in this family are generally tunicate bulbs or corms and very rarely rhizomes. Leaves are sparse, generally basal, and only rarely on the scape (the flower stem). Flowers may be one to a scape, as in many of the daffodils, or numerous in a terminal umbel, like the great purple to lavender globes of an ornamental onion. Their flowers have six stamens, a handy way to distinguish colchicums (amaryllis family) from crocus (iris family).

Iridaceae, the iris family

The iris family, Iridaceae, contains approximately 800-plus species in 60 genera. The flowers, one to several, have six segments. The three outer segments, called *falls*, spread outward or downward and outward. The inner three segments, called *standards*, are erect. They may be showy or very much reduced and bristle-like. Visualize the leaves of such iris family geophytes as *Gladiolus*, *Crocus*, *Crocosmia*, *Freesia*, and *Iris* itself. Mostly basal, they grow in a fan, usually two-ranked. Each leaf is linear to sword-shaped and as such offers a clue that this family includes monocots. Cosmopolitan in distribution, these geophytes may be bulbous, cormous, or rhizomatous. Bulbous iris in the *xiphium* subgenus are found in western Europe and North Africa and have papery tunics. The early spring–flowering *I. histrioides* and *I. reticulata* are dwarf bulbous plants with fibrous, netted tunics. Freesias have corms with a reticulate, netted tunic and are native to South Africa, primarily the Cape Province.

Miscellaneous geophyte families

Although the three families mentioned contain many of our most popular geophytes, some excellent geophytes are tucked away—one here, a trio there—in a handful of families. The aroid family, Araceae, offers *Arisaema*, *Caladium*, and *Calla* to enrich our gardens. All are monocots, and all are vermin resistant, thanks to crystals of oxalic acid that render them unpalatable. The begonia family, Begoniaceae, presents us with tuberous begonia, *Begonia* ×*tuberhybrida*, with its showy flowers, and *B. grandis*, astonishingly hardy and growing quite well in Connecticut and New Jersey. Dicots, begonia seeds each have two cotyledon leaves when they germinate. Then there are monocotyledonous cannas, unique and with a family of their own—the Cannaceae.

The daisy family, call it Compositae or Asteraceae as you wish, is so complex that taxonomists split it into tribes before they get down to genera. From Mexico we get the dahlia, an elegant flower that nearly rivals the iris for the rainbow range of colors found in its flowers. Even the African violet family, Gesneriaceae, manages to include a couple of geophytes: *Achimenes* and *Gloxinia*. While many oxalis are thugs of the worst kind, spreading with territorial ambition, one provides attractive foliage and subdued flowers for container gardening in cold winter regions. *Oxalis regnellii*, with its fuchsia-flushed purple leaves and pale pink flowers, is a member of the Oxalidaceae.

One I would not want to be without, the primrose family, Primulaceae, is home to *Cyclamen*, with attractive foliage and shuttlecock flowers that appeal to every gardener who sees it. Last but hardly least is the buttercup family, Ranunculaceae, wherein we find winter aconite, *Eranthis hyemalis*, as well as several tuberous or rhizomatous anemones.

Bulb families (the splitter's version)

When Linnaeus invented taxonomy for plants, it was based on the appearance of flowers. (One holdout thought it should be based on foliage, but flower power held sway.) Now that DNA testing allows comparison on a submicroscopic scale that gardeners will never see, a massive scramble has ensued to reorganize taxonomic classification of plants. The Royal Horticultural Society's *Manual of Bulbs*, published in 1995, follows the older classification and keeps Liliaceae intact as a major family. The revised families that were split off from Liliaceae, such as Alliaceae, Colchicaceae, Convallariaceae, Hyacinthaceae, and others, are listed in parentheses following the different genera, like so: Liliaceae, *Hyacinthus* (Hyacinthaceae).

In *The Color Encyclopedia of Cape Bulbs* (2002), the revisions to Liliaceae are followed, and South African geophytes are listed within the new families. Of course, this book does not include European, Asian, or North, Central, and South American geophytes. Following is a list of the revised situation for those readers interested in following these transitions.

- Alliaceae, onion family, has been split off from Liliaceae and includes *Allium, Ipheion, Nectaroscordum*, and *Tulbagia*.
- Amaryllidaceae, amaryllis family, now includes *Amaryllis, Crinum, Galanthus, Habranthus, Hippeastrum, Hymenocallis, Leucojum, Lycoris, Narcissus, Nerine, Rhodophiala, Spreklia, Sternbergia*, and *Zephyranthes*.
- Araceae, arum family, includes *Arum, Arisaema, Biarum, Caladium, Colocasia, Dracunculus, Pinellia, Sauromatum, Xanthosoma*, and *Zantedeschia*.
- Begoniacea, begonia family, includes two geophyte species: *Begonia* ×*tuberhybrida* and *Begonia grandis*.
- Calochortaceae, calochortus family, includes *Calochortus*.
- Cannaceae, canna family, has only one member, *Canna*.
- Colchicaceae, colchicum family, has also been split off from Liliaceae and includes *Colchicum* and *Bulbocodium*.
- Compositae, aster/daisy family, includes *Dahlia* and *Liatris*.
- Convallariaceae, convallaria family, was also split off from Liliaceae and includes *Convallaria* and *Polygonatum*.
- Gesneriaceae, African violet family, has two geophytic members: *Achimines* and *Gloxinia*.
- Hyacinthaceae, hyacinth family, split off from Liliaceae, includes the sweetly fragrant *Hyacinthus*, and also *Bellevalia, Brimeura, Brodiaea, Camassia, Chionodoxa, ×Chionoscilla, Eucomis, Hyacinthella, Hyacinthoides, Lachenalia, Ledebouria, Muscari, Ornithogalum, Puschkinia, Scilla*, and *Veltheimia*.

- Iridaceae, iris family, includes *Iris, Babiana, Belamcanda, Chasmanthe, Crocosmia, Crocus, Freesia, Gladiolus, Ixia, Sparaxis, Tigridia,* and *Watsonia.*
- Liliaceae, lily family, has been reduced from its former numerous genera and now is home to *Agapanthus, Cardiocrinum, Erythronium, Fritillaria, Lilium,* and *Tulipa.*
- Oxalidaceae, oxalis family, includes *Oxalis.*
- Primulaceae, primrose family, includes *Cyclamen.*
- Ranunculaceae, ranunculus family, includes *Anemone, Anemonella, Eranthis,* and *Ranunculus,*
- Trilliaceae, trillium family, is another split off from Liliaceae and includes *Trillium.*
- Uvulariaceae, uvularia family, was also split off from Liliaceae and includes *Uvularia.*

World Distribution of Geophytes

While the garden center signs of autumn suggest that the bulbs, corms, and tubers that are offered come from Holland, that refers only to their distribution. Holland may indeed have been where they were grown, but their origins are spread far and wide across the world. The geography of their origins includes Europe and Asia; North, Central, and South America; Africa; and Australia. The underground structures that certain plants developed are a means of getting through the seasonal stress of hard times. These limiting physical conditions include drought or lack of water needed to support growth, and winter cold or lack of warmth necessary to sustain growth. Disturbances such as fire also play a role, especially in grasslands and/or shrubby desert regions such as the *fynbos* of South Africa and the *maquis* of the Mediterranean. (See Chapter 5, "Geophytes for the Mediterranean Garden," for more information.) All geophytes are not created equal. Knowing where a particular geophyte originated offers a gardener more than just its home territory; it provides such details as whether that geophyte wants a dry summer and autumn rains, whether subtropical origins suggest winter protection is necessary, and more.

Certain parts of the world seem to be focal points where more geophytes occur than elsewhere. South Africa gives us such familiar genera as agapanthus, amaryllis, babiana, clivia, crocosmia, eucomis, freesia, gladiolus, kniphofia, lachenalia, nerine, ornithogalum, rhodohypoxis, tulbaghia, veltheimia, watsonia, zantedeschia, and at least as many more. From the Aegean to southern Europe and the Mediterranean come arisarum, arum, bellevalia, bulbocodium, chionodoxa, colchicum, crocus, cyclamen, eranthis, fritillaria, gladiolus, hyacinthella, leucojum, muscari, narcissus, nectaroscordum, scilla, and tulipa, plus a goodly handful of less commonly cultivated geophytes. Some genera extend their range into central and western Asia: arum, biarum, colchicum, crocus, eranthis, fritillaria, gladiolus, hyacinthella, muscari, narcissus, nectaroscordum, scilla, and tulipa, for example. In addition, the steppes of central Asia are also home to belamcanda, eremurus, hyacinthus, and puschkinia. North America is home to arisaema, camassia, erythronium, fritillaria, liatris, sanguinaria, and trillium. Central America and the West Indies were the sources for achimenes, canna, dahlia, gloxinia, hippeastrum, hymenocallis, polianthes, sinningia, sprekelia, tigridia, and zephyranthes.

Understanding regional parameters of winter cold and its duration, summer heat, and rainfall patterns provides a starting place for plant selection and successful gardening. Plants from habitats and climatic zones similar to those of the garden in which they are planted are more likely to thrive than plants from locations that are widely different. Consider the match-up of plants from Japan and the gardens of the northeastern United States: geophytes such as gold band lily (*Lilium auratum*) or the end-of-summer–flowering *L. speciosum*, not to mention such shrubs, trees, and ground covers as Japanese azaleas, flowering cherries, and pachysandra. Spider lily, *Lycoris radiata*, is a familiar geophyte in the southeastern states, as much at home there as in the ditches along rice fields in Japan. Geophytes adapted to the dry, hot summers and mild, wet winters of the Mediterranean thrive in California, but they freeze and rot in New England. Rain—when it comes and how much of it—is an important consideration as the majority of geophytes resent wet conditions, especially if the excess moisture arrives during their dormant season.

Soil types also have a major impact on plant growth. Consider a deciduous woodland. One acre of a mixed deciduous forest drops anywhere from a ton to a ton and a half of leaves and litter in an annual replenishment of organic matter. Its loamy soil is composed of particles small enough to hold on to nutrients and moisture, yet large enough to drain freely. Contrast this with a coniferous forest, where the annual jettison of resinous needles takes far longer than a year to decay. The soils are constructed of a dry, sterile duff, low in nutrients and having a low, acid pH. Where conditions are suitable for the growth of broad-leaved evergreen trees such as southern magnolias with their large and glossy leaves and thickets of evergreen rhododendrons, the soil may also be impoverished. The actual decay of such robust leaves is slow, and the climate's warmth and rain promotes rapid breakdown of organic matter that is in the soil.

Tropical rain forests have their biomass tied up in growing plants and a rapid recycling of fallen organic matter. Once large acreage is cleared for grazing animals, the tropical forest does not regenerate, in large part because the mineralized subsoil that is now exposed cannot nourish young seedling trees. Compare this situation with the temperate eastern United States. Space that is opened for crops or pasture quickly reverts to woodland within a human lifetime. Grasslands—meadows, prairies, steppes, and even lawns to some extent—are composed of herbaceous plants that die back at the end of the growing season, creating a humus-rich layer as leaves and stems rot down. Prairies in the Midwest have rich, black loam that may be 6, 7, or even 10 feet (1.8 to 3 m) deep, a striking contrast to temperate woodlands with a layer of humus-rich soil that is measured in inches.

Arid regions, dryland sites, have neither the organic bulk nor the moisture necessary to assist in decomposition. Their soils are mineralized, consisting of sands and gravel that are generally low in nutrients and quickly drain whenever water is available. Geophytes adapted to these regions, having taken up water during the damp winters and springs, store it through the dry summer months. Tulips from the steppes of Central Asia begin the formation of their root primordia from just such reserves of moisture stored within their bulbs. Geophytes from Mediterranean regions such as Turkey, Iran, Iraq, and Israel or the South African Cape region flower in winter and early spring when moisture is available. Their life cycle is nicely timed. When the stressful, dry summer weather arrives, they are aestivating (sleeping), dormant below the soil's surface until suitable conditions return with the seasonal rains.

What Makes a Garden?

Just what is a garden? What qualifies, defines, and determines that this place with plants fits the definition?

Gardening is the imposition of human desires as to which plants shall be allowed to grow in a particular space and which shall be removed. This applies equally to horticulture as to agriculture, from a cornfield or orchard to a herbaceous border of perennials carefully selected and placed for color and composition. The difference is the aesthetic effect: gardens are expected to be beautiful, while the beauty of an orchard or bulb field, though undeniable, is happenstance. Sometimes, however, it is recognized. Years ago, my brother, Ben Orlove, did some anthropological field research in Mexico. He mentioned that the villagers around Lake Pátzcuaro in Michoacán often talked about how their fields were *bonito* (pretty) when they were free of weeds and the maize plants were all of uniform height as opposed to having patches of scrawny plants. Beans and squashes interplanted with the maize were okay; the fields could still be pretty.

The natural cycle of growth is often interrupted as ornamental plants are clipped, pinched, trimmed, or trained in a manner to suit the gardener. Ruthless deadheading denies plants the opportunity to set seed. Aberrant forms, grotesques that need the gardener's nurturing and coddling to survive, are called rare, unique, and special—anything with variegated foliage; perennials with double flowers, unusual colors, or dis-

Is this attractive pairing of grape hyacinth (*Muscari armeniacum*) and sunny yellow dandelions happily growing in turf a garden or merely an unkempt lawn? It depends on your point of view. Photo courtesy of Brent Heath/Brent and Becky's Bulbs.

torted petals; and dwarf, weeping, or columnar trees and shrubs.

Gardening, it becomes apparent, is by its very character an artificial manipulation of nature. Just as decisions must be made on a pragmatic basis (is the plant suitable for the existing soil type, moisture level, sun to shade, summer heat, or winter cold that the site provides?), aesthetic choices are also necessary—not merely those affecting the emotional responses of attraction to a plant, but its suitability to the style of the garden. Fortunately, there is a garden style to suit any fancy, from formal to casual to country to naturalistic, those based on *feng shui*, of a single color, on a mountaintop rock garden, and whatever else you can think of. But the garden should have plants. Concrete with gazing globes and a fountain might be trendy, but without plants it doesn't fit the definition of *garden*: 1.) a plot of ground, usually near a house, where flowers, vegetables, or herbs are cultivated. 2.) A piece of ground or other space commonly with ornamental plants, trees, and shrubs, used as a park or other public recreation area, or as an arboretum.

Native, naturalized, exotic

Plants are the material; garden design is the method. While the plants that are selected for a garden will have some influence, they do not dictate the design as much as the gardener's preference for a particular style inspires the selection of plants. Formal gardens declare themselves with clipped hedges and topiary and symmetrical planting of paired herbaceous borders in carefully chosen color themes along a paved path backed by brick walls. Maintenance is high, what with deadheading spent flowers, staking floppy-stemmed plants, and careful pruning and tending of both shrubs and herbaceous plants. But a suitable native shrub can be grown as a hedge, evergreen *Ilex opaca* for example, just as readily as some exotic selection such as yew, *Taxus baccata*.

Naturalistic garden style takes its form from the natural—that is, the wild—landscape. Unfortunately, much of what we see around us is a bastardized amalgam of remnant natives mixed with naturalized escapees from abroad. In some instances, these foreigners have so infiltrated into the warp and weft of our landscapes that they are frequently mistaken for native plants. Grassland plants such as ox-eye daisy, *Leucanthemum vulgare*; yarrow, *Achillea millefolium*; and clovers are common examples that the novice often mistakes for native wildflowers. Let us, then, first define our terms for plant origins.

Native refers to plants that originate where they are found growing wild. Although there is debate over the time frame, which is most generally accepted in North America as pre-European settlement on the East Coast, no geographical boundary has been set. Some authorities are extremely restrictive. John Diekelmann and Robert Schuster, in their excellent book *Natural Landscaping: Designing with Native Plant Communities* (2003), discuss "the integrity of genetic makeup of local species [that] may be compromised by the introduction of plants from distant areas." The suggestion is that local plants, over millennia, adapt to local conditions, whereas the same species growing elsewhere might not be as suitable. Their suggestion: "The safest and most ethical answer to this problem is to make every attempt to use plants from populations growing within 50 miles of the site to be planted. Not only will they be more likely to thrive, they may help insure the preservation of locally adapted species." True, a tree with excellent fall foliage color may be programmed to turn from green to blaze orange earlier in the colder portion of its range than in the milder climates. The latter can be caught short, still green, by the advent of cold weather.

Plants that originated elsewhere but have settled down, woven themselves into the local tapestry and function as if native, are called *naturalized*. They never applied for a green card but have made themselves very much at home. The meadow plants mentioned earlier and others, such as yellow flag iris, *Iris pseudacorus*, thriving in wet ditches in Connecticut and elsewhere are good examples. However, the ebullient "May all your weeds be wildflowers" has a dark side, and certain plants from abroad make their escape from the confines of the garden to become vicious thugs. In the United States, consider kudzu, *Pueraria lobata*, in the South; multiflora rose, *Rosa multiflora*, in the Northeast; tamarisk, *Tamarix pentandra*, in the arid Southwest; and foxglove, *Digitalis purpurea*, lining roadsides in the Pacific Northwest. Intentional introductions as plants to enhance our gardens, they have become unwelcome guests running rampant, crowding out the natives. What oriental bittersweet (*Celastrus orbiculatus*), multiflora rose, and other such invaders have in common is the ability to adapt without fuss or bother, coupled with ease of propagation. Such herbal terrorists are creating a very real threat not merely in our gardens but in the larger landscape. Perhaps the optimistic view of weeds as wildflowers needs to be taken with a grain of salt—or perhaps a spritz of herbicide. Choosing the plants to use in our gardens is more than a matter of aesthetics and suitable growing conditions. If you accept the premise that only one plant can grow in any given space, it is easy to understand why we need to be concerned.

Keep in mind that a lag time, a decade or two, often occurs before the invasive nature of a new introduction becomes apparent. Once birds and small mammals discovered how tasty are the hips of multiflora roses, they dispersed the seeds far and wide. While I do not remember the book in which I read it, I do recall the author's advice on how to plant a hedgerow: Set up posts, and string wire between them where you want the hedgerow. Perching birds will deposit the seeds of what they have been eating, creating a mixed hedge of what's already in the neighborhood. This will be lovely if it is flowering dogwood, *Cornus florida*, but not so welcome if they have been feasting on Russian olive, *Elaeagnus angustifolia*.

Then there are *exotics*, plants that thrive in a garden setting but seem unable to move beyond the garden gate. Two-hundred-year-old lilacs that persist by the cellar hole of a tumbledown house or daffodils that thrive in a similarly abandoned garden are able to grow on their own but do not extend beyond their original site.

Design style

Unless you want a Keukenhof garden of your own, the bulbs, corms, rhizomes, and tubers that you plant will mingle with herbaceous perennials and woody plants. They can do so in a formal, regimented manner or in a casual style, something that provides a natural feel to your garden. Do plants drive the garden style, or does the garden set the tone? Consider the various ornamental onions—*Allium* species and cultivars. Their flowers are arranged in an umbel, grouped at the top of the flower stalk, each flower on a stem of equal length. The result, for many of the popular larger ones, is a substantial purple soap bubble tethered by its stalk, uncluttered by foliage that often withers away by the time the bulb is in bloom. Such a high-tech and artificial-appearing flower must belong in a refined and arranged garden, right? Not necessarily so. In her classic English country garden, garden maven Rosemary Verey chose *Allium aflatunense* to join the yellow daisies of Caucasian leopard's bane, *Doronicum orientale* (syn. *D. caucasicum*), under the archway of laburnum with its trailing clusters of flowers, like yellow wisteria. Landscape designer and nursery owner Kurt Bluemel created a marvelously casual yet colorful meadow-style planting of bold *Allium giganteum* with *Achillea* 'Coronation Gold' amidst grasses. In my first BelleWood Garden, I combined the soft, mauve flowers of *Allium karataviense* with *Geranium* 'Johnson's Blue' and the soft, silver foliage of *Artemisia ludoviciana* 'Valerie Finnis' and deep purple-black violas. Ornamental onions are popular with flower arrangers. They have a "high-style" look (and no onion smell) and are attractive even as they finish blooming and go to seed. Clearly, it is the design that suggests how plants—including bulbs, corms, rhizomes, and tubers—will be used.

At Kurt Bluemel's garden in Baldwin, Maryland, a meadow-style planting combines the floating purple globes of *Allium giganteum* with ornamental grasses, *Achillea* 'Coronation Gold', and other perennials. The surrounding plants disguise the ornamental onions' lack of foliage, withered away by the time they are in bloom. Photo by author.

At BelleWood Garden, a soft combination of colors matches the pale mauve flowers of *Allium karataviense* with the silver foliage of artemisia and the deep-toned flowers of *Geranium* 'Johnson's Blue' and dark purple violas. Photo by author.

Naturalistic gardens

How to define and describe naturalistic style? I do not consider it to be a slavish replication, a recreation of the wild landscape. Suggestions that homeowners with a townhouse in Chicago follow the prairie paradigm makes little sense to me—the prairies are vast and a townhouse garden is minuscule by comparison. Plants mentioned in the original plats of the area might offer suggestions, as for the Chicago Botanic Garden's wonderful reconstituted prairie. A botanical garden's or a nature center's focus differs from that of a homeowner. The preferred method of maintaining prairie gardens is to burn them, something sure to upset the neighbors in a condominium community. What the homeowner could employ is a suitable design that suggests a prairie. Grassland equals grasses, so grasses become the warp of the design. Color is provided by *forbs*, herbaceous plants that are neither grasses nor grasslike. Many forbs are *composites*, daisy family plants with many small flowers grouped together in a head, looking like a large single flower. So use a mix of grasses and flowers such as black-eyed Susan (*Rudbeckia fulgida*), prairie coneflower (*Echinacea purpurea*), and others. Add non-composite forbs such as gay feather (*Liatris spicata*) and butterfly weed (*Asclepias tuberosa*).

In addition to the grasses and forbs, prairies are also home to geophytes that live from year to year underground. Turk's cap lily, *Lilium superbum*, is a lovely lily native to damp meadows from Georgia and Alabama north to Massachusetts and New York, and west to Minnesota. It can grow 8 feet (2.5 m) tall, which might be problematic in a garden of modest proportions. However, since the intent in naturalistic design is merely to provide a sense of prairie-ness, it is possible to accept a substitute. For example, the Mid Century Hybrid Asiatic lilies flower in early to midsummer and are generally about 2 to 2½ feet (60 to 75 cm) tall, with upward-facing, bowl-like flowers; *Lilium* 'Enchantment' is a vigorous, easily grown cultivar with black-freckled, orange flowers.

The grasses, forbs, and geophytes create the feel of a grassland. Aesthetics are satisfied with the pleasing color range of dark-eyed yellow daisies, orange-centered pink daisies, lavender spires, and brilliant orange lilies, all intermingled with the grasses. In addition to providing a haven from urban life, forbs and geophytes can furnish flowers for cutting and can even attract butterflies.

Some might call this a cottage garden, with that tousled casual look of intermingled perennials and annuals, vegetables and herbs, shrubs and vines—the rose-covered thatched cottage so popular in Aga saga novels. I believe that naturalistic gardens are different from cottage gardens because the former takes its design style from natural plant communities. But there are similarities. While subtler than the maintenance required in a formal garden, both naturalistic and cottage gardens require a certain modicum of control. While annuals and perennials, even shrubs, are granted more freedom to complete their growth cycles—self-sowing foxgloves and larkspur, columbines, and flowering tobacco in the cottage garden—floppy plants such as Turk's cap lily or fall-blooming asters are supported by their neighbors rather than stakes or a trellis. Nevertheless, anything goes when it comes to choosing plants for the cottage garden. Cabbages next to climbing roses? That's fine. In naturalistic gardens, the paradigm is the natural plant community, with appropriate substitutions for plants that might be expected to grow there being permissible, as the previously mentioned Asiatic hybrid lily for the native. Additionally, nonnative plants from corresponding habitats might be introduced— European hellebores in an American woodland garden.

As it becomes more popular, naturalistic gardening based on plant communities— a meadow garden, woodland garden, and other types—often confuses the material (the plants) with the method, or design style. It is the "feel" of grassland and woodland habitat indigenous to a region that creates the naturalistic garden design style, rather than merely the use of native plants. The natural landscape that I might expect to see around me—mixed deciduous forest, meadows, and wetlands in a region with cold winters, warm summers, and rainfall around the year—is the template against which I must match both plants and design of my naturalistic garden.

Consider traditional Japanese garden design. Japan is the only country of which I am aware that relies on native flora for its gardens. Compare and contrast this to the

This superb pairing of ornamental onion and perennials shows just how effective good garden design can be. The intense reddish purple of drumstick allium, *Allium sphaero-cephalon*, is a color complement to the rich yellow daisy flowers of *Coreopsis verticillata*, while the softer yellow of *Hemerocallis* 'Siloam Bo Peep' displays a touch of the same reddish purple to tie the trio together. Photo courtesy of Brent Heath/Brent and Becky's Bulbs.

garden history of England, where historically the worldwide empire shipped American, Asian, and African plants back home to adorn gardens and glasshouses. In Japan, native plants have been traditionally used in extremely stylized gardens. The plants used—from trees and shrubs to ground cover plants, vines, and perennials—are native Japanese plants. Historically, the garden styles are very formal, high in maintenance, and ritualized in the shaping, training, and placement of plants, and it is the careful maintenance that makes the garden. A quick clip with a hedge trimmer would be an anathema—pines should be carefully candled by hand, tweaking the new growth each spring. I clearly remember taking two Japanese friends to visit Millstream, the garden of Linc and Timmy Foster in Falls Village, Connecticut, and a Mecca for rock gardeners from across the United States, Europe, and Great Britain. The Fosters had transformed the mountainside with plants from around the world grown in an informal, naturalistic manner. A sunny alpine meadow of creeping *Phlox subulata*, *Iberis sempervirens*, hardy geraniums, columbines, and small bulbs carpeted a sloping, rocky site adjacent to the millstream. The woodlands were filled with an assortment of American, European, and Asian species, so carefully sited and well grown that they all looked indigenous. As we drove away, Nihei-san turned to me and said, "In Japan we would not call this a garden." Too natural, it did not provide the visual clues that he expected, which would define "garden" in Japanese terms, where careful maintenance is the delineation. In 1997 I was a student at the first intensive seminar sponsored by the Kyoto University Research Center for Japanese Garden Art. During a lecture, one of our professors said that if you took a piece of woodland and tended it—raking and clipping, perhaps doing some weeding but without additional planting—it would, over time, look like a garden. Clearly, the Japanese think of maintenance as the benchmark of a garden. I believe many American gardeners think in the opposite direction, that it is the plants that make a garden.

If your personal preference is for native plants, if the property in question belongs to a nature center with a mission statement that requires this, or if this is some site where landscape restoration is the goal, then yes, natives only. Naturalistic design using only native plants in a manner similar to the way they would grow in nature is certainly an option. But this is only an option, not a mandate. I do not see native-only as a requirement for naturalistic, plant-community–based design. Native plants can also be used in a formal, traditionally designed garden. Think of *Echinacea purpurea*, *Liatris spicata*, and other prairie plants of the American Midwest that are part and parcel of the formal and/or cottage garden as well as in a naturalistic, plant-community–based design. Equally carefully chosen nonnative plants can weave themselves into the tapestry of a naturalistic garden.

Let us define some more terms. For me, *garden* implies a more intimate space. An orchard, a vegetable garden, or a flower garden are places where plants for a specific purpose are grown. My garden is an art form in four dimensions, adding the influence of time to height and breadth and depth. *Landscape* is a grander concept. It encompasses the regional sense of place that transcends a lifetime. Used in a cultural context, *landscape* can be applied to urban sprawl and agricultural farmlands. I look at the local crop fields of corn and soybeans, wheat and hay, which roll over the surrounding gentle hillsides of western New Jersey. In the less than a decade we have lived here the fields have changed as "McMansions" sprout up. This puts a burden on my garden to become even more a place of peace and sanctuary, solace and contemplation. I think of my garden as a place to loosen my mind and come to my senses, appreciating the sight, scent, sound, touch, and taste of the plants.

As a geographical entity, *landscape* can be used to describe the community of plants adapted to a particular region—which brings us back to naturalistic design. Unfortunately, what we typically see around us is homogenized, placeless landscape design. We do not adapt to the environment but instead cultivate plants at the expense of spirit of place. Just as the same ubiquitous stores may be found in American malls from coast to coast, we find irrigated lawns in the arid West replicating the greensward of wetter regions. Gardeners transplanted to Florida want to grow tulips and daffodils that languish, diminish, and die without their winter chilling. My brother in California is nostalgic for the lilacs that grew in Brooklyn, New York, where we were children. Even when regionally appropriate plants are grown, the ecology of a plant community is fragmented. We ignore the structure of a woodland with its canopy and understory trees, shrubs, and herbaceous plant layers, or a grassland's complexity. A foundation planting packs shrubs against the house while a specimen tree stands isolated in the lawn, and perennials grow in the flower garden's arbitrary arrangement of colors and shapes.

So, having decided on a naturalistic design based on plant communities and not restricting the palette of plants to locally native species, what else should we consider when choosing plants? Obviously, they should at least look as if they were native to the area. Seasonal fall color shift aside, I expect the majority of plants I see around me, woody or herbaceous, will have green leaves. Variegation is the exception, rather than the norm. Red, gold, gray, or silver is outlandish in terms of naturalistic design. Wild-type plants will have single, rather than double flowers. Single flowers provide better rewards of nectar and pollen to bees, butterflies, and hummingbirds. Consequently, such plants stand a better chance in the reproductive marathon, with a greater likelihood they will produce seeds and, along with the next generation of plants, food for birds and beasts. But prudence and caution are needed when dealing with exotic plants.

Some exotic plants have successfully moved into the neighborhood, to the point where they are sometimes mistaken for natives. Tawny daylilies, *Hemerocallis fulva*, line the roadsides, while ox-eye daisies (*Leucanthemum vulgare*), red and white clover

(*Trifolium pratense* and *T. repens*), yarrow (*Achillea millefolium*), and other nonnative plants have become naturalized residents of grasslands in the Northeast. Then there are absolute thugs from abroad such as garlic mustard, *Alliaria petiolata*, who take over the neighborhood and crowd out the residents. Any exotic, nonnative plants that I introduce to my garden must be good neighbors to adjacent plants and should also be stay-at-home plants that will not stray outside the property line. Not only should they look as if they belong, they must be well behaved. Modest to moderate self-sowing within my garden is acceptable; invasiveness within the garden and, more definitely, outside its boundaries, is not. Nor is aggressive cloning, nonsexual reproduction such as practiced by crow garlic, *Allium vineale*, permissible. Gardeners need to recognize their influence not merely within the garden but also on the larger ecosystem outside the garden gate. No matter how attractive, there is no excuse for introducing plants that have the potential to cause problems. This is not solely an American problem. In 2001, South Africa issued a three-stage set of restrictions for invasive alien weeds. The most restrictive list is a register of plants that must be removed and destroyed at once. The intermediate category requires a permit for those plants to be grown, and the third category lists plants that may not be sold, planted, or grown but allows existing mature specimen plants to remain.

~~~~~~

CHAPTER 2

Geophyte Care and Cultivation

Geophytes are, on the whole, a category of plants I would call "easy keepers." Acquire them, get them in the ground, and up come flowers. Children love geophytes since even the smallest ones are easily managed by little hands. In *The Secret Garden*, by Frances Hodgson Burnett, published in 1909, little Mary finds out just how reliable some geophytes are. Discovering some sharp, little green points pushing through weeds and grass in a neglected Yorkshire garden, she clears out around them with a piece of wood. Later that day she asks Martha, a young housemaid, what "those white roots that look like onions" might be. "They're bulbs," Martha tells her. "Lots o' spring flowers grow from 'em. Th' very little ones are snowdrops an' crocuses an' the big ones are narcissus an' jonquils an' daffydowndillys. Th' biggest of all is lilies." Mary asks, "Do bulbs live a long time? Would they live for years and years if no one helped them?" And Martha's answer explains part of the charm bulbs have for me and for every gardener who grows them. "They're things as helps themselves, that's why poor folks can afford to have 'em. If you don't trouble 'em, most of 'em'll work away underground for a lifetime an' spread out an' have little 'uns." That is, I think, the essence of their popularity—the magical reappearance of geophytes in the spring after their winter rest. Others perform in summer and fall.

Planting Techniques

Choosing and using geophytes adapted to your region will give the most satisfactory long-term results. As well, attention given to their initial planting followed by a modicum of aftercare is more likely to result in generous bloom than haphazardly cramming them into the ground and ignoring them. Obviously, your goal is to choose and use the best geophytes you can find. I purchase them anywhere and everywhere I find them: from wholesale and retail stores, "big box" discount stores, garden centers and nurseries, and mail-order specialty vendors. My favorite source would be a quality nursery offering a decent range of bulbs loose in bins. Fondling the merchandise is part of my makeup. It allows me to choose the biggest, plumpest, soundest bulbs; quality corms; and firm tubers. One caveat: loose in the bin means potential mix-ups as a child picks up a tulip bulb, is told to put it back, and yellow lily-flowered 'West Point' ends up in the bin with vivid 'Red Shine'. Better if they drop it in with daffodils, because tulips and daffodils are easy to tell apart. Tulip bulbs are always singletons and have one flatter side and the other more rounded, covered in a smooth tunic of chestnut or ruddy brown. Daffodils may be singletons, but the larger cultivars are often double-nosed, joined at the base. They are shaped more like an elongated onion, with a tattered, pale brown tunic.

Regardless whether you are planting true bulbs, corms, rhizomes, or tubers, bigger is better. The larger size is an indicator of greater food reserves in storage, healthier growth, and better flowering. Within a particular genus will be variations. The biggest bulb of *Narcissus rupicola*, a charming rush-leaved daffodil with a dainty yellow flower or two per stem, is never going to reach the size of *N. cyclamineus*, parent of the Division 6 cultivars, let alone that of a Division 1 trumpet daffodil. Your goal is to secure the top size available for that genus and species or cultivar. The one exception would be hyacinths. The top size hyacinths, 7 inches (18 cm) in diameter, produce super-full flower stalks that, when used in the garden, are prone to falling over. They are better for

Surrounded by stacked bins and baskets of bulbs in the M & G/Van Eeden Brothers warehouse, the author and Leo van Tol examine some colchicum bulbs. Photo by Arnoud Bosveld.

potting and forcing. Smaller, landscape-size bulbs, 6 to $6^{1}/_{2}$ inches (15 to 16 cm) in diameter, have smaller, self-supporting flower stalks and need no staking.

As the saying goes, if you insist on paying peanuts, you should expect to get monkeys. Your goal in selecting bulbs should be quality, not merely the cheapest price. You'll notice a price spread—buy 10 crocus, daffodils, or tulips, and each costs more than it would if you purchase 50. One hundred is an even more moderate in price per unit, and a thousand will be the most economical bargain—if, that is, you have space, time, and energy to plant that many. Geophytes that never get planted are a waste of money. And there is a large difference in the effort needed in planting 1000 crocus or planting 1000 daffodils.

Queuing your geophytes

You would not expect to leave bare-root perennials sitting in a bag for a couple of weeks, which is something that happens to geophytes more often than not. While bulbs, corms, rhizomes, and tubers are more resistant to drying out than fibrous-rooted perennials, there are limits. Every spring, plaintive questions appear on Internet bulb forums: "I did not plant my [choose one or more: tulips, daffodils, hyacinths, crocus] last fall. Can I plant them now, or should I wait until next fall?" An onion purchased at the grocery store is not expected to last more than a few weeks; why should other geophytes, simply because they are grown as ornamentals rather than edibles, be expected to be less perishable?

Gardeners often buy bulbs by fives and tens, and think 100 extravagant. This warehouse full of bulbs suggests that there are enough to go around, even if we plant by an order of magnitude more. Photo by author.

Seduced by the economy of quantity purchasing or discounted end-of-season bargains, what happens if you cannot get everything planted in an afternoon? Let's call it prioritizing rather than triage, as a successful outcome for all is certainly possible. Begin with the understanding that the best place for geophytes is in the ground. Nature never intended that they would leap forth from the soil, lay around on the surface for a few weeks or months, and then dive back underground again. However, not all geophytes are as obliging about coping with these conditions—digging, curing, storage, shipment, and then a further wait to be planted—as your common tulip. So how to decide which ones can wait more successfully than others? Bulbs and corms store some moisture, even when conditioned for shipment and storage. On the other hand, tubers such as *Anemone blanda* and *Eranthis hyemalis* shrivel into hard, woody scraps. They'd really rather not wait any longer than necessary before getting back into nice, moist ground. The best course of action is to plant, and generally sooner is better than later. If you have purchased more geophytes than can be planted in an afternoon, a weekend, or a week, you need some triage system to decide who has preference.

Tubers such as *Anemone blanda* and *Eranthis hyemalis* arrive at the stores drier than bulbs and corms, so they go to the head of the queue. Geometry also enters into the delay sequence. Relatively speaking, smaller geophytes have proportionally more surface to volume than larger ones, so they dry out more rapidly. Send smaller geophytes

A bin full of guinea hen flower, *Fritillaria meleagris*, at the Amsterdam street market. A true bulb, they are rather small, with just a few scales and no tunic; it should be clear that these little bulbs could easily dry out past the point of viability. Photo by author.

to the head of the planting queue. The next consideration is for bulbs that have no tunic, such as guinea hen flower, *Fritillaria meleagris*, which will lose moisture more quickly than a crocus, which has a nice, brown tunic wrapping. Bulbs without a tunic should be planted earlier than bulbs that do have a tunic and ahead of corms, since they all have tunics.

While they are waiting to be planted, store geophytes in paper bags or cardboard boxes, rather than in plastic bags that hold moisture, which can lead to mold. Tubers versus bulbs and corms, tunics versus no tunics, small versus large—we're making progress sorting them out.

Lilium have permanent fleshy roots that should not dry out. If dormant lilies cannot be planted promptly, keep them packed in barely damp peat moss at cool temperatures. Another bulb that resents delay is the large, fleshy, tunic-less crown imperial, *Fritillaria imperialis*. Dog's tooth violets, *Erythronium*, are subject to drying out and also bruise quite easily. Fall-blooming geophytes resent being out of the ground at this time, so *Colchicum* and fall-flowering crocus also need prompt planting. So who can wait? Tulips are better planted late than early to prevent untimely leaf growth. November is just fine in the Tri-State area of New York, New Jersey, and Connecticut, and even December is okay, provided the ground is still digable (unfrozen).

Refrigeration is not necessary unless you are planting "out of zone": by that I mean

Crown imperial, *Fritillaria imperialis*, is a large true bulb without a tunic. It starts to root in mid- to late summer. These roots may look as though they are reaching for the sky, but that is only because the bulb was left upside down in the bin. Photo by author.

Dutch hybrid crocus have a somewhat large corm (for a crocus, that is). The papery tunic wraps the surface, but they can still dry out relatively quickly. Photo by author.

Dog's tooth violet, *Erythronium* 'Pagoda', has a bulb that looks rather like a dog's canine tooth. Since they lack a tunic, it is easy for the bulbs to dry out and/or bruise. Photo by author.

gardeners in mild winter regions who are determined to have daffodils and tulips in the spring. Since these geophytes require a winter chilling, the refrigerator stands in for Mother Nature. Advice is usually given to store bulbs away from ripening fruit, which, it is suggested, gives off ethylene gas that can blight the flower bud already formed in hyacinths, tulips, daffodils, and other true bulbs. One day at the supermarket I noticed boxes of "ethylene-absorbing baking soda," containing baking soda, zeolite, and some potassium compound. Before I started filling the refrigerator with bags of bulbs and boxes of this product, I thought I should question how well it might work. Henk Gude of Applied Plant Research (the former bulb research center) in The Netherlands provided the following information: "Sachets of absorbent material such as zeolite are used to trap ethylene gas, which is oxidized by potassium permanganate inside the grains. The sachets are used in storage rooms to delay ripening of fruits and vegetables. In tulip bulbs, the ethylene damage threshold is much lower than in fruit, so the sachets are less effective. (They don't catch the last ethylene molecules.) With respect to the combined storage of refrigerated bulbs and fruit, I don't expect that the ethylene trapping material will be necessary (or useful) in this case. At temperatures below 10°C, the fruit will produce little ethylene, and the sensitivity of the bulbs for ethylene is also much lower than at room temperature." The answer appears to be that A) it wouldn't work too well for flower bulbs, but B) it is not necessary anyway. Since a refrigerator in good operating order should hold somewhere between 38° to 42°F (3° to 6°C), gardeners need not be concerned about apples and flower bulbs stored in the same crisper drawer. Still, if it makes you feel more secure, use one bin for your produce and the other for your bulbs.

Tools and techniques

Planting day arrives. The important decision is matching geophytes to their appropriate sites. Sometimes it takes me longer to decide where to plant than to do the actual work. Always be mindful of your garden's various conditions of sun and shade, well-drained or soggy places, exposed or sheltered. If you have good soil—that gardener's holy grail of high organic, moist, yet well-drained—then planting is easy and can be accomplished with a trowel. If it is heavier clay, then hand tools won't do. It is better to improve an area rather than individual holes, and a shovel is more suitable. Here in New Jersey where the soil is clay-based and rocky, I use a mattock.

First dig over an area big enough for a group of geophytes and also improve the soil by incorporating a layer of compost 2 inches (5 cm) thick. If the soil is sandy, as is the case in parts of Massachusetts, compost remains a suitable improvement. Should the site be wet, choose only those geophytes that tolerate such conditions (see Chapter 8, "Geophytes for Damp to Wet Places"), create a raised bed, or plant somewhere else. One useful technique for geophytes you know will need digging and replanting is to plant them with a thin layer of yellow sand over their tops, before back-filling with soil. That way, when you dig them up, the yellow sand reminds you that you're getting close and should excavate more carefully. When cherry tomatoes and berries came in perforated one-pint plastic baskets, I would use them to plant cyclamen and other small treasures. Again, the idea was to make it easy to dig the buried geophyte without damaging it or losing offsets.

I never use the tin-can-on-a-stick, the so-called bulb planter tool. For my soil, it is too flimsy, and I do not like the "one-size-fits-all" approach, where little crocus, moderate tulip, and huge crown imperial bulbs are all supposed to manage with identically sized holes. A sturdier version called a "naturalizer tool" is available that should work

Though useful in any site, the naturalizer tool on the left is the best choice in heavier soils with tree roots and stones or for plugging bulbs into ground covers. The heavy-duty bulb planter on the right, with its sturdy stainless steel tube, is intended for use in better prepared, more open loam soils.
Photo courtesy of Brent Heath/Brent and Becky's Bulbs.

satisfactorily in good—that is, a light, loamy—soil. It is a fish tail–shaped steel tool mounted on a sturdy shaft with a crossbar toward the base. I jab the tool's points in the ground, jump onto the crossbar with both feet, ram it into the ground, step off, wiggle it back and forth, and a nice hole opens up for small- to moderate-sized geophytes. Mine has been used so much that the red paint is worn off to the depth I drive it into the soil.

Where I want to prepare an area rather than just individual holes, an 8 pound mattock works quite well in my heavy soil. It has a wide, flat blade for turning soil and mixing in amendments at one end of the metal head, and at the other end a more pointed shape is handy for prying up rocks and roots. I know some people swear by electric augers, which are like oversized drill bits. If you have a smaller garden with decent soil, one of these would probably work well. Because too many rocks and tree roots are in my soil, and I don't have an extension cord long enough to reach down into the woods where most of my geophytes are planted, this method doesn't work for me. A cordless drill is more portable than the plug-in kind, but it will frequently will run out of juice before all your geophytes are planted. Plan on having a back-up battery, fully charged and ready to go. Nell Jean Campbell in Colquitt, Georgia, uses a post-hole digger if she has only a few dozen geophytes to plant. Given her sandy soil, this is a feasible technique. The tool, with a pair of wooden handles at the top and a pair of curved, vertical scoops at the bottom, makes a big enough hole for two, three, or four geophytes to nestle closely together. When she has more to plant, like several hundred, Nell gets serious and uses a power-take-off hole-digger on her tractor. It makes a hole 8 inches (20 cm) in diameter, big enough for her to put in three, four, or five geophytes. Now, clearly, two people working together with one to dig and the other to drop in the geophytes will really speed things along. Even so, using hand tools with my unimproved soil and working by myself, I can plant about 100 daffodils or 500 small geophytes in an hour.

Dr. Barad drills and Chris Stout does the planting as two pairs of hands and an electric auger make light work of planting tulip bulbs in well-prepared soil. Photo by author.

Fertilizers

Often, the only fertilization I give geophytes grown in a casual manner in my woods is that which is supplied at planting time. Of course, when overcrowded groups are dug and divided, I'll rejuvenate the site with more compost and add some granular fertilizer at this time. It is important to understand the growth habits of different geophytes in order to understand the most suitable way to fertilize them. One major difference in geophytes is between those that flower in early to mid-spring and then go dormant and those that grow in summer. Nutrients in the soil are available to plants when microorganisms are active, usually around 52°F (11°C) and above. The early geophytes are making their growth while the soil is still cooler than this and are drawing on the reserves stored within the bulb, corm, or tuber. Nitrogen is important for leaf growth, but the elements most closely associated with root and shoot growth, overall plant health, flowering, and fruit production are phosphorus and potash (potassium). Phosphorus and potash remain relatively static in the soil, so I believe it is important to get them down where the roots will be growing. Incorporating fertilizer at planting time is the best option. I often use a 5-10-10 or 10-20-20 general fertilizer. If I am using single-element fertilizers, I then use muriate of potash and superphosphate. Their nutrients are more quickly available to plants. Since chemically they are salts, these inorganic fertilizers can also burn roots and the basal plates on bulbs and corms. It is important to incorporate these fertilizers with the compost-amended soil at the bottom of the planting holes, and then cover it with a thin layer of soil before planting the geophytes. Organic gardeners can use various rock dusts, green sand, and other mineral supplements.

Notice that I have not mentioned bone meal. Even if it were an excellent fertilizer (which it is not), using bone meal in the garden is probably not a good idea. The way I understand it, in olden times bone meal was manufactured from fresh bones that still had some meat scraps attached. Today, bones are steamed to extract fat from the marrow, which is used to manufacture who knows what, soap perhaps. As well, the bones are mechanically scraped clean of meat scraps to be used for other by-products. Then bone itself is processed for gelatin. So much of what previously would have been incorporated as plant nutrient is removed; what is left is nearly pure calcium phosphate, which is just about insoluble. I believe that bone meal is a poor fertilizer, low in nutrients, and attractive to every dog and skunk in the neighborhood. They will come digging for the bones they think are buried and in the process uproot the geophytes. These days, though, there is more to concern the gardener than the efficacy or lack thereof of bone meal as a nutrient or the nuisance value of attracting skunks and dogs: it might just kill you. Bovine spongiform encephalopathy, BSE for short, is a rare, brain-rotting disease thought to be primarily transmitted from the brain tissue of infected cattle. Jim Shields, who enthusiastically grows bulbs as an avocation, explains the risks thusly:

"Putting on my professional hat (biochemist, protein chemist), I would say that there has to be a possibility of contracting BSE through bone meal. The agent is a prion, a rearranged version of a normal body protein. The rearranged form, actually refolded, is then pathogenic. Steam does not inactivate it; and neither, obviously, do digestive enzymes in the gut. Breathing the dust should work even better than eating it if you want to contract the disease. Its manifestation in humans is known as vCJD, or the variant of Creutzfeld-Jacobs Disease. People who want to sell you bone meal and other animal byproducts will vigorously dispute this. There are also people who dispute that we are undergoing global warming. In cases where future personal profits are involved, the value of the opinions offered should be seriously questioned. I have banished all forms of bone meal from my garden, permanently. It is not worth the risk. Even though that risk should be very small, it is not equal to zero. Getting vCJD would be a really unpleasant way to die." Even organic gardeners should look for an alternative fertilizer.

In the occasional situation when I think geophytes that flower in spring need a "pick-me-up," my preference is for water-soluble fertilizer with a 10-30-20 ratio. Though available to the plant only for a short time after application, liquid fertilizers are quick acting and can be absorbed as a foliar feed, through the plants' leaves—a useful attribute when the soil is still too cool for microorganisms to be active. It is better to use a liquid fertilizer for foliar feeding on a sunny day with relatively low humidity. If the liquid stays on the leaves for an extended period (as would be likely on a humid, overcast day), the chances of fungal diseases are increased. Rather than a single, concentrated dose, I use liquid fertilizers at half the recommended strength. If the label suggests one tablespoon to a gallon of water, I either mix one-half tablespoon to a gallon of water or a full tablespoon to two gallons. I apply the first half-strength feeding when the leaves are fully developed, with a second feeding (still half-strength) just before the flowers open. Should time permit among the rush of other springtime activities, and if I made a note on my calendar, the geophytes get a third feeding two weeks after the flowers fade. I also use the half-strength liquid fertilizer when feeding seedling geophytes and when transplanting geophytes that are in active growth. This just gets sloshed on from a water can, pouring it over the leaves and adjacent ground.

Into the ground

When you think about it, it becomes obvious that geophytes possess the power of "vegetable locomotion." How else could their seed fall to the ground and the bulb, corm, rhizome, or tuber that eventually forms find its way down into the dirt? Even though geophytes will adjust their depth by means of contractile roots that pull them deeper into the soil, a good start from the gardener remains helpful.

The general rule of thumb is to plant geophytes two to three times as deep as they are tall. A bulb or corm 1 inch (2.5 cm) high would have 2 to 3 inches (5 to 7.5 cm) of soil over the top. Where the soil is light and sandy, you can plant more deeply. In a heavier clay loam, plant more shallowly. A few exceptions should be noted: Madonna lily, *Lilium candidum*, for example, prefers to grow with the top of its bulb barely below the soil surface. Other lilies, including both species such as *L. superbum* and cultivars such as the Mid Century Hybrids, are stem-rooting. In addition to permanent roots at the base of the bulb, stem-rooting lilies produce seasonal roots on the buried portion of the stem. Clearly, the deeper they are planted, the more roots they will produce to nourish the bulb.

For anything other than formal bedding, where the geophytes are arranged in orderly rank and file, spacing can be a quandary. In an attempt to create a natural look, do not toss them into the air and plant where they fall. The usual result, I've found, is that a couple hit me in the head, a few land at my feet, and the rest disperse into the fallen autumn leaves, successfully camouflaging themselves against retrieval. Instead, plant a group in a tapered oval drift, narrowing to a more-or-less point. If you have large numbers of one kind, think of a school of fish. Have your groups all swimming in the same direction. Make some groups larger than others. If you plant 100 snowdrops, most of the groups should contain 10 to 15 bulbs, with three or four, 5-bulb group-ings. The effect will be of established colonies with a few smaller, immature groups.

Another technique I remember reading in Marion Rombauer Becker's 1971 book, *Wild Wealth*, is her suggestion to think of a coarse net thrown over the landscape. Its meshes would crumple together in the hollows, and there the geophytes would be planted closely. On a slope where the imaginary mesh was able to spread out, they

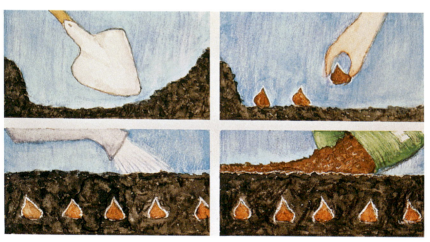

Planting bulbs is as easy as one, two, three, four: dig a hole; set the bulbs, corms, or tubers in place; cover them with soil and mulch; and then water. Drawing courtesy of the Netherlands Flower Bulb Information Center.

would be more widely spaced. Yet a third technique, used by my friend Sandy Snyder when she was planting little species tulips in her buffalo grass lawn, was to plant the bulbs along a spiral. We easily recognize straight lines or a grid, yet a spiral of flowers in grass does not present an immediately recognizable pattern to our eyes and so looks more random than it actually is. In the herbaceous border, plant daffodils and tulips in groups of ten. Set six or seven bulbs around the perimeter and the remaining three or four in the center of the group. I think it looks better when all the tulips or daffodils in each group are of the same cultivar. Each group might be different—ten white 'Mount Hood' next to ten 'Dutch Master' adjacent to ten 'Spellbinder'. The effect is stronger than three 'Spellbinder' with four 'Dutch Master' along with three 'Mount Hood' inter-mingling in one clump. When planting geophytes in a herbaceous border, keep in mind that the spring-flowering ones will be dormant in the summer when the perennials are flourishing. Rather than have too many bare spots to fill with annuals, allot the geo-phytes perhaps 10 to 15 percent of the space. If you plant tulips and daffodils adjacent to perennials such as peonies, Siberian irises, or daylilies, their expanding foliage will conceal the aging geophyte foliage as well as filling the gap left by the dormant bulbs.

In spring, Sydney Eddison's herbaceous border is a delight as daffodils and tulips har-monize with a backdrop of forsythia. When the bulbs are dormant, their absence will be concealed by peonies, daylilies, and other perennials that also share the garden. Photo by author.

After the geophytes are in the earth, they will begin rooting, something that may start as early as August (late summer) in those planted in previous years. Unless it is raining as you put your tools away, it is important to water geophytes after planting. The final touch is a layer of mulch to retain the moisture in the soil, help insulate it, and hopefully disguise the area so squirrels will not dig in the freshly turned soil. If the squirrels dig anyhow, an old window screen laid on the ground may deter them, as will thorny lengths of cane pruned from rose bushes or holly leaves with their sharp prickles raked from under the tree and scattered on the soft ground.

Out of sight should not mean out of mind; watering is important, especially if the weather is dry. Photo courtesy of the Netherlands Flower Bulb Information Center.

Propagation

Most home gardeners are not interested in producing large numbers of additional geophytes. But the magical process of raising new plants from seed, or cloning a few more from an existing one, is part of the never-ending adventure waiting down the garden path for those who are willing to explore and try.

Raising geophytes from seed

Gardeners who think nothing of sowing seed to raise annuals, vegetables, and even perennials often hesitate at the idea of raising geophytes from seed. There is nothing extreme or terribly exotic about raising bulbous, cormous, or tuberous plants from seed; all it takes is some patience. Brent Heath of Brent and Becky's Bulbs mentioned in a lecture that, typically, most geophytes flower in three to five years from seed. Dutch growers find it easy to raise species alliums from seed, and the blue shades of *Anemone blanda* are raised from seed, as is *Arum italicum*, some species of *Chionodoxa*, and more. If you do sow the seed, in a few years you will have flowering-sized geophytes. If you don't sow the seed, in a few years you'll have nothing. One thing to keep in mind, though: only species may be raised from seed. *Cultivar* is short for *cultivated variety*, and cultivars may keep their name only when propagated by asexual means such as division, chipping, or tissue culture.

Some points to consider that are different for geophytes as compared to marigolds and lettuce: Seedling geophytes will be in the same pots for an extended period of time, perhaps a couple of years. One very useful hint is to standardize the size of pots you use, rather than use a mixed assortment of yogurt containers, styrofoam coffee cups, and round and square pots in mixed sizes and various materials that will require individual attention to watering. Generally, a $3^1/_2$ or 4 inch (9 or 10 cm) pot is the most useful size for anything other than tiny quantities of seed.

Since the immature geophytes will be in the same container for an extended period, sturdy, long-lasting labels are a necessity so you will know what is growing in which pot. Anodized aluminum is the longest lasting material, with UV-resistant plastic an acceptable alternative, especially if the plastic label is pushed well into the potting medium where it is less likely to be broken off or pulled out. Use an old-fashioned lead pencil, which is longer lasting than "indelible" markers. It was Linc Foster, doyen of rock gardening, who taught me that there was a right way and a wrong way to write a label and that much more than the name of the plant should go on the label. Before you write, place the point of the label to the right. This way, since you are writing left to right, you cannot unexpectedly run out of label before you finish. Begin with the name of the plant. Perhaps it is *Arisaema thunbergii* subsp. *urashima*, which is written along the length of the label. Turn over the label, and write down the source of the seed. In this instance, it might be the North American Rock Garden Society seed exchange, abbreviated as NARGS. This is written across the width of the label, as is the third piece of information, which is the date the seed was sown. If the seed is large in size and modest in number (a likely scenario for arisaema), I also like to include the number of seeds sown. Additional information will become available in the future, such as the date germination was observed, if or when the seedlings were repotted, and the number of seedlings that were pricked out. Extra pots each receive a new label.

In general, you need to consider whether the seed should be sown fresh—as is the case for *Sanguinaria canadensis* and trilliums, for example—or if the seed requires a maturation or curing period. Another point to keep in mind, especially for Mediterranean climate geophytes: If it comes from an area with winter rainfall, it is better to sow the seed in the fall. If it should come from a region with summer rainfall, sow the seed in the spring. Gardeners in the Northern Hemisphere can more easily adapt Southern Hemisphere geophytes to the topsy-turvy summer/winter cycle by growing them from seed rather than trying to convince a bulb that January is winter and time to rest rather than summer and time to grow.

Monocot geophytes—anything in the Liliaceae, Iridaceae, Alliaceae, and Amaryllidaceae—germinate with only a single grasslike seedling leaf. Dicots generally have two seed leaves, except when they do not. Cyclamen, for example, begin by sending up only one leaf, and the same is true for trillium and arisaema. The other "leaf" is underground, making the first small attempt at a tuber. When seed germinates, it follows one of two patterns: In *epigeal* germination, which is the most familiar type and common in many geophytes, cotyledon leaves emerge at the same time as the roots. In *hypogeal* germination, found in peonies, some lilies, and certain other geophytes, though roots are growing below ground, the cotyledons do not appear above ground and nothing appears to be happening the first season. Leaf growth will occur in the second season. Seeds may have a lag time between sowing and germination. Annuals from desert regions need to have an inhibitor washed from their seed coat by winter rains if they are to germinate well. Plants native to cold winter regions often need a chilling period, called *stratification*, before they can germinate. Some seed, notably trillium and bloodroot (*Sanguinaria canadensis*), have a fleshy structure called an *eliasome* that is attractive to ants who carry the seed away in a distribution method named *myrmecory*. Keep a close eye on the progress of ripening seed on these plants or the ants may gather it before you do.

The seeds of some geophytes from fire ecology regions (*fynbos* and chapparal) germinate better with smoke. Smoke-impregnated paper discs are available, which are soaked in water that is then used to water the seed pots and improve germination rates. Diana Chapman of Telos Rare Bulbs in Arcata, California, uses fire and smoke with spectacular results for *fynbos* geophytes. She says, "I sow the seeds as usual in a clay pot in a sterile mix (Supersoil plus decomposed granite) and cover the seeds with about a half inch of decomposed granite. I then pile dry material on top of and around the pot on my driveway and set it on fire. I have tried different dry material, such as leaves, grass, twigs, and, when sowing Australian seeds, I add a lot of eucalyptus, but I'm not sure it makes much difference what you use. It probably is a good idea to mix in several different materials, though. Usually I keep adding more material as it burns. Also, after the fire has started burning really well, I add some green material to make it as smoky as possible. I try to keep it burning for about 10 or 15 minutes. After the pot has cooled off, I remove all large pieces of unburned material and water the pot thoroughly.

"I should add that I have used other methods, and they haven't worked as well. I've used the "Smoke Plus" papers from Kirstenbosch Botanic Garden, and I used smoke by itself from my bee smoker. That worked almost as well as firing the pots off, supporting the thesis that it is the smoke, not heat, that effects germination, though I have found that firing the pots was somewhat more effective than smoking them with a bee smoker. But this was also dependent on how long I could keep the fire going and how smoky it was. I usually tried to keep things smoking for about 15 minutes.

"I sowed some Australian seeds a couple of years ago, and divided them into four groups of the same species. I used smoke water on one, smoke water and scarification on another, fire on the third pot, and left one pot untreated as a control. The fire pot was spectacularly more successful than the others, and interestingly enough, the pot using smoke water had the least germination!

"Although it is theorized that the heat from fire makes little cracks in the seed coat thereby hastening germination, generally it is felt that it is actually the smoke itself that stimulates germination. There has been some research done in Australia regarding this. There are hundreds to thousands of volatile components in smoke, and it is theorized that some have the same effect (because they are chemically similar) to gibberellins, which have profound effects on seed germination and plant growth. Gibberellins are a group of plant hormones—there are at least 40 that are known. They are naturally found in the tissues of plants, bulbs, and seeds. I have also used gibberellic acid (GA3) on seeds with very good results, and the various gibberellic acids are extensively used in agriculture.

"I have tried using my fire technique on several other genera, not because they would naturally experience it in their native haunts, but on the principle that the heat and smoke seem to exert some stimulatory effect. It worked spectacularly on *Veltheimia*, of all things! I had a batch of 100 seeds that I treated this way, and every seed germinated on the same day about three days after I fired them off! It hasn't worked with everything, though."

Since the seedling geophytes will remain in their original pots for such a long time, it is important that they be sown thinly enough so that they have room to grow without crowding. I use a loose, open potting mix consisting of equal parts by volume of sterilized potting soil and one of the "peat-lite" mixes made up of peat moss, perlite, and vermiculite. Since the various potting soils differ from one another, if the resultant blend seems heavy I add sand to lighten the mix further. Next I water the seed pots by standing them in a pan of water to half their height. When the surface looks damp, I take them out and let the pots drain. Afterward, I usually top the pots with a thin layer of fine gravel, either crushed granite chick grit or aquarium gravel.

Asexual propagation

Those geophytes that naturally propagate vegetatively are easy to multiply. True bulbs such as daffodils and snowdrops make numerous offsets, which over time form congested, overcrowded clumps that flower poorly. If the clumps are dug in late spring as the foliage begins to wither, the bulbs may be separated and replanted. Keep in mind that the replanting takes more effort than digging up the congested clump. This natural increase provides the gardener with additional plants to use elsewhere in the garden or share with a friend.

In some instances, extra bulbs can be encouraged to form through special handling; it is magical. Not only can geophytes be propagated simply by dividing a crowded cluster of bulbs or corms, but more arcane, yet simple, methods also work. A single scale broken off a lily bulb has the potential to produce a whole new bulb. Slice and dice a daffodil from top to bottom, and as long as each fragment includes a bit of the basal plate and a smidgen of two scales, each piece can regenerate into a new bulb.

Division

The easiest way to multiply geophytes is by division. Dig up an overgrown clump of daffodils or snowdrops, separate them one by one, and as many as 50 separate plants may result. Dig and divide after flowering while the leaves are yet green. Brent Heath of Brent and Becky's Bulbs prefers to wait until the leaves begin to fade to yellow. (After all, he points out, you wouldn't like it if someone took your dinner plate away.) Remember that it is the foliage growth that nourishes the geophyte for the following year's performance. One mass of *Narcissus* 'Telamonius Plenus' (formerly 'Van Sion') daffodils gave me five or six flowering-sized bulbs and more than 40 offsets (none of which I could bear to discard). Prepare the new planting area with compost and fertilizer, if possible before the geophytes are dug up. Of course, if some are going back into the same site this is not feasible. Since the geophytes are in active growth, they must be replanted promptly.

Daffodils, snowdrops, crocus, gladiolus, and lilies are just a few examples of geophytes that frequently make offsets that can be detached from the mother bulb or corm to begin life on their own. This type of increase is rather obvious and occurs naturally without any outside effort on the part of the gardener. Daffodil offsets will remain attached to the mother bulb's basal plate for a couple of years. In crocus, crocosmia, acidanthera, and gladiolus, miniature corms called *cormels* or *cormlets* develop at the basal plate as the old corm withers and a new one forms after flowering. Generally, shallow planting encourages cormel formation, while fewer develop with deep planting. Cormels are easily separated from the flowering-sized corm, but they need to grow on for another year or two before they reach flowering size, which they will do more quickly if they are removed from the parent corm and grown on separately in a nursery area. Small gladiolus cormlets, especially, can become somewhat dried out over winter storage and are then slow to come into growth when planted the following spring. Soak them in several changes of cool water for a day or two, then store them in damp peat moss until the first roots appear, and then plant promptly. Or store them over the winter in barely damp peat moss to keep them plump and prevent the tunic hardening. Giant lily, *Cardiocrinum*, is monocarpic, and the bulbs die after flowering. The mother bulb, which took 10 years from seed before reaching flowering size, disintegrates but first produces numerous nonblooming-sized offsets. *Lilium regale* naturally forms two to four daughter bulbs above the mother bulb's base, the old bulb disintegrating in the process. It is when we want more new geophytes than develop unaided, or when it does not readily occur unaided, that intervention is necessary.

I usually propagate double bloodroot, *Sanguinaria canadensis* 'Multiplex', by simple division—dig as the leaves begin to yellow in late summer or early autumn, and separate the branching rhizomes so that each piece has a fresh shoot-tip for next spring's growth. It's been said they can be even more quickly increased from 1 inch (2.5 cm) sections sliced from the rhizome. The cut edges should be seared over a candle flame to coagulate the orange sap and then dusted with a fungicide and planted out in a nursery bed. It will take about two years for these small propagules to reach flowering size.

Chipping and bulb scaling

Other techniques for propagating bulbs require that the gardener perform some surgery. Hyacinths make a few offsets at the basal plate. For commercial purposes, this rate of increase is too slow, so growers wound the basal plates to encourage more offsets to form along the injured portion. The bulbs are dug after the foliage has withered away in late spring and then washed free of soil. Either an *X* is cut into the basal plate or the center of the basal plate is scooped out with a tool resembling a melon ball cutter. The cuts must be deep enough to go through the plate, and the wounded tissue is dusted with a fungicide. The bulb is then placed—right side up—so the base is only an inch (2.5 cm) or so deep in some dry, sandy soil in a flowerpot. Callus tissue will form. Commercial growers keep the hyacinth bulbs in a darkened area at 70°F (21°C) for a couple of weeks, gradually raising the temperature by 15° to 20°F (8° to 10°C). Over the next two or three months, the bulbs are stored at high humidity. Large numbers of small bulblets form around the wound. In autumn, these bulblets, still attached to the mother bulb, are planted out. The bulblets grow luxuriant foliage in spring, and generally the mother bulb disintegrates and dies. When the bulblets leaves yellow off, they are dug, separated, and planted out in rows in a nursery area, where they reach flowering size in about four years.

Crocus, which are corms rather than bulbs, are done the other way around, from the top. And most crocus (at least those that are not eaten by squirrels, mice, or chipmunks) usually do well enough on their own to satisfy most home gardeners. For rarities such as *Crocus sieberi* 'Bowles' White' that are often slow to increase, gently pluck out the main growing point on the upper surface and dust with a fungicide. Four or five cormlets will form from dormant buds on the surface of the corm. Of course, it takes nerve and a steady hand to mutilate something that's both expensive and difficult to obtain in the first place!

Narcissus are chopped, sliced, and diced in a technique called *twin-scaling* that also works with other bulbs such as *Galanthus*, *Hippeastrum*, *Hymenocallis*, *Lycoris*, and *Nerine*. Stand the bulb up on its basal plant and, cutting vertically, divide it in half. Each half is again cut in half. Continue cutting each piece into smaller wedges. Cleanliness is important, so dip or wipe your knife in a 10 percent bleach solution (one part bleach to nine parts water). A daffodil can be cut into eight or ten sections. It is important that a fragment of the basal plate remains attached to each piece. If the bulb has numerous scale rings, it can be further fragmented into segments of two or three scale segments, but each must have the all-important piece of basal plate. The smaller the pieces, the higher the failure rate, which can be as high as 50 percent for twin-scale pieces. Set each scale section vertically in a pot with a 50/50 mix of peat moss and sand, allowing the tips to protrude above the surface. Gentle bottom heat often helps things along. New bulblets begin to form between the scales within a few weeks. At this point, they can be moved along to a flat or pot filled with a soil-based potting mix. This technique is used to work up large stocks of a new cultivar.

Some growers feel that chipping a non-blooming, somewhat immature bulb gives even better results than using one that has flowered. Cut the bulb apart, and get the pieces growing. Once a new bulb has formed but before it reaches flowering size, chip it again. On consideration, this is akin to making stem cuttings of coleus or pelargoniums, where nonflowering shoots are preferred. The plant's focus should be on growth, not on bloom.

Lilies can be propagated by a somewhat different scaling technique. When newly purchased bulbs arrive, they are often accompanied by several detached scales that fell off while in transit. Each individual scale can be encouraged to form a new bulb. This can be done in the autumn or after bulbs have flowered in midsummer. In the autumn, dig the bulbs and remove several individual scales from the outside of the bulb. Take only a few—no more than the outer layer or two of scales so the bulb itself is not weakened. Dust the scales and the wounded area of the bulb with a fungicide. Very finely powdered sulfur, called *flowers of sulfur*, is an old-fashioned broad-spectrum fungicide, but I've heard of other gardeners using powdered charcoal as well. Put the scales in a plastic bag with several times their volume of a 50/50 mixture of barely damp peat moss and sand. Close the bag and keep it at room temperature (65° to 70°F, or 18° to 21°C) for about six weeks. Three to five bulblets will form at the base of each scale, but they will not form leaves until after a chilling period. Refrigerate the bag for about two months, after which time the individual bulblets can be detached from the scales. If growing conditions in the garden are suitable, they may be lined out in a nursery area. If conditions are still inclement, pot the little bulblets individually and keep them in a cool greenhouse or under grow lights. If scale propagation is done in summer, the scales may be stuck in a pot of sandy soil, upright and with the upper half of the scale exposed. Small bulblets will form at the base of the scales in about three to six weeks. Transplant to a nursery row without separating the individual bulblets. Grow on for a year, and then separate and replant. Alternatively, scales can be summer planted directly in a nursery row where the soil has been amended with sand to make it fine and light. Leave the scales in place for a year, after which they may be dug and the individual bulblets detached and replanted.

Another technique used for lilies takes advantage of the fact that some lilies, such as *Lilium longiflorum*, form bulblets along the stem on the portion buried below ground level. These form throughout the summer, and the 30-day period between mid-August and mid-September is the best time to harvest them (in North America). Pull the entire stem out of the bulb with a twisting motion. If only a few stems are to be propagated, heel them in a small trench, laying them horizontally and covering them with a thin layer of light, sandy soil or a mixture of peat moss and sand. Occasionally, give the trench a light sprinkling of water to keep the soil just damp. In mid-October, when the little bulblets have hardened off, they should be dug, separated from the remnants of the stalk, and lined out in a nursery area. They will reach blooming size in about two years. Some lilies, such as *L. bulbiferum*, *L. lancifolium*, and *L. sargentiae*, form aerial bulblets (more properly called *bulbils*) in the leaf axils. The number of bulbils that develop will be increased if the lily's flower buds are pinched off as soon as they begin to form. You sacrifice one year's flowers to gain more bulbs down the road. Some lilies that do not ordinarily form bulbils can be induced to do so. Disbud, and then, just a week or 10 days later, cut the stem back by half. *Lilium candidum*, *L. chalcedonicum*, *L. ×hollandicum*, *L. ×maculatum*, and *L. ×testaceum* all respond favorably to this treatment.

Interestingly enough, the hardy begonia, *Begonia grandis*, forms aerial bulbils (more correctly called *tubercles*) in the leaf axils. In mild winter regions these often fall to the ground and produce new plants on their own. Alternatively, they may be collected and planted out that same autumn where new plants are wanted. Where the begonia is hardy but at the colder edge of its range, the tubercles should be collected and stored over the winter in a refrigerator, packed in a plastic bag filled with barely damp peat moss, and then planted out in spring. *Pinellia cordata*, a charming arisaema relative that is not at all aggressively invasive as are its cousins, also forms a little tubercle at the juncture of each heart-shaped leaf and its petiole.

Propagation from cuttings

Another incredible technique for propagating lilies is also possible through stem and leaf cuttings. This is best done in summer, soon after flowering. Stem cuttings produce small bulbils in the leaf axils, as will leaf cuttings that are taken with a small heel of the old stem. Either of these techniques requires a moist, buoyant, humid atmosphere—either a mist system or a shaded, enclosed plastic box to keep the leaf and stem from drying out. The small bulbils that form must be handled with care, as described previously.

Muscari, *Hyacinthus*, *Veltheimia*, and *Lachenalia* can be propagated from a somewhat different technique utilizing leaf cuttings. A mature, vigorous, still green leaf is cut from the bulb. A complete leaf can be cut into two or three pieces. Each is placed, oriented as it was growing, in a peat moss and sand rooting medium, with the lower edge buried a couple of inches (5 cm) below the surface. Keep moist—high humidity and bottom heat are both necessary. In two weeks to a month, small bulblets will form on the bottom of the leaf, after which they can be planted on in a soil-based potting mix.

Dahlias propagate quite nicely from stem cuttings, much as you would multiply a coleus. When new shoots begin to grow in spring, take a tip cutting with three or four pairs of leaves. (The lower portion of the stem will "break" and produce two new shoots.) Remove the lower two pairs of leaves close to the stem. Dust the cut surfaces with rooting hormone and place the cutting into a pot filled with a 50/50 peat moss and sand mixture. Bury the cutting up to the remaining pair of leaves. Lightly dampen the rooting medium, and cover with a plastic bag. Keep in bright light but away from sunlight. New roots will quickly form, and the cutting can be hardened off. Planted out in the garden, it will flower the same summer. What's more, tubers will form underground, and these may be lifted and stored over the winter for next year's growing season.

Trillium present gardeners with an ethical dilemma. They are beautiful and we want to grow them in our gardens, but many of the plants offered for sale are collected from the wild, since they can take 10 years from seed to reach blooming size. While still too slow to satisfy the numbers a production nursery requires, home gardeners can easily increase the number of plants in their garden. First, get your trillium. Some native plant societies offer trillium plants for sale, which are either propagated from their own material or obtained as rescues from a construction site. Trilliums grow along the leading edge of the underground stem, dying away at the back. Dormant buds appear along the underground stem, held in reserve—in case of emergency, if you will. If you remove the growing point, the dormant buds will start to grow. Do this carefully enough, taking a small portion of the rhizome together with the growing point, and you may be able to salvage the tip and get it to grow. Use a fungicide on all cut surfaces. Another technique calls for cutting a shallow groove two-thirds of the way around the tip, leaving it still attached to the rhizome. Dust with rooting hormone. New growing points will form along the wounded portion. If you have a large rhizome with several obvious growth rings, try slicing them apart into individual fragments. Dust all cut surfaces with fungicide, and pot up in a sterile growing medium such as perlite. A winter chilling is necessary to vernalize the dormant buds and bring them into growth, so it can easily take a year before anything appears to be happening.

Coping with Deer

I well remember how thrilled I was the first time I saw a deer in my garden. Of course, that was a number of years ago, and where I used to tiptoe out with my camera I now charge forth, hurling invective and rocks. These days, whether or not you plan on attracting wildlife to the garden, the entire Bambi family may come to dine. Not only are these creatures found in the wilds of Montana or rural areas—these days deer trot across Main Street in broad daylight. Their admiration for tulips is more gustatory than aesthetic, and the goblet-shaped blossoms are eaten the day before they would have opened. Deer also like lilies. I believe they appreciate the taller stalks, since they need not bend down to dine on the buds. Dahlias are another favorite, only in this case the deer will eat the leaves and stems before the flowers are even buds. Repellent sprays are one option, but they take repeated effort if they are to work. A three- to four-week rotation through different sprays—a scent repellent based on putrescent egg solids, sewerage sludge, strongly odoriferous soap, or bone tar oil, alternating with a taste repellent such as a capsaicin-based hot pepper spray. When you cycle back to a scent-based spray, choose a different one than that which was previously applied. I don't mean to imply that the repellent is applied only once a month. As plants grow, the tender new shoots must be protected, and heavy rain will reduce their effectiveness, so repellents need to be applied if and when they are washed off by rains.

Deer are high jumpers rather than broad jumpers—they can easily clear a fence as tall as 6 or 7 feet (2 m). Unless the lower edge is tight to the ground, deer can get down and wiggle underneath in a commando-style crawl. Two things I've learned over the years: deer do not willingly jump blindly, and if the fence is solid—a stockade or board-butting-to-board style—they won't leap over it into unknown territory. Another option is to use lower fencing about 3 to 3^1/$_2$ feet (1 m) high, but set up the fences as a pair. They must be too close together for deer to jump over the first fence, have room to land, and jump over the second one. You could pair up one utilitarian wire fence with an inner hedge or a more decorative wooden fence. If the pair of fences are made of high-tensile wire, string the strands at different heights on the different fences. Deer have poor binocular vision and will have difficulty distinguishing which wire is where. High tensile wire can be electrified; use a fence charger intended for use with sheep rather than cattle or horses. Deer have hollow hair that insulates to a certain extent, and a strong charger designed for woolly sheep is more effective.

These various repellents and fencing options are not guaranteed solutions. I find it is easier to grow plants, including geophytes, that white-tailed deer generally don't eat. (That's not to say that groundhogs or rabbits may not go after something that the deer do not.) Considering that my garden is not fenced and deer look in the kitchen window, I don't do too badly.

Deer-resistant geophytes

Many deer-resistant bulbs are found in Amaryllidaceae, the amaryllis family. Poisonous, and seemingly immune to browsing by deer, these include daffodils (*Narcissus*), snowdrops (*Galanthus*), and snowflakes (*Leucojum*). Gardeners in California and similar Mediterranean regions can grow *Amaryllis belladonna*, the true amaryllis, commonly known as naked lady. Other tender amaryllis family members include crinums, *Hippeastrum*, *Nerine*, *Zephyranthes*, and another naked lady also known as surprise lily or magic lily, *Lycoris* species and cultivars.

Aroids, plants in the Araceae, or arum family, contain oxalic acid crystals in all parts of the plants. Accordingly, all Jack-in-the-pulpit (*Arisaema*) species, whether native North American or exotic Asian; caladium; arum (*Calla* species and cultivars); and calla lily (*Zantedeschia*) are distasteful to deer. Perhaps because many of the Ranunculaceae, or buttercup family, are poisonous, geophytes in this family are usually ignored. Winter aconite, *Eranthis hyemalis*, is disregarded, as are various anemones such as spring-blooming Grecian windflower (*Anemone blanda*) and the woodland *A. nemorosa*.

Though Liliaceae, lily family, bulbs such as lilies and tulips are preferentially favorite food for deer, they ignore a few bulbs in this family, including ornamental onions, (*Allium* species and cultivars), every *Camassia* I ever planted, and the pretty little blue-flowered glory of the snow, *Chionodoxa luciliae*. Spring-flowering squills such as *Scilla siberica*, *S. mischtschenkoana*, and *S. bifolia* are also unharmed. Every fritillaria, from the stately but skunky smelling crown imperial, *Fritillaria imperialis*, to the charming and checkered bell flowers of guinea hen flower, *F. meleagris*, are also left alone. Grape hyacinths (*Muscari* species and cultivars) grow and flower unhindered. Confusingly called naked lady (seems to be a popular name) or fall crocus (which it is not), the poisonous fall-flowering *Colchicum* species and cultivars remain unmolested. Though hyacinths do not always do well in subsequent years in all gardens, since deer don't eat them they cannot be the cause for hyacinths' decline. Deer will, however, occasionally chew the tips off wood hyacinth, *Hyacinthoides hispanica*, leaves. Four o'clock, *Mirabilis jalapa*, is another geophyte that is rarely, if ever, bothered by deer. And a few more random genera that deer ignore include *Canna*, *Oxalis*, and *Cyclamen*. For more information on deer-resistant geophytes, see "Quick Picks" in the back of the book.

Plant Partnerships

Gardens are places where plants come together, hopefully with the result that they look better together than they do separately. Herbaceous perennials, trees and shrubs, ground covers and annuals, and, of course, geophytes form a living tapestry that changes through the seasons. That's not to say that only one predestined, correct, appropriate marriage exists for each plant, or we'd have little choice in the matter. If such were the case, a simple set of lists would suffice, and having selected plants from column A, a gardener would need only obtain the match-up plants on column B. How boring, and how sad that would be.

Perhaps I like naturalistic and you like formal. Some of those design style differences may be managed through placement of plants, but in part it is also their selection. More obviously, one gardener loves jazzy, hot, vibrant color combinations: bold *Canna* 'Tropicanna', with peach, orange, and red on its sizable leaves, crowned with apricot-orange flowers joining fire engine–red flowers of *Crocosmia* 'Lucifer' and *Monarda didyma*, and the soft, lavender-violet spikes of gay feather, *Liatris spicata*. Perhaps that's too much after a hard day at the office and you'd rather come home to something more subdued and soothing. In that case, pair *Canna* 'Tropicanna' with the copper-bronze foliage of *Pennisetum setaceum* 'Rubrum', some lime-green *Coleus* 'The Line' with a thin reddish purple streak down the center, and *Lysimachia nummularia* 'Aurea' to make a carpet of chartreuse foliage. Imagine a quiet summer evening sitting out on a shaded patio with a glass of Chablis, and the subtle moonlight appeal of *Caladium* 'Candidum' or 'June Bride'. Their white leaves are easily visible, ghostly in the moonlight, accentuated with the fragrant white flowers of the August lily, *Hosta plantaginea*, and a sprinkling of white impatiens. Even if it is winter, if the garden is not buried in snow it may still be awake. The deep green arrowhead leaves of *Arum italicum* 'Pictum', the veins traced out in gray-silver, stand out against the white trunks of birch trees and the bright stems of red twig dogwood, *Cornus alba* 'Elegantissima'. Then in summer the shrubby dogwood's white-edged leaves still pair attractively against the birches, and white caladium provide a seasonal accent.

Consider the garden habitat. Are you dealing with shade, whether woodland or created by buildings? In that case you could scatter a carpet of little geophytes under shrubs and trees. An assortment of ground covers are also useful, such as running myrtle or periwinkle (*Vinca minor*), pachysandra (*Pachysandra procumbens*), sweet woodruff (*Galium odoratum*), or evergreen creeping phlox (*Phlox stolonifera*).

The range of herbaceous perennials to partner with geophytes might include hosta and hellebores, ferns and astilbes, or Siberian bugloss (*Brunnera macrophylla*) and a diversity of others. In sunny sites, choose peonies and Siberian iris, daylilies and summer phlox, yarrow, artemisia, ornamental grasses of moderate size, and more.

In a casual, naturalistic, cottage, or country-style garden, self-sowing annuals can provide the perfect partnership for spring-flowering geophytes. As the geophytes are going dormant, the annuals are coming into growth. The annuals not only draw attention away from the yellowing foliage on bulbs, corms, and tubers, but they provide interest at a later season. Begin by sowing seed over the area. In some climates this may be done as the soil cools off in late fall or early winter. Otherwise, spring is an option. Loosen the soil, rake lightly, and scatter the seed. Often, sowing half the seed in one direction, call it left to right, and the remaining seed top to bottom gives better coverage. Firm the soil lightly.

If young plants are available in your area, they may be spring planted. Plants, even small annuals, will be more costly than a package or two of seeds but will give more predictable results. Remember that if you want the annuals to return year after year, spent flowers must be allowed to mature and produce seeds. Daisylike flowers, such as calendula (*Calendula officinalis*), annual coreopsis (*Coreopsis tinctoria*), and annual gaillardia (*Gaillardia pulchella*), are easy, as are nigella (*Nigella damascena*), woodland forget-me-not (*Myosotis sylvatica*), larkspur (*Consolida ajacis*), and green-flowering tobacco (*Nicotiana langsdorfii*). Low-growing annual candytuft (*Iberis umbellata*), sweet alyssum (*Lobularia maritima*), California poppy (*Eschscholzia californica*), and Shirley poppy (*Papaver rhoeas*) can also be useful.

Texas gardeners make use of Texas pride, *Phlox drummondii*, a half-hardy annual native to that state, with white to pink, primrose-yellow, scarlet, crimson, rose, or lavender flowers. Some are accented with a dark or white eye, while others are evenly colored. Growing anywhere from 6 to 18 inches (15 to 45 cm) tall, they make a great partner for geophytes (and perennials, too) such as gladiolus, with skinny ankles that look kind of bare at the bottom.

Mary Sue Ittner's garden is on California's north coast. She looks for partnership plants that match her growing conditions and work with the geophytes she grows—plants that come from nutrient-poor soils and don't need a lot of summer moisture. A little trefoil showed up, and she is encouraging it. It is dormant from fall until spring, coming back into growth as cover for the geophytes as they are dying back. As the lotus dies back in late fall, Mary Sue cuts it back. Several species of *Lotus* are variously native to the United States; others have naturalized from their European, Canary and Cape Verde Island, or Tenerife origins; and still others come from Portugal and the Mediterranean. The low-growing, mat-forming species are spring and summer growing, with pealike flowers in yellow, orange-red, to scarlet or purple. Another plant Mary Sue likes is a low-growing *Zauschneria* (formerly *Epilobium*) with silver leaves and bright red-orange flowers. It is probably California fuchsia, *Z. californica* (*E. canum*), a charming, much-branched shrublet that Mary Sue cuts all the way back in winter when it starts to look scruffy. *Zauschneria californica* 'Dublin' (syn. 'Glasnevin') is a cultivar 8 inches (20 cm) tall with bright orange-red flowers. Gardeners looking for something more subdued could try white-flowered *E. hirsutum* 'Album', or pale pink *Z. californica* 'Solidarity Pink'.

Another plant that seems to be working well is muntries, *Kunzea pomifera*, from Victoria, Australia. A mat-forming evergreen shrub with stiff, smooth, and tiny leaves less than 1/4 inch (0.5 cm) long, it makes a pleasant carpet about 6 inches (15 cm) tall that spreads out as much as 4 feet (1.2 m) wide. What Mary Sue appreciates is the fact that the geophytes can come up through it since muntries doesn't root down as it goes. Small, white, feathery flowers in dense clusters are followed by edible purple fruits. As well, she uses lots of California annuals such as farewell-to-spring (*Clarkia amoena*) and others from South Africa such as *Ursinia*, which reseed themselves each year and come into bloom as the geophytes are fading. Origanums are also useful, as they are low when the geophytes are flowering and come into bloom later on.

I cannot emphasize too strongly how important it is to be aware of your local conditions. Not only does the Atlantic coast differ from the Pacific shores across North America, and the chilly northern tier of states differ from tropical Florida, but states and provinces have their own regional variations. California, for example, is a diverse state, with strongly varying conditions from north to south, coast to inland, sea level into the mountains. At Marguerite English's gardens, at an altitude of 3700 feet (1128 m) in the mountains of southern California, temperatures range from a winter low of 15°F (-9°C) to a summer high of 90°F (32°C), with extremes swinging 15°F (7°C) lower and 20°F (10°C) higher, with a few days of snow in winter and several days of extreme heat in August and September. Winter ends and spring begins with rainy, cloudy days. Gophers are a real pain, as are ground squirrels and pack rats. Marguerite grows several pest-resistant geophytes such as narcissus in the open garden, and she cultivates

Geophytes are available for gardeners everywhere—from the familiar assortment of cold-tolerant bulbs, corms, and tubers that are planted in autumn and flower in spring, to the equally diverse array of summer-blooming, tender geophytes that want mild winters (or storage indoors). If you plant them, they will bloom. Drawings courtesy of the Netherlands Flower Bulb Information Center.

many more in raised beds or cages made from hardware cloth or ¹/₂ inch (1 cm) aviary wire to protect them from the rodents. She partners the geophytes with sturdy perennials that can tolerate her challenging conditions: hardy *Geranium*, perennial *Alyssum*, perennial evergreen candytuft (*Iberis sempervirens*), several *Penstemon* species, and low-growing evergreen *Dianthus*.

Jane McGary is also in the mountains, but her garden is at 1600 feet (488 m) elevation in the foothills of the Oregon Cascades. Her exposed and windy, informal, naturalistic garden is in the maritime Pacific Northwest. It receives, on average, 45 inches (114 cm) of rain each year, mostly between October and June. Rodents such as deer mice and voles are a problem, as they tunnel and eat various bulbs and corms. As might be expected with that amount of rain, slugs are common and leave their slimy trails around as they devour flowers. Jane pointed out that many geophytes from the Mediterranean and American West naturally grow under trees and shrubs. Muscari, which she finds to be invasive given her garden's conditions, are restricted to sites under trees and shrubs and places where nothing else will grow. Jane recommends geophytes from steppe and desert regions as appropriate in a rock garden, in partnership with the herbaceous plants and small shrublets that would typically be used there. Others, such as large scillas and daffodils, and, Jane supposes, trilliums can grow up through ground covers. Living as she does in the country, Jane points out that a formal garden would look silly: "My garden extends into and blends with the surrounding forest and fields, and, unfortunately, the weeds and predators extend into the garden. I have little time to garden, and anything that survives here has to be able to fend for itself to some extent. I do select sites related to the preferences of wild populations. My garden has a wide range of slopes, exposures, and microclimates. There are sunny areas and both deciduous and coniferous shade. There are parts that I don't water in the summer and others that I do. I also have a large rock garden where I grow many species. In the rock garden and the bulb frames I do keep the environment under control." Jane casually notes that she grows around 1100 species of geophytes in bulb frames, moving some into the garden for trials as stock permits.

The best fertilizer for the land, it has been said, is its owner's footsteps. And, perhaps, our eyes can help. See where the snow stays and where it melts away more quickly. Watch where the leaves pile up in windrows each autumn, and where the ground is kept clear by the wind. Keep a garden journal—even something as simple as notes on a calendar—of temperature, rainfall, and what is in bloom. It will provide important information in gardening seasons to come. Visit gardens, public and private, to see what others are growing. It's not plagiarism; it's research. And remember, above all, that gardening is supposed to be fun. Enjoy yourself.

~~~~~~

CHAPTER 3

Geophytes for Temperate Woodland

Winter's grip relaxes ever so little and the first geophytes emerge from frozen ground. Snowdrops, *Galanthus nivalis*, push forth their white bells, and yellow buttercup-like flowers of winter aconites, *Eranthis hyemalis*, enrich the garden. Our native geophytes, sensible plants that they are, will wait a little longer. After all, it will be weeks until spring, and it is a certainty that frosty nights and days are still to come. This variable time frame depends on the wintry weather that precedes it. Should the winter be mild, these first geophytes awaken early. Growth will be later when winter clenches its icy grip on the land. Cold coupled with consistent snow cover provides kinder, gentler conditions than those that occur when such an insulating comforter is absent. Of course, the snow may have another effect: Michael Ruggiero, senior curator at The New York Botanical Garden, remembers one winter when the snow cover was so reliable that the snowdrops grew, bloomed, and finished before they saw the light of day.

Though their bulbs, corms, and tubers—even their flowers, stems, and leaves—may congeal with the cold, some sort of vegetative antifreeze protects these geophytic plants of spring, and that is truly remarkable to me. When I was newly married, the refrigerator in our apartment had delusions: it thought it was a freezer. You can imagine what this did to vegetables. Onions thawed to a soft, odoriferous mass. Geophytes that adapt to winter can freeze in the ground, but not in the freezer. Snowdrops become so stiff with cold that their stems snap when I pick them for a dainty bouquet. Stately stems of crown imperial (*Fritillaria imperialis*) that are 3 feet (1 m) tall will slump to the ground and then hoist themselves back up again with the mid-morning thaw.

These dainty harbingers of spring provide welcome assurance that winter is on the wane. They arrive, bloom, and then depart until the following year. It is, therefore, necessary to provide the appropriate partners for the seasonal dance—plants that, while perhaps not in flower as early as the geophytes, provide visual interest when the geophytes are dormant. At the same time, such plants should not overwhelm the geophytes—snowdrops are swallowed up and scarcely visible when buried in a coarse,

The early bulbs of spring must have some form of vegetative antifreeze within their tissues, for they seem impervious to snow and cold. Every year, March snows descend on *Narcissus* 'Rijnveld's Early Sensation' in my garden, yet it blooms unscathed. Photo by author.

Relative scale is important, and the giant snowdrop, *Galanthus elwesii*, is marginally tall enough to appear above the carpeting ground cover of English ivy. Pachysandra would have concealed it altogether. Photo by author.

mid-green mat of pachysandra (*Pachysandra terminalis*) and are much more effectively paired with a glossy, dark green carpet of running myrtle, *Vinca minor*. And it is important to look beyond the first and second spring to shade-tolerant herbaceous perennials and a handful of geophytes that arrive to enhance the autumn woodland garden, even, in a few instances, remaining through the winter.

Give some thought to where these springtime messengers should be planted in your garden. While you might be willing to trudge through the snow to see some early flowers, other family members might not be so enthusiastic. So plan on at least a handful that will be visible from a window, as advertisement of the garden's bounty. When planting smaller geophytes—snowdrops and such—I'd advise a minimum of 25, but even 100 is not excessive. And on my larger property I strew them around by the thousands. They are planted like schools of minnows, with groups of 25 swimming in the same direction, and smaller groups of 10, like sprats following along. Larger geophytes, perhaps narcissus, will make a nice display with 10 as a minimum number. Plant 6 or 7 in a circle with the remainder in the center and you'll have a good note of color. And by the same way of thinking, plant the group of 10 with only one cultivar. The effect will not be as fine when 3 yellow, a few bicolor, and a couple of white daffodils are coming and going a week or so apart. Remember that you are not dropping lollipops from a passing airplane. What's wanted is an informal scattering that folds over the contours of the land, suggesting a natural increase of an established colony and natural proliferation.

Geophytes for the Temperate Woodland

First spring, in my estimation, arrives with the first flowers in the open garden. Oh, I know all about the arbitrary calendar date of the vernal equinox in North America as the third week ends in March. But consider this—calendar advice is arbitrary. "Plant peas on Saint Patrick's Day," we are soberly advised, and some years it works. Some years you need dynamite for the planting holes. Phenomenology, studying the phenomena of nature, is more reliable. Moreover, it allows for regional differences. "Plant corn when the oak leaves are the size of a mouse's ear." Well, yes, it is difficult to climb an oak tree with a little mouse clutched in your fist, eyes bright and whiskers quivering, but you get the idea. Accordingly, I find that my phenomenological spring in western New Jersey arrives any time between early January and early March, depending on the winter cold, snowfall, and night and day temperatures.

That is, by the by, one of the drawbacks of the USDA hardiness zone map system. It takes into account merely the low temperature, not its duration or following daytime temperatures. Any gardener could tell them that there is a huge difference between nighttime temperatures that dip down into the 20s Fahrenheit (minus single-digits Celsius), followed by above freezing temperatures each day, and the contrasting situation where temperatures remain below freezing, night and day, for a week or more. Soil type also plays a role. There is a large difference between an open, sandy loam that is quick to warm up, and heavy, wet clay. Here in New Jersey my clay is not as bad as some types of clay but it does stay damp and cold. My garden in Connecticut had loamy soil high in organic matter, moisture retentive, yet well-drained. In retrospect, some of the horticultural talent I attributed to myself as a gardener had more to do with the site and perhaps less to do with my capabilities. Now that my planting tool is a mattock, rather than my hands, I understand the differences far better. And I know how important it is to know the garden—its sheltered nooks and exposed crannies, where drainage is better or worse, where the wind blows bare and where it piles the windrows of leaves. Make use of the microclimates to stretch the gardening seasons. And enjoy the geophytes that welcome first spring, others that close out the gardening year, and those that perform in between.

Snowdrops

"Rose is a rose is a rose is a rose" wrote Gertrude Stein in *Sacred Emily*, in 1913. While I myself love snowdrops, I'd be hard pressed to differentiate among a mixed planting of them should their labels be removed. However, the true galanthophile (to give them their formal name) can discern minutia not apparent to other gardeners. Proportions

A snowy drift of common snowdrop, *Galanthus nivalis*, sprawls at the base of an oak tree in the author's Connecticut garden. As attractive as they appear en masse, it is time to dig and divide the congested conglomeration of bulbs before they go into a decline. Photo by author.

of the outer three petals, gently cupped like a tiny Victorian cream spoon, and the inner, smaller three petals, which form a tube and are marked with green, the green or grayish green color of the leaves, whether flat, plicate, or convolute—this is the stuff of taxonomists. No matter; all are charming, and all are welcome in my garden. Three species of *Galanthus* are good doers, happily growing and increasing in the garden. The common snowdrop, *G. nivalis*, is readily obtained; another, the giant snowdrop, *G. elwesii*, is moderately available; and the third, *G. woronowii* (syn. *G. ikariae* subsp. *latifolius*), is the least readily available of these three but worth the search.

In the United States, snowdrops are sold in autumn along with the general miscellany of other dormant geophytes. Their little bulbs, looking much like miniature versions of daffodil bulbs, tolerate this treatment but would prefer to relocate while in active growth—"in the green," as the British phrase it. Of course, if transplanted in the spring, snowdrops need the same gentle handling you would expect to provide any other herbaceous plant with active root and shoot growth. They cannot sit around for a week or two or more, as can dormant geophytes. If a generous friend offers to share, or if your own planting is overcrowded and needs division, spring is the ideal time. Decide where the new planting is to be. Prepare the site with some compost and a judicious amount of fertilizer. Separate the crowded clump, and settle each bulb into place with a good watering; then mulch.

I have not found seedling snowdrops in my gardens. They readily multiply by offsets, though, forming such dense clusters of bulbs that they sometimes heave themselves out of the ground to lie around on the surface like little white pearls cast from some earthy oyster. I've discovered that snowdrops' bulbs, when dug fresh from the earth, often lack the papery vestments of purchased bulbs. When dug and treated for storage and shipment, they have nice, brown parchment jackets. Scoop them up from where they are exposed and replant, or just toss some compost over them to conceal them from view—either treatment seems equally appreciated.

Galanthus nivalis has two flat, gray-green leaves, each less than $^{1}/_{2}$ inch (1 cm) wide and pressed flat against each other as they emerge. The single pendant flower has green chevron markings at the opening of the flower's tube. *Galanthus elwesii* has glaucous, gray-green leaves, with one wrapped around the other when they first appear. Earlier into growth and larger overall than the common snowdrop, the giant snowdrop also has larger flowers. This species can readily be distinguished from the common snowdrop by means of the second green marking at the base of the flower's inner tube. In some clones, the two green markings fuse together as a solid blotch. *Galanthus woronowii* is a small snowdrop, with fresh, bright green leaves. As they emerge, the two leaves wrap one around the other.

Native to woodlands and forested places from western Europe to the southern Balkans, to the Caucasus Mountains and the Caspian Sea, snowdrops are easily satisfied and lend themselves to many places in the woodland garden, provided they have some sunshine in spring and are not parched, even when dormant in summer. These requirements eliminate conifers, Norway maple, and beech as companion trees. Choose deciduous trees that offer dappled shade, or in gardens with broad-leaved evergreens, such as those in the American Southeast, plant them at the woodland's edges or in glade openings. Suitably nestled against the roots of a large oak, snowdrops look charming.

A neighbor has a large star magnolia, *Magnolia stellata*, whose smooth, gray bark and sheltering branches create a pleasant frame for the giant snowdrops that are in bloom well before the magnolia's buds even begin to swell. If you want to provide a background, running myrtle or periwinkle (*Vinca minor*) is suitable in scale, and has the dark green leaves that provide a polished contrast to the snowdrop flowers. And a combination of magnolia, periwinkle, and snowdrops would create just the kind of design that complements both a casual or formal garden, suitable for town or country. I find shrubs such as deciduous rhododendrons and enkianthus are also suitable. Another friend has giant snowdrops in her lawn, at the shady edge next to a terrace. They grow and bloom, return year after year, but do not seem as exuberant as those elsewhere in her garden. It is not that they are mown down, because she is cognizant of the fact that geophytes need to complete their cycle of growth. Perhaps the turf itself is simply too much competition.

Of course when I moved from Connecticut to New Jersey, many geophytes made the move with me. It was like a treasure hunt, digging for buried bulbs, corms, rhizomes, and tubers that were by now dormant, basing my activities on recollections of where they had appeared in previous springs. The other complication was deciding where to plant them in the new garden. Since they had to be planted promptly, like right now, they went in harum-scarum. *Galanthus woronowii* got sprinkled along a rough path or track. (I suspect it was originally created by construction equipment, its appearance now softened by the years.) The result has been surprisingly successful, with a handful here, another there, planted as I worked my way uphill with the basket of bulbs. Shrubs along the way include witch hazel, *Hamamelis virginiana*, and spicebush, *Lindera benzoin*, which are native on the site. I planted some pulmonaria, which is now seeding about; a few hellebores, *Helleborus orientalis*; and ferns for later in the season.

Galanthophiles, snowdrop aficionados, possess an almost obsessive devotion to the minutia of plant variation, selecting and naming forms with small differences. Once graced with a cultivar name, of course the price goes up. Some you are likely to see in specialists' catalogs include the following: Handsome, early flowering, and stately (this is relative; remember snowdrops do not tower over other plants) *Galanthus* 'Atkinsii' starts the snowdrop season and often flowers in mid- to late January for me. 'Magnet' is another popular cultivar. It is a sturdy snowdrop with a nice-sized flower characterized by a long, slender pedicel that allows the flower to sway to and fro as it dangles. And then there is very popular 'S. Arnott', often mistakenly called 'Sam Arnott' or 'Samuel Arnott'. A substantial flower with a rounded, somewhat compact appearance, it is carried on a sturdy stem, good for cutting if you have an appropriate vase. (A tip that I read in one of Beverly Nichols's books is to place the vase of snowdrops on a mirror, thus allowing a glimpse of their inward beauty.) *Galanthus nivalis* Scharlockii Group is a snowdrop with an unusual form. Appearing as two narrow, leaflike green extensions above the flower, the spathe valves look like a pair of tiny donkey ears extending above the flower. *Galanthus nivalis* 'Viridapicis' accidentally showed up in my first garden. I had ordered 100 *G. nivalis*; what flowered the next spring were mostly doubles, and a few, five or less, had green markings on the outer segments. These proved quite vigorous, making numerous offsets and multiplying rapidly. It has quickly become a favorite and has traveled with me from garden to garden.

Obtaining the uncommon snowdrops is not an easy matter. When offered for sale in some British specialty catalogs, they are priced as you might expect. If a friend in the U.K. offers you some snowdrops from his or her garden, it is not as simple as packing them up and entrusting them to the postal service. With the intention of protecting them from overcollection in the wild, galanthus, along with cyclamen and sternbergia, are protected under the Convention on International Trade in Endangered Species (CITES) Appendix II (which means that although they are not yet threatened with extinction, trade is being watched). Going to a notary and swearing your friend's galan-

Even with a fluffy coating of snow, the green-tipped petals of *Galanthus nivalis* 'Viridapicis' make this cultivar one of the more easily distinguishable. Photo by author.

thus are bulbs of cultivated, propagated origin is not sufficient. Governmental-level documentation is required for both export and import. A permit from the Ministry of Agriculture and Fisheries, Plant Health Administrative Unit, is needed to get them out of the country. A matching permit from Animal and Plant Health Inspection Service (APHIS) PEQ / Permit Unit is required to bring them into the United States. And additional requirements are necessary for a phytosanitary certificate. Fortunately, some domestic mail-order sources make life easier for the serious amateur collector in the United States.

The rarest snowdrop I ever had was the autumn-blooming *Galanthus reginae-olgae*. Her October visits and mysterious disappearance are described in Chapter 10, "Geophytes for the Autumn Garden."

Double snowdrops are a problem for me. My ideal is the delicate grace owned by the single flower, and the doubles all too often remind me of an excess of ruffled petticoats. That said, the Greatorex double *Galanthus* 'Desdemona' does have a certain appeal. H. A. Greatorex of Norwich was an English galanthophile who raised a number of double-flowered snowdrops from *G. plicatus* in the 1940s: 'Cordelia', 'Desdemona', 'Dionysus', 'Hippolyta', 'Jacquenetta', 'Lavinia', 'Nerissa', 'Ophelia', and 'Titania'. Some are said to be better than others, but the only one I am familiar with is Othello's unfortunate spouse. I think they need the right site, next to a path in an obviously cultivated setting, rather than off in the woods pretending to be wildings.

The straight species, *Galanthus plicatus*, is a fine snowdrop. The two leaves press flat against each other as they emerge from the ground, and when they mature they display a unique backward roll along the edge. Leaf color varies from bright green, similar to *G. woronowii*, to mat green or even somewhat glaucous. Nina Lambert of Ithaca, New York, finds that the "clumpers," particularly the doubles, need to be lifted and divided and/or drenched with a fungicide. She has lost all of the doubles to fungus attacks, though the three older gardeners who gave her the bulbs did not have similar troubles. She also has trouble keeping *G. elwesii*, and doesn't know why, except that it does not reappear after a winter with prolonged snow cover.

Charming as they are, many more snowdrops are out there than are actually deserving of a cultivar name. Just consider what Dr. John Lonsdale has to say about this, and keep in mind that it comes from a man passionate about bulbs. Edgewood, his extraordinary garden spilling down a Pennsylvania hillside shaded by mature oak trees, is filled with little bulbs he has raised from seed. He has a greenhouse filled with cyclamen, species crocus, rare iris, a diversity of *Narcissus bulbocodium*, and more—again, that he has raised from seed and nurtured to maturity. Withal, he refuses to be stodgily pedantic. In fact, when it comes to dealing with the classification and identification of more than 700 named species and varieties of snowdrops, he finds the whole thing rather funny.

"I defy anyone, especially *Galanthus* experts, to accurately identify more than 5 to 10 percent of any of the snowdrops put in front of them. It would be great fun to have the equivalent of a double blind, placebo controlled 'clinical trial' using snowdrops as the 'drugs.' The results would be hilarious, and no FDA panel would recommend approval of any more novelties. Every genetically distinct snowdrop is unique. They just don't need naming. They might deserve to be grown, but most will never get into general circulation. Those that do will soon be hopelessly mislabeled and misidentified. They will never again be correctly identified, because they are so intrinsically variable and similar to the zillion other unique ones that look just like them. I love the use of phrases such as 'most likely to be the latter as it is more readily available.'"

Snowflakes

One spring day when we still lived in Wilton, Connecticut, I was visiting my friend Judy Restuccia. Over a cup of tea and mixed with some garden chitchat, I mentioned that my snowdrops were in bloom. Hers were also, she told me, and with teacups in hand we strolled out to take a look. Great excitement, for her "snowdrops" were instead spring snowflake, *Leucojum vernum*. Flowering as early as the main flush of galanthus—which is to say, in early spring (March in Connecticut)—the spring snowflake has a bell-like flower, white with a green dot at the tip of each of the six fused petals. The

A combination for early spring (late March in New Jersey) pairs spring snowflake (*Leucojum vernum*) with Christmas rose (*Helleborus niger*) for a frosty play of white on white in the garden. Photo by author.

leaves are a rich green and emerge as the flowers are just expanding. Spring snowflake has one or rarely two flowers to a stem, and it prefers somewhat damper conditions than do snowdrops.

The reason behind my jubilation is that when ordering spring snowflake, all too often the unwitting gardener receives instead the summer snowflake, *Leucojum aestivum*. (Snowflake species are conveniently named for the season of their bloom: *vernum* relating to the vernal season of spring; *aestivum* referring to aestivale, or summer season; and—you guessed it—*autumnale*, the autumn-blooming snowflake.) Clearly, these had been planted by the previous owner, now deceased, so there was no one to ask where the bulbs had first come from. So off to the toolshed for a trowel and a pot, and a precious start of this delightful bulb came home with me. They settled down and began multiplying, as bulbs will when they are happy with their growing conditions. Fortunate that Judy had shared with me, because a couple of years later her septic system failed and what the backhoe didn't dig up, it rumbled across and compacted into the ground. Happily, I was able to share back some snowflakes. Naturally, some moved to New Jersey with me. I tucked them in along the banks of the intermittent drainage creek, with small deciduous ferns to hold the space when dormant (bare ground being an inducement for weeds to grow or absent-minded gardeners attempting to plant something else). Snowflakes prefer a moist soil, something Nina Lambert and I agree on. The higher portion of her Ithaca, New York, garden has sandy soil, and she notes that "keeping *Leucojum vernum* has been a consistent problem. Only the ones that have come from you have done well. They want more moisture in the spring than most people realize. By the way, Dick Redfield [a skillful and experienced rock gardener in Scotland, Connecticut] has found them to self-sow by his stream. Gorgeous."

By whatever means you have obtained them, plant spring snowflakes in groups of 10 or more. A partly shaded site is preferred—one that does not get too dry in summer. As with other woodland geophytes, dig some compost or leaf mould into the soil before planting. Set the small bulbs twice as deep as they are tall, about 2 or 3 inches (5 to 7.5 cm) below the soil surface. Water and then mulch the area with shredded leaves or composted wood chips. Spring snowflake can be moved just as the flowers wither, replanting as soon as possible after digging them up.

Winter aconite

According to W. E. Sherwell-Cooper in *The ABC of Bulbs and Corms* (1951), winter aconites "look very charming indeed when growing among other plants in the shrub border in a half-shady place, or in fact, almost anywhere." I give that an enthusiastic second, since winter aconite, *Eranthis hyemalis*, is not only one of the earliest of spring-flowering geophytes, it is one of my favorites. (But I say that about all of them.) Winter aconite is in the Ranunculaceae, or buttercup family, and in common with other poisonous plants in that family is untroubled by the range of vermin that devour other geophytes. Only a couple of inches (5 cm) high, sunny yellow buttercup flowers—each bedecked with a frilly, green, leafy ruff like that of Toby in a "Punch and Judy" puppet show—spangle the ground in late winter or earliest spring. While it is a good doer once established, accomplishing this if you are starting with commercially obtained tubers in the autumn is not easy. When geophytes are prepared for shipment, they are given a drying or curing period. For the majority of them, especially corms and tunicate bulbs, this merely firms up their tunic, makes them sleepy, and readies them for the journey. Bulbs without a tunic are fine if they are planted promptly after receipt. Certain tubers, including winter aconite, are very unhappy about this. They dry to the point of desiccation. And, in my experience, many winter aconites do not survive the experience. Plant 100 of these inexpensive little tubers, wizened and looking rather like the trash that's left over after screening compost, and perhaps 20 will appear and flower the following spring. You can up the odds a bit by rehydrating the tubers before planting. Two caveats: Moisten the tubers with an overnight stay in damp peat moss; tossing them in a bucket of water is not as satisfactory. Second, once they are moistened, the tubers must be planted the very next morning, since otherwise they will quickly begin to rot. Since it is not possible to tell which side is up (if, indeed, it makes any difference whatsoever), I just loosen the soil and set the tubers an inch (2.5 cm) or so deep. Let them figure out which way to send their roots and shoots.

Those that flower in spring will afterward make a nice quantity of pale tan, tiny seeds, which germinate quite well the next spring. Once they have reached flowering size in two or three years and have in turn begun to reseed, the planting will quickly bulk up. Soon you can scoop up a trowel-full of winter aconite and distribute them around the garden with almost 100 percent success. Sometimes I collect the seed and sow it in a shallow plastic nursery flat that is left out in the garden. This gives me more winter aconite to plant (and share) without disturbing the existing plantings. But I am still a piker in this activity.

Elizabeth Lawrence wrote a wonderful book, seminal in my development as a gardener and in my affection for geophytes. Published in 1957, *The Little Bulbs: A Tale of Two Gardens* is the story of her garden in North Carolina and that of Mr. Krippendorf, her friend in Ohio. In it he mentions that one spring after the winter aconite had flowered, he "gathered and sowed sixty thousand seeds." Miss Lawrence said she did not doubt his planting but was dubious about the counting. He replied that "he had counted a thimbleful, and used the thimble as a measure for the rest." In 1971 she wrote a small booklet about "Lob's Wood" for the Cincinnati Nature Center, which had acquired Mr. Krippendorf's property in 1965. In it she writes, "And after more than fifty years (though no new tubers have been bought) they have seeded themselves, with the help of Mr. Krippendorf, all over the woods, and bloomed everywhere in drifts and sheets and patches." Quoting from one of his letters, she mentions how he wrote, "I hope I get a quart of seed this year. It will give me such pleasure to sow them. I scatter the seed on the ground without any preparation, and I love to see tens of thousands of seedlings with only one or two leaves, even though it will be eight or ten years before they carpet the ground." Over time and in a more modest garden, this same proliferation can be a nuisance. Nina Lambert finds that winter aconite seeds so prolifically in her Ithaca, New York, garden that it makes a solid ground cover in early spring, which is a problem for other, less vigorous, geophytes and small perennials.

I've not seen *Eranthis pinnatifida* offered for sale in western countries. It is native to woodlands on the island of Honshu. In Japan, it is poetically called *setsubun*, a name that means the eve of the beginning of spring. The finely dissected ruff of leaves and white flowers quickly distinguish it from the other species. A Japanese friend sent me some fresh seed. It germinated well, and I saw the first flower a couple of years later. An ethereal white flower balances on a finely snipped, gray-green leaf. The C-shaped stamens ring the center, with a dot of yellow pollen at each end. And a central cluster of violet stigma cluster in the center. I've been told that it is tricky to grow, susceptible to late spring frosts, and resentful of transplantation. Perhaps my expeditious sowing of seed directly in the ground (compensating for my sometimes neglectful oversight about watering seed pots) was a fortuitous compensation for difficulty in moving plants. As for the rest—well, my soil is a silt loam, and very acid, pH 5.1, on the slope above the

creek-side flats where the *setsubun* are growing. I'll collect seed from this year's flowering and sow it in another couple of places, a safeguard against frost, floods, and other natural hazards. When this second generation is up and growing well, perhaps then I'll see if it wants to move as tubers or only as seed. Meantime, I'll enjoy what I have.

Persian violet

Most gardeners are familiar with cyclamen as a tender pot-grown plant offering flowers in the midst of winter. That others are hardy in Zones 5 and 6 comes as a pleasant surprise. Persian violet, *Cyclamen coum*, flowers in earliest spring, along with winter aconite and snowdrops. The smooth, brown tuber with a

With translucent white flowers, *Eranthis pinnatifida* is an uncommon cousin of the more familiar yellow winter aconite, native to the woodlands of Japan. Photo by author.

gently rounded bottom produces both foliage and flower buds in fall. Roots appear at the bottom of the tuber, shoots from the upper surface. The round to kidney-shaped leaves, red flushed on the underside and dark green with variable silver markings on the surface, remain through winter's cold and snow. So do the buds, which will not unfold into plump badminton shuttlecock flowers until early to mid-spring. Most commonly, the flowers are a bright magenta or soft pink, with a darker blotch at the base of the petals, but a white form also exists. Once established, *C. coum* is quite drought-resistant and will thrive even under beech trees and conifers. In The New York Botanical Garden's rock garden is a lavish grouping of this cyclamen happily growing, flowering, and reseeding under some contorted pines on a rocky knoll at the back of the garden. Charming in appearance, cyclamen captivate those who see them. The difficulty is obtaining plants.

Nancy Goodwin of Montrose Nursery in North Carolina sent me a postcard in May 1990 that read, "If you still want those *Cyclamen purpurascens*, I think I can send you 10. No, I did not send my collectors to Turkey. What I did was to go through the stock on the top of the bench in the little greenhouse." The reference to collectors in Turkey is tongue-in-cheek, since cyclamen are under CITES Appendix II in an attempt to protect the genus from overcollection in the wild. One compelling reason Nancy opened her nursery was to offer a wide range of cyclamen raised from seed. Though Montrose Nursery is no longer in business, other specialty nurseries such as Seneca Hill Perennials—

At Rita van der Zalm's nursery, a plump tuber of *Cyclamen coum* sits at the appropriately opened page of the *International Checklist of Hyacinths and Miscellaneous Bulbs*. The small pink nubbins of shoots indicate the tuber is ready to get growing once it is planted. Photo by author.

Ellen Hornig's nursery in Oswego, New York—do sell propagated cyclamen. Or you can raise them from seed yourself.

The major hurdle to propagation by seed is that cyclamen seed is not widely available. In fact, unless you belong to organizations such as the North American Rock Garden Society or the Hardy Plant Society, which offer extensive seed lists to their members, it is hard to come by. Fresh seed is best, since old seed takes longer to germinate, but fresh seed is difficult to obtain unless you are already growing cyclamen. However, gardeners are determined and resourceful. Let's assume that somehow you managed to acquire cyclamen seed. Soak the light brown seed for 24 hours in some tepid water to which a drop or two of dish detergent has been added. This removes the sticky coating on the seed, which inhibits germination. Rinse the seed, and then sow thinly on the surface of a gritty soil mix. Barely cover with soil, and top with a layer of coarse grit or aquarium gravel. Water, and keep dark, damp, and (if possible) on the cool side. Fresh seed will germinate in a matter of weeks. Older seed can take a year. Keep checking periodically, as once germination occurs the young seedlings need light. Fluorescent grow lights are quite satisfactory. The first seed leaf, only one, is plain green. I usually keep the young plants undisturbed in the original pot for a year or more after germination. They soon form a tiny, tender, pale pink tuber. Keep the seedlings growing as long as possible. When they do go dormant, give them an occasional drop of water but do not keep constantly wet. Another method is to set the pots in a tray of sand, which is kept somewhat moist. Some seedling plants will flower their second growing season. When time comes to plant the tubers of *Cyclamen coum* in the garden, set them rather shallowly. Since roots form at the bottom of the tuber (except for *C. hederifolium*, discussed in Chapter 10, "Geophytes for the Autumn Garden," which roots at the top of the tuber), amend and improve the soil below planting depth, and mulch lightly. Cyclamen do not like wet conditions. Keep in mind that the natural cycle of a woodland renews mulch in autumn, which persists through winter, breaks down in spring, and is a thin, remnant layer in summer. Gardeners tend to maintain a constant mulch layer year-round, and this may not be what all woodland plants desire.

Tucked up against some tree roots, a vivid, cerise-pink *Cyclamen coum* lends color to the drab February scene at BelleWood Garden. Photo by author.

Crocus

Crocuses are commonplace in spring gardens. The Dutch hybrids, with their larger, chalicelike flowers in a rich array of lavender, striped, and white or yellow, pop up in lawns. Species with smaller flowers display themselves in rock gardens. They all open wide in sunshine and fold close their petals at night or on rainy days. What they don't like is shade—except, that is, for *Crocus tommasinianus*. Native to southeastern Europe—the Balkans, Hungary, and Bulgaria—in the wild it is found in light dapple

Tommy crocus, *Crocus tommasinianus*, spills like a smoky haze across a hillside at Winter-thur in Delaware. The only crocus that willingly grows in shade, it is also a good doer that easily and quickly multiplies, creating this sort of lavish display. Photo by author.

woodland shade, an easy explanation for why it does so well in a similar garden setting. It is happy under deciduous shrubs and small trees and weaves around under a low ground cover such as running myrtle, *Vinca minor*. Deer will eat it, but I think the crocus just keeps going along. Crocus have their ovary below ground, so once the flower is pollinated, even if it is bitten off by a deer the subterranean seed capsule will continue to develop and then emerge to scatter its seed. And this small crocus seeds itself about with happy abandon. While providing a welcome attribute in a larger garden (especially one such as mine with what might be called a casual or laissez-faire design style), in small gardens this habit can make it something of a pest. As well, it makes quantities of offsets.

Typically, crocus close their flowers on dull and overcast days, a means of keeping their pollen dry. The outside of the petals is quite often dull colored. When sunshine dappling through still-bare branches coaxes them into opening, the effect is far richer, with the warm lavender to lilac interior on display, contrasted with orange stamens. The straight species has flowers of a translucent mauve. Named forms with stronger hues include *Crocus tommasinianus* 'Barr's Purple', with a rich, lilac-purple interior and a grayish exterior; dark, reddish purple 'Ruby Giant' and 'Taplow Ruby'; and 'White-well Purple', with a purple-mauve exterior and silvery gray-mauve interior. I've seen the white ones, 'Eric Smith' and *C. tommasinianus* f. *albus*, only in pictures, so I cannot say from personal experience if this is really any improvement over the mauve to lilac and shades of purple that contrast so nicely with the brown scurf of last year's sodden leaves carpeting the ground. A handful or more of the small tan corms, each snugly wrapped in a fibrous tunic, tucked here and there into a corner of the garden, along a path, and under some shrubs will make a surprisingly showy, happy greeting to winter's end and the early days of spring.

Chionodoxa

It has never been quite clear to me why there is a quest for blue roses. Frankly, it's not a color that sounds alluring for a rose. Did I not read something about gene modification? The plan was that they'd splice delphinium genes into roses to obtain the desired result. No matter. What I find equally puzzling is the absence of an equal passion for the handful of already blue flowers, which includes several spring geophytes. Consider glory of the snow, *Chionodoxa luciliae*. If you want to see what can be accomplished with a grand planting of this simple bulb, what was done with vision and the time to achieve it, you could do no better than to visit Winterthur in Wilmington, Delaware, and stroll along the paths of the March Bank in the month that names it. Henry Francis du Pont painted with plants. He used them to create great landscape pictures, from the carpet of plants underfoot to towering trees overhead. And the March Walk, with its oceans of blue, is a sight to behold. At Winterthur, glory of the snow flowers in mid-March, with each bulb producing a few upward-facing, ethereally blue flowers that are paler toward the base of each petal. The petals fuse at the base to form a cup, and the stamens are a soft, creamy white, like old ivory. Now picture them by the thousands as they were planted and the tens of thousands they have become, given time to self-sow and multiply.

You don't need deep pockets or have to wait more than a few months to enjoy glory of the snow in your own garden. Buy 100 or so (they're small, quick to plant even by the thousand, and inexpensive) and tuck them in groups to enhance early shrubs such as winter jasmine (*Jasminum nudiflorum*) or the early Korean rhododendron (*Rhododendron mucronulatum*). Native to western Turkey, Crete, and Cyprus, *Chionodoxa luciliae* bloom as the snow melts and retreats up the mountainsides. Its blue flowers, with just a softening hint of lavender, are enhanced by a white eye. They are quite hardy and flower in my garden as spring is getting well established, in March.

Chionodoxa gigantea is an earlier, now invalid name for the species now called *C.*

The March Walk at Winterthur is more of a river, as scilla and chionodoxa pool beneath the trees. These little bulbs easily arise, flower, and then go dormant before the trees spring into competitive growth. Photo by author.

luciliae Gigantea Group. Usually only one or two flowers appear per 6 inch (15 cm) high stem, but they make a really fine display when grown en masse. If they are raised from seed (as happens when they start to self-sow) a surprising range of variation occurs. The typical blue with a white center is of course the most numerous, but others will display more white with only a blue tip to the petals, and some have more of a lilac to lavender cast. A white form is available on the market as *C. luciliae* 'Alba', but this has been a weaker grower for me. Confusion reigns between *C. luciliae* as it was originally described by Pierre Edmond Boissier in May 1878 and the form that has been trundling around gardens under that name. Let us refer to the latter as "*C. luciliae* of gardens" for the moment. At 10 inches (25 cm) it is taller, and it carries as many as 12 or 15 flowers. Taxonomists are having a great time deciding whether this is *C. forbesii* from southwestern Turkey or *C. siehei*—or maybe the two are synonymous. The flowers are blue-violet, with a prominent white eye. *Chionodoxa* 'Pink Giant' has clear, luminous pink flowers. It is a vigorous form that grows well in woodland shade where it retains its pinkish hue. I like it in combination with *Helleborus orientalis* subsp. *abchasicus* Early Purple Group, with its plum-colored flowers. Best with some shade, under sunny conditions, 'Pink Giant' fades nearly to white.

Even more intense color is found in *Chionodoxa sardensis*, which has an intensity of blue that must be seen to be believed, its concentration unadulterated by any white. One easy way to distinguish this from the *luciliae/forbesii/siehei* crowd, even while still in bud—the flower stem of *C. sardensis* is 6 inches (15 cm) tall and purplish brown. Four to twelve flowers per stem provide an abundant display from even a handful of bulbs. In a lightly shaded site at the edge of the woods I planted a goodly number, 50 or more, with 10 *Narcissus* 'Rip van Winkle'. The dwarf daffodil, a cheerfully tousled, ragged mophead of a double, like an exaggerated dandelion, makes a charming contrast to the blue puddle beneath them. The two kinds of bulbs have been coming back year after year, so I think it is a happy marriage.

As chionodoxa are finishing their display, the electric blue flowers of *Scilla* are beginning to open. Where the two genera are planted in proximity, they occasionally cross-pollinate. Then the bigeneric hybrid ×*Chionoscilla allenii*, a naturally occurring cross, with *Chionodoxa siehei* and *Scilla bifolia* as the parents, may occur. Flower color is a darker blue to lilac to rich violet-blue, becoming more violet as they age, and the flowers resemble those of its chionodoxa parent in that the petals are fused at the base. Those of scilla are separate. The stamens are blue, like those of its scilla parent, a helpful means of distinguishing chionoscilla from chionodoxa, which has white stamens. As with other bigeneric hybrids—animals as well as plants—it is sterile, so propagation is through offsets or twin-scaling. (See Chapter 2 for information on propagation.) It was first described in the late 1800s by James Allen, noted for his work with snowdrops, when it showed up in his garden in Shepton Mallet, in Somerset.

Scilla

Scilla is another genus of early-flowering bulbs for the shady or woodland garden. At first glance it is easy to confuse scilla and chionodoxa. Both are blue, both are small, and both have more or less cup or bell-like flowers in early spring with some overlap of their bloom time. Easy to compare and contrast if you have an example of both genera, but what if you are asked for a name when only one is available on which to make a diagnosis? Keep in mind that scilla have petals separate from the base and blue stamens. The petals on chionodoxa are fused at the base, and the stamens are ivory white. Another difference is that scilla have threadlike stamens, while those in chionodoxa are flattened and lie close together in a small cone. Some scillas are a glowing, nearly electric blue, while other species have quite pale flowers. They are deer, rabbit, and rodent resistant and—where happy—will gladly seed about and make more.

Most commonly seen in gardens is blue squill, *Scilla siberica*. It grows in light to dappled shade, under deciduous shrubs and small trees such as Japanese maples and dogwoods, as well as thriving in sunny lawns. Thousands flow, spill, and pool along the March Walk at Winterthur. The bulbs have a blue-violet tunic, quite rich looking and offering promise of the electric-blue flowers to come. The deepest flower color is found in 'Spring Beauty', a readily available cultivar. Another time, in a different garden and in a sunny site, I planted at least 100 scilla beneath 10 water lily tulips, *Tulipa kaufmanniana*. In full sun, the cream and rose tulips would open wide, creating the scene I had imagined of water lilies floating on a pool of blue.

Nina Lambert enjoys *Scilla siberica* when it is growing outside the boundaries of her back garden. She mentions that "it has self-sown into little swatches here and there down one of the little gorges nearby. It is fine growing in pachysandra in the front yard here." In the rock garden, she finds that scilla requires some restraint. "The scilla and chionodoxa get rooted out periodically, particularly where they share quarters with trillium and the less invasive species that inhabit the rock garden. They are wonderful (as are the *Galanthus nivalis*) in the wood lot sections of the yard across the road. There they are growing on a berm and a bank that are not watered and get dry in summer, and where the tree and shrub roots have made it impossible for the various cycles of new home owners to 'garden.' Yet they refused to maintain themselves here when planted under a large viburnum. *Scilla mischtschenkoana* [syn. *S. tubergeniana*] has had to be thinned often since the foliage is gross and smothers its neighbors. Several of the clumps have had to be reset often as either the bulbs have tended to wash out (due to wash on the slope) or else they have tended to grow (or heave) upward. The same for the large pink chionodoxa, which I think is 'Pink Giant'. The pink form of *S. bifolia*, unless carefully sited, is too washy to be appreciated."

I agree with Nina. The two-leafed scilla, *Scilla bifolia*, with its one-sided racemes of starry, soft blue little flowers is another species of which I am quite fond. Growing only a couple of inches (5 cm) tall, sometimes reaching 4 inches (10 cm), it mixes quite nicely with other geophytes that flower at the same time, such as *Crocus tommasinianus*. But I reserve my affection for the blue ones. The pink form is pink only in bud, and the best I can say about the flowers when they open is that they are not white, so dingy is the color.

Scilla mischtschenkoana is a bulb of another color. The name is a problem, since when plant names change they never seem to alter to shorter, more pronounceable versions but always morph into something more difficult to say and spell. I have no idea how to pronounce it. Sneeze, and I suppose you'll be close enough. The papery tunic is whitish gray-beige, an easy distinguishing characteristic that differentiates it from the red-violet tunic of *S. siberica* when both are still in bags or boxes. Also, in this case tunic color reflects flower color. Rather than an intense blue, the flowers of *S. mischtschenkoana* are a pale tint of barely blue, the color of skim milk with a turquoise line penciled

down the back of each petal. It needs careful siting if it is not to appear washed out. Place it so spring sunlight streaming through still-bare tree branches can illuminate the early flowers. Only 3 to 4 inches (7.5 to 10 cm) tall, this little scilla blooms before its rich blue cousins. In fact, it starts to bloom as it pushes through the soil a good three weeks before its electric-blue cousin. It is *hysterogenus*, meaning the shiny, bright green leaves follow the flowers out of the ground.

The only bulb with which it might be confused is *Puschkinia scilloides* var. *libanotica*. Not only do the two bulbs look alike, their range in the Caucasus and northern Iran overlaps. They are easy to distinguish if you see them side by side, for puschkinia has a short spike of drooping, bell-like flowers, and those of the scilla are fewer, somewhat larger, more open, and more widely spaced on the stalk. It is when only one example is present and a visitor to the garden says "What's that?" that uncertainty may set

So eager to bloom that the buds are scarcely above ground, *Scilla mischtschenkoana* opens its pale, skim-milk blue flowers before the leaves are fully developed. Photo by author.

in. A close look at the flowers will distinguish the two: in *Scilla mischtschenkoana*, the petals are separate to the base of the flower, while those of puschkinia are fused into a bell-like tube at the base. Named for Count Apollo Apollosovich Mussin-Pushkin, a 19th century Russian chemist and geologist who collected plants in the Caucasus and Ararat regions, puschkinia also has watery blue, bell-like flowers.

There is precedent to any confusion about which bulb is which. In the 1920s, Georg Egger, German consul in Tabriz, a town in northwestern Persia, offered to collect bulbs for the Dutch firm of Van Tubergen. What he told them he would collect was a very beautiful chionodoxa. Rather than trek into the mountains himself, he sent a "trust-worthy person," who, misunderstanding Herr Egger's directions, went to the wrong place. And did so two years in a row. However, each time, along with the unwanted puschkinia, he collected five or six bulbs of a previously unknown, very floriferous, early-blooming scilla. The unfamiliar little bulb was named *Scilla tubergeniana* and introduced in 1931, later to undergo a name change to *S. mischtschenkoana*.

Corydalis solida

If you like the color purple, the spring-flowering fumitory, *Corydalis solida*, is going to be a favorite. It grows from an odd sort of little fleshy yellow tuber, pointed at the bottom and flattened at the top, which, now that I think about it, resembles a miniature turnip. They don't appreciate being out of the ground and should be planted promptly upon receipt, as they quickly start to dry out. Dormant tubers are sold in autumn, and the choicer cultivars may also be had as actively growing potted plants in spring. In spring, plants send up two or three feathery, dissected, glaucous, gray-green leaves, reminiscent of those on American native dicentra species, and a stem of anywhere from a few to as many as 20 long-spurred, mauve-purple flowers. Unlike dicentra with their two-spurred flowers, corydalis flowers have only a single spur, looking more like a larkspur's flower. While in growth they form a loose mound, perhaps 8 inches (20 cm) high. After flowering, the plants go dormant and quickly retreat underground.

Native from Europe into Turkey, Lebanon, and western Asia, spring-flowering fumitory is a widespread, common plant of deciduous woodlands. Plants have been exceedingly happy in my woods, making sheets of color in front of green, pink, and deep purple flowered plants of Lenten rose, *Helleborus orientalis*. I'm thinking of spreading them under a star magnolia, where they could mingle with scilla and chionodoxa. Not only do the tubers multiply well, but plants reseed generously. Clearly spring-flowering fumitory is best in casual, rough woodland situations where they have room to romp around. Rod Leeds, author of *The Plantfinder's Guide to Early Spring Bulbs* (2000), would have you banish the "forms with very muddy purple flowers to the wilder parts of the garden" or dispose of them altogether. Either mine are not so muddy, I'm less discriminating, or I merely have more space to fill with plants and welcome spring-flowering fumitory for its generous bloom and undemanding nature. I agree with Leeds that various cultivars with better flowers exist, but these are still scarce and considerably more expensive when they are available, a situation that places them into the accent plant rather than "filler" category.

Corydalis solida subsp. *solida* 'Blushing Girl' has rich pink flowers. A single spring-planted tuber had multiplied into two by the end of the same summer, giving me hope of a small colony in the near future. 'Snowstorm' is a compact, creamy white–flowered cultivar, and 'George Baker' has rich, salmon-red to brick-red flowers—but at $10 for a single tuber, I cannot afford to plant large swatches. These cultivars do not appear to seed about at all, let alone with the prodigality of the species.

Corydalis cava (syn. *C. bulbosa*) is another, larger, spring-flowering, tuberous fumitory for the woodland garden. Rather than a little turnip-shaped tuber, this one gets bigger each year, also pulling itself deeper into the soil and over time becoming larger, rather corky, and hollow in the center. If you care to excavate an older tuber, it can be successfully divided provided each bit has a growing point. This species has two pale green, ferny leaves, and either purplish red or white flowers.

Wood anemone

Wood anemone, *Anemone nemorosa*, is a charming little flower of spring, with one or rarely two, six to eight petalled, daisylike flowers on a stem 3 inches (7.5 cm) tall. It flowers for me in early May, making a fine, if transient, carpet since it quickly disappears as it goes dormant. Typically, this wide-ranging woodlander has white flowers with the reverse of the petals flushed with blue. Found all over Europe and in northern and western Asia, various selected forms are available. 'Allenii' has especially fine, rich blue flowers, distinguishable from 'Robinsoniana', which has soft, blue-lavender flowers with a rosy flush on the reverse. 'Vestal' is somewhat later blooming with white petals surrounding a neatly tufted, petaloid center. Given the somewhat dampish, shaded condition that it prefers, the branching rhizomes spread reasonably quickly.

Wood anemone would be far more popular and common in gardens were it not for the fact that the slender, glossy, chestnut-brown rhizomes dislike digging, drying, and trans-Atlantic travel. Once established within a garden they are easy to transplant or even share with a gardening friend in the next town, provided you do so as the leaves are yellowing. Wood anemone dislikes disturbance while the leaves are yet green. Commercially, the rhizomes need careful handling, packed with some wood shavings or barely damp peat moss to keep them from drying out. And early planting is also important. Just like winter aconite, *Eranthis hyemalis*, wood anemone must head up the planting queue. Brent Heath is considering offering them for September shipment only. Pair it up with a light ground cover, perhaps periwinkle, *Vinca minor*. Japanese painted fern, *Athyrium niponicum* 'Pictum' is another good partner.

A buttercup-yellow woodland anemone, *Anemone ranunculoides*, has solitary, deep yellow flowers that make an attractive pattern over the medium, deep green leaves. Pair it up with pale yellow *Primula vulgaris* for a subtle combination, or choose lavender-flowered *Viola labradorica* with its somber, deep purple-green spring leaves for stronger contrast. (The violet's leaves lose the purple tones as the woodland canopy fills in.) Also found in damp meadows and moist woodlands across most of Europe and

A tangle of bare branches laces over the *Anemone nemorosa* that carpets the ground. Together with *Narcissus* 'Mount Hood', these early geophytes create a garden picture while most other plants are still asleep. Photo courtesy of Brent Heath/Brent and Becky's Bulbs.

western Asia, the little buttercup anemone has been grown in English gardens long enough to have crept into the countryside and naturalized in several places. Where the range of *A. ranunculoides* and *A. nemorosa* overlap, in sites such as Silesia, a darling hybrid occurs naturally between the two species. *Anemone ×lipsiensis* has delicious, pale sulfur-yellow flowers. I see it blooming in The New York Botanical Garden's T. H. Everett Rock Garden each spring and covet it anew, only to forget to order it each fall.

Anemone flaccida is an attractive spring-flowering rhizomatous anemone from Japan, with skinny, polished, dark brown rhizomes and exquisite flowers, their white petals surrounding a boss of golden stamens. Shy flowering, the patch in my wet woods near the drainage creek produces only a few blooms. Each stem has two buds, and the flowers open in sequence. The tidy clump of three-parted leaves, the two outer ones themselves two-parted, are dark green, marked with a silvery dot at the notch of each lobe. They seem to prefer constantly moist conditions and rather heavy shade, as they wilt quickly in hot weather before summer dormancy sends them back underground. As well as Japan, this species is native to eastern Russia and northern China.

The most commonly available anemone is the Grecian windflower, *Anemone blanda*. Its foliage, similar to that of a buttercup, is a pleasant foil to the daisy-like flowers of 2 inches (5 cm) in diameter in shades of blue, pink, or white. Their natural range is from Greece through Asia Minor to the Caucasus and Kurdistan. I have the blue shades planted along the driveway, where they happily flower in late March, well before the trees leaf out. Apparently content with their situation, they've even begun to self-sow. They seem untroubled by the occasional off-road event in winter when the pickup

Grecian windflower, *Anemone blanda*, grows from knobby tubers. The paler tubers on the left are how one purchases them, while those on the right have plumped up nicely following an overnight soaking in some damp peat moss. Photo courtesy of Rob Cardillo.

truck with snowplow veers a little off the pavement. (I think he perhaps uses the reflective driveway markers as a guide, since the tire marks go right over them—and the dormant anemones.) Rather than the thin, sticklike rhizomes of the other woodland anemones, Grecian windflower grows from a tuber. They arrive in a hardened, dried-out state and respond well to an overnight soak in wet peat moss. Two caveats: Once soaked, plant the tubers the next day. Rehydrated but unplanted tubers quickly become moldy and rot. Secondly, don't use a bucket of water as a quick substitute. The wet peat moss is definitely preferable. Several named forms are available: 'Atrocaerulea' has deep blue flowers and grows from small, buttonlike tubers. 'White Splendour' has large white flowers and grows from large tubers, usually offered as cut-up chunks. 'Radar' is an expensive selection with intense, cerise-pink flowers.

Wood hyacinth, *Hyacinthoides*

The taxonomists have had a revisionist hack at wood hyacinth, also known as bluebell. The two most familiar species began their career as *Scilla hispanica* and *S. non-scripta*, later being shifted over to *Endymion* before ending up in their current classification of *Hyacinthoides*. Whatever the name, what grows are spikes 12 to 20 inches (30 to 50cm) tall, drooping blue bells whose petals reflex somewhat at the tip, bloom-

Early in spring of 1973 I made my first visit to The Netherlands. The park across the street from Hotel Bel Air in Den Haag was filled with a carpet of wood hyacinths, *Hyacinthoides non-scripta*, growing and blooming beneath mature beech trees just starting to bud. Photo by author.

ing in mid- to late spring. Both species grow from a fleshy white bulb with an all-but-absent thin membrane of a tunic. The English bluebell, *Hyacinthoides non-scripta*, is recognized by its flowers that are arranged on one side of the stem, nodding gently at the tip. I have not found it to be a sturdy plant, but rather one that mopes along. Perhaps the warmer, even hot summers, chilly winters, and heavier precipitation in New Jersey are not to its liking. This is the bluebell of folk tale and children's stories, enchanted and made magical by fairies who would gather for their midnight revels, called to the dance by the sound of bluebells ringing. Nightfall was the dangerous time: children who wandered into a bluebell glade would be captivated by the fairies, and adults became pixilated until another mortal could guide them out. Children used to gather bluebells by the bunch as part of May Day celebrations, and even today the bluebells in bloom at Wisley, garden of the Royal Horticultural Society outside London, are appreciated as a token of the early May Bank Holiday. My friend Hilary Cox told me that her grandfather on her mother's side, Edward 'Ted' Brick, "was a rosarian of some repute in Hampshire. Some of my childhood memories involve riding in his car through the countryside and villages of Hampshire on a Sunday afternoon in spring. We'd stop by the woods' edge to pick huge baskets of bluebells and primroses. I can remember the fragrance still." And while she cannot grow primroses, English bluebells do really well in Hilary's Indiana garden. Rampant collecting of English bluebell bulbs from the wild offered a serious threat to wild populations, and legislation was enacted to halt the practice. However, these days cross-breeding with garden populations of the Spanish bluebell, *H. hispanica*, is even more of a problem. (See the appendix, "Bulbs Going Wild.")

Wood hyacinth, *Hyacinthoides hispanica*, is a charming bulb for larger gardens but can be somewhat of a thug where space is limited. Not only does it reproduce through offsets, but it also seeds about with gay abandon. Where space is limited, rigorous deadheading

A scene suitable for a larger garden, mixed colors of *Hyacinthoides hispanica* ramble though a woodland. The ferns make an attractive companion planting, not only while the bulbs are in growth but also for interest when they are dormant. Photo courtesy of Brent Heath/ Brent and Becky's Bulbs.

as the flowers fade will control the latter tendency, and the gradually increasing clumps are not as serious a problem. The fleshy white bulbs have a barely there, inconspicuous tunic. Over time they descend deeper into the earth than originally planted, which can make it difficult when you want to relocate or evict them. Shiny, mid-green leaves make an upright tuft, from the center of which arises a stalk laced with well-spaced bells. The typical color is a soft, medium blue. Cultivars such as 'Alba', 'La Grandesse', 'Mount Everest', and 'White City' have clean, white flowers; 'Queen of the Pinks' is a deep pink; 'Rosabella' is soft pink; and 'Rose' is violet pink. Good luck in finding these named cultivars. However "white" and "pink" forms are reasonably easy to obtain and are satisfactory for those merely looking for flower color other than blue. Here at Belle-Wood Garden I planted hundreds of blue wood hyacinths along the banks of the intermittently flowing drainage channel, mixing them in with Virginia bluebells (*Mertensia virginica*), lungworts, ferns, hellebores, and hostas. Along one smaller rill that feeds into the channel during periods of heavy rain I planted white wood hyacinth in between clumps of dark green Christmas fern, *Polystichum acrostichoides*, for a very crisp and appealing spring combination. The idea is to partner the wood hyacinths with leafier perennials to disguise the yellowing foliage as they age into dormancy in early summer.

Daffodils

Were Gertrude Stein to parse one of our favorite spring bulbs rather than the rose, it might have become "Daffodil is a narcissus is a jonquil is a buttercup." Late in the 16th century, Mathias de l'Obel developed a system of plant classification that focused on foliage. *Narcissus* included the wide-leaved *N. tazetta*, *N. poeticus*, and trumpet daffodils, while narrow-leaved kinds included *N. bulbocodium*, *N. jonquilla*, *N. juncifolius*, *N. triandrus*, and others. The 21 woodcuts used to illustrate these narcissus were also used in books by other authors. Even earlier, in 1557, Charles L'Escluse (whom you might better know as Carolus Clusius, of tulip fame) and Rembert Dodoens used the term "pseudonarcissus" in *Histoire des Plantes*. Then in 1585, when L'Escluse's book *Rariorum Plantarum Historia* was published in Antwerp, several of the woodcut illustrations were captioned as pseudonarcissus and others as narcissus. Pseudonarcissus, or bastard daffodils, had a trumpet as long or longer than the petals. All the "true" daffodils had a cup or chalice-like center.

In his *Metamorphoses*, Ovid relates the myth of Narcissus, a handsome Greek shepherd lad who was given the gift of eternal youth and beauty—but only if he never saw his own reflection. When he spurned the affections of the nymph Echo, she retaliated with the help of Nemesis, goddess of retribution and vengeance. As Narcissus sat beside a clear pool, he saw his reflection, became transfixed, and turned into a beautiful flower. As to *daffodil*, the most frequent suggestion is that it is a corruption of

Asphodel, though I find it difficult to learn when, where, or how the change was arrived at. What matters whether it was *affodil*, *daffodil*, or *daffodyl*? By 1629 when Parkinson came along with his *Paradisi in Sole Paradisus Terrestris*, things were in a right muddle. Rather snobbishly he chides the "many idle and ignorant Gardiners . . . doe call some of these Daffodills Narcissos, when as all know that know any Latine, that Narcissos is the Latine name, and Daffodill the English of one and the same thing. . . . " This linguistic befuddlement continues into modern times. The current catalog of a wholesale Dutch bulb vendor offers trumpet daffodils but large-cup, cyclamineus, and small-cup

Daffodils at The New York Botanical Garden brighten the spring landscape. Later on, the grass will be mowed selectively, avoiding the daffodils' leaves until they have matured. They are needed to nourish the underground bulbs for next year's display. Photo by author.

narcissus. In the southern and southeastern United States, any yellow daffodil, irrespective of its parentage, is in the vernacular called a *jonquil*, while in Arkansas the true jonquils (*N. jonquilla* and its cultivars in Division 7 that have *N. jonquilla* as a parent) are called *buttercups*. At its simplest, then, *Narcissus* is used today as the Latin name for the genus while *daffodil* is the common name.

As a member of the family Amaryllidaceae, daffodils are pest-resistant and generally avoided by deer, rabbits, woodchucks, voles, mice, chipmunks, and other furry fiends. Many are long-lived perennials. Some cultivars are great in regions with cold, snow-covered winters; others thrive in southern California or the American Deep South. There are daffodils for the formal bedding scheme *à la* Keukenhof, for informal naturalistic planting, for cut flowers, for the rock garden, and even potted for coaxing into early bloom while winter lingers outdoors and gardeners are greedy for spring. Daffodils are perfect geophytes for the novice or absent-minded gardener. I'm thinking of some that are growing in the front yard of a burned-out house a couple of roads over from where I live. They receive no care, no fertilizer, and no water. Yet every spring they reward the passer-by with cheerful yellow flowers. Their raggedy yellow and green double flowers in early spring suggest to me that they are *Narcissus* 'Van Sion', first introduced in the 1500s under the name of *N. telemonius plenus* and now registered as *N.* 'Telamonius Plenus'. It was Vincent van Sion, a Fleming living in London, who first grew the bulbs in England in 1620. As a cultivar, a cultivated variety of garden origin deemed worthy of a name of its own, the only way bulbs of this specific daffodil can be propagated is asexually, cloned through offsets or some other human intervention. This means that the bulbs of 'Telamonius Plenus' I dug from the shabby, weed-strewn, unkempt property (with permission, I hasten to add) share the same genetic identity as the bulbs Vincent planted all those several centuries ago.

The digging was relatively easy. Enthused by the opportunity, I dug three clumps; staggering with the bushel-basket-sized earthy lumps to my station wagon, I heaved them onto the blue tarp carefully covering the cargo area and headed homeward. What I should have remembered was the digging at the other end, when all the bulbs and their babies would need to be separated and replanted, each and every one. Unlike daffodils in autumn, carefully prepared for transit and storage, these were in active growth. The bulbs had roots at one end, leaves at the other, and would not take kindly to time out—out of the earth that is. Fifty or more bulbs clung on each of the three clumps. Perhaps five in each clump were of blooming size, with the remainder too small to flower. Remember that the offsets cannot crawl away from mother. They remain nestled snugly up against her, all competing for the local area nutrients and moisture. No wonder many were stunted. The replanting was not as much fun, especially toward the end of the 150 or so bulbs. But each one got its ration of compost, some fertilizer, and a gentle soaking to settle it into place. The following spring I noticed a modest increase in the number that flowered. After all, they'd been wrenched from the earth and replanted, so they focused more on reestablishing roots than providing energy to the nascent flower bud cradled with the bulb. By the third spring, two years after the move, the number that had reached blooming size were significantly greater. So the answer is that overcrowded bulbs are worth the effort if you are willing to dig and delve, and wait.

Daffodils grow well in light to dappled shade, and they also thrive in sunny meadow situations. When grown in a woodland, I've noticed that daffodils tend to face toward the sun. Pay attention to the orientation of your paths when planting daffodils, or you may find that those on one side are showing you their backs. While in active growth, daffodils will accept a surprising amount of water but dislike wet, soggy conditions while they are summer dormant or in winter. Daffodils look best, to my mind, when planted in groups of 10 or more, all of the same variety. I dislike the so-called naturalizing mixes, a random grab-bag of different kinds. If you want an assortment, choose the kinds you prefer, keep them separate, and plant with some attention to arrangement. Having tall, yellow trumpet daffodils in the same clump with bunch-flowered double yellows, a couple of yellow and red bicolor long cup, white triandrus, and other mismatches gives a thin, spotty, jumbled effect.

Use six or seven bulbs in an approximation of a circle, with the remainder in the center of the group. Plant approximately three times as deep as the bulb is high, more shallowly in a heavy loam and deeper in a light, sandy soil. Daffodil bulbs come in different sizes. Single-nose bulbs have one growing point. Double-nose bulbs have two flowering-size bulbs sharing one basal plate, and triple-nose bulbs have three. Not all classifications of daffodils produce double- or triple-nose bulbs; some come only in singles. But if you find an advertisement for a cultivar known to produce doubles or triples at a suspiciously low price, they are most likely smaller size, single-nose bulbs. You may have the same number of units, but they'll produce fewer flowers. As well as using daffodils in the garden, they are great cut flowers. Remember that when freshly cut, they ooze a substance into the water of a vase that causes tulips sharing

Dormant bulbs are easy to forget. Someone did not remember that daffodils were planted here and paved right over them. No matter; the daffodils pushed up and flowered anyhow. Photo by author.

the same water to deteriorate rather quickly. Condition the daffodils, keeping them in a separate container for a day or two before joining them with tulips. And some daffodils are good for coaxing into early bloom, flowering as potted plants indoors while it is still winter outdoors.

With so many daffodils, whole books have been devoted to them. Daffodils are classified into 10 divisions based on their appearance and parentage, with an additional, separate category for wild species. Other than the species, all daffodils are cultivars, or cultivated varieties of garden origin.

Trumpet daffodils are in Division 1, with a single flower on each stem and the trumpet or corona equal to or longer than the petals. They are reliably stalwart in cultivation, increasing at a moderate rate. Their flowers are instantly recognizable as they come into bloom in April and May in Zone 6, earlier in the southeastern United States and later in the northern and northeastern parts of the country. Many cultivars are available, with flowers of yellow, white, bicolor in yellow and white, and orange to red-orange. They vary in height from 12 to 18 inches (30 to 45 cm) tall. These are good daffodils for cooler climates, better in the U.S. Northeast, the northern tier of states,

At BelleWood Garden, poeticus daffodils line an old farm path. Their mild fragrance is more apparent when massed like this, making a welcome addition to my garden. Photo by author.

the Midwest, and Canada than in the Deep South. Use trumpet daffodils for more formal bedding-out schemes; in the perennial garden mixed with peonies, daylilies and Siberian iris; in large-scale informal designs; and in combination with trees and shrubs. I find that yellow daffodils make a better show when viewed from a distance than do white ones. Here is where the golden daffodils of William Wordsworth's poem "Daffodils" may be found, such as clear yellow 'King Alfred', which typifies our image of what constitutes a daffodil. The true 'King Alfred' is rarely offered these days, and its more vigorous look-alike 'Dutch Master' is a frequently unacknowledged substitute. 'Unsurpassable' is another "King Alfred type," with showy, golden sunshine yellow. 'Arctic Gold' is a warmer goldenrod-yellow, while 'Best Seller' is a softer primrose-yellow. Color is not a criterion for classification and excellent white and bicolor daffodils are available in Division 1. Today wider trumpets and rounder petals are more fashionable, but 'Beersheba', with a narrower trumpet and pointed petals, introduced in 1923, continues to be a personal favorite of mine. 'Mount Hood' is lovely, a classic with white petals and a creamy, yellow-white trumpet that ages to white. When 'Spellbinder' opens, the flower is a cool, lemony yellow. Then the flower undergoes an even more dramatic color shift as it ages and the trumpet pales to white. 'Mrs. R. O. Backhouse' is a daffodil with a pink trumpet, but its color is best under cool conditions and when the flowers first open. Not all trumpet daffodils flower at the same time, and 'Rijnveld's Early Sensation' is a yellow trumpet that blooms for me in late February or early March, standing up to the end-of-season snowfalls that often blanket it.

Large-cup daffodils, with one flower per stem and the trumpet reduced to a cup that is more than a third but less than equal to the petal length, are in Division 2. They bloom somewhat later in the season. There are good yellows such as 'Camelot' and ever-popular, two-tone yellow 'Carlton', which does well in most places and is even good in warmer regions. 'Ambergate' is a glowing bicolor, with rich, deep yellow petals and a bright red cup. 'Carbineer' is a subtler version, with lemony yellow petals and an orange-red cup whose color deepens as the flower ages. 'Flower Record' is a softer bicolor, with white petals and a yellow cup edged with red. 'Spring Queen' has a pale, lemon-yellow cup and white petals. 'Ice Follies' is high on the list among the most popular daffodils, with extra large flowers, white petals, and a soft, light yellow, flat cup. 'White Plume' has white petals and a white cup. There are pink large-cup daffodils, such as 'Louise de Coligny', 'Salome', and 'Pink Charm'. Both large- and small-cup daffodils bulk up well.

Small-cup daffodils in Division 3 also have one flower per stem, and the cup is reduced in size to a third or less of the petal length. They usually flower later than trumpet and long-cup daffodils. Some of these are good landscape choices, useful both for formal bedding or in casual, more relaxed designs. 'Barrett Browning' has yellow petals and a tidy, ruffle-edged, red-orange cup. Blooming early for this classification, it is a good choice for forcing. 'Audubon' has a pale yellow cup edged with orange-red, and white petals. 'Birma' is a deep yellow, with a rich orange cup deepening to red at the edge. It tends to bleach if grown in full sun, and dappled or partial shade, especially at midday, is better. 'Sinopel' is a fragrant small-cup daffodil that looks remarkably like the Division 4 poeticus cultivars. It has pure white petals that overlap at the base and a short little green cup edged in yellow.

Division 4 includes all the double daffodils. Since they can arise from any of the other groups, some have multiple flowers on a stem while others are single, and the proportion of petal to cup is not a consideration. In the garden, those with the fullest flowers tend to be a problem—when it rains they soak up water like a sponge, become heavy, and fall over. Doubling can occur in the petals or in the cup. Some are neat and tidy; others look blowsy and ragged. Personal preference will decide if you do or do not like double daffodils. They were quite popular in the late 19th and early 20th centuries. Several heirloom varieties in the Phoenix line are described in Chapter 7, "Geophytes for the South and Southeastern United States." 'Van Sion', now registered as *Narcissus* 'Telamonius Plenus', has already been mentioned. Another heirloom variety is *N.* 'Eystettensis', or Queen Anne's double daffodil, mentioned by L'Obel in 1581. It was named for Bessler's herbal, the *Hortus Eystettensis* published in 1618, and in which it is first portrayed. It grows a modest 7 inches (18 cm) tall, and the cup has been replaced by six gradually increasing layers, giving it the look of a tidy, six-pointed star. Confusion easily sets in. This is the double daffodil named for Queen Anne of Austria. However, the double daffodil named for Queen Anne of England, called Queen Anne's double jonquil (*N. jonquilla* 'Flore Pleno'), is a more rounded double flower, late-blooming, and 6 to 8 inches (15 to 20 cm) tall. *Narcissus* 'Pencrebar', introduced by Alec Gray in 1929, looks identical. Since he found it growing in a Cornish garden of the same name, I suppose there is the possibility that it and Queen Anne's double jonquil are one and the same.

Narcissus 'Cheerfulness' and 'Yellow Cheerfulness' are fragrant, bunch-flowered, creamy yellow and richer yellow daffodils with pompom centers, derived from tazetta daffodils. 'Bridal Crown' is a loose, open double with several somewhat larger creamy white and saffron-yellow fragrant flowers to each stem, that is earlier in bloom. 'Rip Van Winkle' is a cheerfully tousled little double, like a raggedy dandelion. 'White Lion' is waxy white with a few pale yellow petals in its heart, and 'Golden Ducat' is a sport of 'King Alfred'. Double daffodils always look gardenesque to me and seem more appropriate in a formal setting than in a naturalistic planting.

Triandrus daffodils, in Division 5, are classified based on their parentage—they must be derived from *Narcissus triandrus*. These cultivars have two or three nodding, fuchsia-like, drooping flowers to each stem. The flowers' petals are reflexed and flare somewhat back from the perpendicular with the trumpet, and the flowers are fragrant. They bloom late in the season and grow anywhere from 10 to 14 inches (25 to 35 cm) tall. Many triandrus cultivars, especially the earlier selections, have white flowers. Angel's tears is a common name attached to a species' form, *N. triandrus* 'Albus'. Apocryphally it is told that the name derives from that of Angel Gancedo, a Spanish boy. Tired and in a temper after a difficult climb collecting bulbs for nurseryman Peter Barr in 1887, he supposedly burst into tears.

Introduced in 1916, *Narcissus* 'Thalia' has long been a standard, with starlike, reflexed petals and a relatively large cup. Michael Jefferson-Brown, in his book *Narcissus* (1991), writes that some daffodils, including 'Thalia', are weakened by a virus that has infected commercial stocks. 'Tresamble' has wider petals, which overlap at the base. 'Liberty Bells' has flowers of a rich golden yellow, while 'Petrel' is milky white and 'Ice Wings' is a soft ivory white.

Cyclamineus daffodils in Division 6 are readily distinguishable by the reflexed petals that are the hallmark of *Narcissus cyclamineus*. The species flowers have the petals so strongly reflexed that they are in line with the little trumpet, "like a mule about to kick" according to one old book. Cyclamineus cultivars are among the earliest to bloom and have one or two flowers on stems 7 to 10 inches (18 to 25 cm) tall. They multiply well, their flowers are long-lasting, and I find them to be appealing, with great presence and personality. They are great in my woodland gardens.

Narcissus 'February Gold' (which never blooms in February for me, but a month or so later) works well together with such native plants as blue cohosh, *Caulophyllum thalictroides*. Blue cohosh starts into growth as the daffodils bloom and then fills the bare space with attractive summer foliage and pretty blue berries in autumn. Hellebores are another choice. Some cyclamineus cultivars are relatively short, and their aging foliage may be quickly concealed by smaller hostas, pulmonaria, and other perennials of modest size. 'Peeping Tom' is another good yellow, with an extra-long trumpet. 'Jenny' has white petals and an old ivory, creamy white trumpet. 'Dove Wings' is another lovely white once it ages; though the petals are white from the start, the trumpet is yellow when the flower first opens. 'Jack Snipe' is a bicolor, with a yellow trumpet and softly flared back white petals. 'Tête-a-tête' is a modest 6 to 8 inches (15 to 20 cm) tall, with two or even three yellow flowers to a stem. As well as for garden use, it is a good choice for potting up and coaxing into early bloom.

Jonquillas, *Narcissus jonquilla* hybrids, are in Division 7. Two to six sweet, strongly scented flowers to each 8 to 18 inch (20 to 45 cm) stem appear later in the season than do trumpet, long-cup, or cyclamineus daffodils. The short petals are flat, at right angles to the cup, and the dark green leaves are rather rounded and rushlike. Jonquillas are more heat-tolerant and can readily be grown in the U.S. South, where many other daffodils fail to thrive. They are very prolific and multiply freely. *Narcissus* 'Trevithian' usually has two sweetly scented, lemony yellow flowers on a stem 18 inches (45 cm) tall. A group of these, fronted by the smoky blue flowers of grape hyacinth (*Muscari armeniacum*), makes a strong yet not strident or overpowering color combination in the spring woods. *Narcissus* 'Baby Moon' is much smaller, only 5 to 6 inches (12.5 to 15 cm) tall, with buttercup-yellow flowers in mid-spring. Several jonquillas are named for birds: 'Quail' is soft golden yellow and 'Pipit' has flowers that open a soft lemon-yellow and the cup fades to white. Both are deliciously, sweetly fragrant, with the sort of perfume that wafts across the garden on a spring breeze and cajoles you down the garden path.

Division 8 is for the tazetta daffodils, bunch-flowering hybrids of *Narcissus tazetta*. Sun-lovers, they are discussed in Chapter 5, "Geophytes for the Mediterranean Garden."

More than any other group of daffodils, the poeticus cultivars are stamped by their ancestor, *Narcissus poeticus*, all of them exhibiting the crystalline white petals and

Poeticus daffodils in the Alps. Such a beautiful image of bulbs in the wild—nothing more can be said. Photo courtesy of Brent Heath/Brent and Becky's Bulbs.

much reduced cup banded green, yellow, and red. Some short-cup daffodils in Division 3 look very much like poeticus, but since the hybridizers are allowed to decide where (within reason) a new introduction is to go, I can only assume that they have their reasons. Poeticus cultivars are among the last to flower, blooming in late spring. The species is native to Europe, from central and southern France and northern Spain through the Alps and down to southern Italy, through the Balkans and into Greece. Only a limited number of cultivars are available: 'Actaea', introduced in 1927, continues to be strongly popular. 'Cantabile' is a more recent arrival but not by much, having been introduced in 1932; clean, white petals overlap around a shallow, little, ruffled yellow cup, rimmed with red and having a green eye at its center. 'Felindre' and 'Milan' date from around the same time and are similar in appearance.

Asian *Arisaema*

Arisaema, *Arum*, *Arisarum*, and *Pinellia* are all in the Araceae, or aroid family. Accordingly, the tubers, leaves, spathe and spadix, and seed pulp contain crystals of oxalic acid, rendering them unpalatable. Critters such as deer, rabbits, mice, voles, and chipmunks who come to your garden to dine will leave these plants alone. *Arum* is discussed in Chapter 10, "Geophytes for the Autumn Garden."

A marvelous correspondence exists between plants of eastern North America and those of Japan, Korea, and nearby portions of China. Not only are they close Asian relatives, but many of these counterparts of our native plants thrive in North American gardens. Since they are exotic, we find them interesting, often more fascinating than our native plants. And nowhere is this better shown than with the popularity of Asiatic relatives of our native Jack-in-the-pulpit. These tuberous woodland plants with their bizarre flowers are fashionable and sought after accents for the shady garden. Foremost of these is snow rice-cake plant, *Arisaema sikokianum*. A stately, chocolate-brown hood tips gently over the pure white spadix,

The showy, contrasting chocolate-brown spathe and white spadix of *Arisaema sikokianum* at BelleWood Garden. Photo by author.

which is flattened at the tip. The common name is a transliteration of its Japanese name, *yuki mochi so*, which references the cakes of pounded rice that are a seasonal celebratory part of the rice harvest. Native to the Japanese islands of Honshu, Shikoku, and Kyushu, *A. sikokianum* has been hardy in both my Connecticut and New Jersey gardens. Starting into growth in mid- to late spring, flowering-size plants have a pair of three- or five-parted leaves, sometimes enhanced with a central silver blotch. It is lovely with the lacy silver-gray fronds of Japanese painted fern, *Athyrium niponicum* 'Pictum', or the rosy pink flowers of *Primula sieboldii*.

Mature plants produce tremendous numbers of seed, as much as 500 on one plant. Seed sown in autumn and kept indoors under grow lights will germinate without a chilling period. Keep growing through the winter and encouraged growth by watering regularly with half-strength fertilizer. If the little leaves show no signs of yellowing on their own, gradually dry off the containers in late winter (mid-January in North America) and give the plants a six-week-long resting period. Start into growth again in spring, thus achieving two cycles of growth in one year. The second actual year and third growing cycle should yield a few flowering-size plants, with more the following year. Be aware of a debilitating rust disease, also found on North American native species. Orange-red pustules appear on the undersurface of the leaves. A mild case may be treated with flowers of sulfur, using a spreader-sticker to help the solution adhere, as arisaema leaves are somewhat water-repellent. Repeat at least weekly, more often in rainy or humid weather. Severely infected plants should be dug and destroyed by burning.

Sometimes called cobra lily for its domelike spathe that is rolled over into a hood, *Arisaema ringens* has a somewhat sinister appearance. Two large, shiny, three-parted leaves appear, rising above the greenish or brownish spathe. Native to the coastal forests of Honshu's Kanto district and westward, cobra lily is also found on Shikoku and Kyushu, as well as in Ryukyu, China, and South Korea. It is considered rather tender in England, emerging early enough to be caught by a late frost. In my experience, our colder temperatures keeps it safely dormant until the weather is more settled.

The cobralike hood of *Arisaema ringens* makes a relatively late appearance in the garden, a fortunate situation that avoids frost damage to the spathe and large, glossy leaves. Photo by author.

Another species I am especially fond of is *Arisaema thunbergii* subsp. *urashima*, which I would grow for its foliage even if it never flowered. Each dark green leaf is finely divided into 12 or more narrow leaflets in a *pedatisect* manner, arranged with the lateral lobes cleft into two or more segments and palmately divided, similar to the fronds of maidenhair fern, *Adiantum pedatum*—which, by the way, makes a pleasant companion. The unusual bittersweet chocolate–brown spathe has a long extension at the tip; however it is not as long as the whiplike flagella at the spadix, which is so long it trails on the ground. This is a vigorous species, with tubers forming many bumpy off-sets and lots of seed, which germinates irregularly—some reasonably promptly and the rest taking their time.

In a Japanese folk tale, Taro Urashima was a kind-hearted young fisherman. One day he found some children tormenting a sea turtle. When he rescued it, the turtle, a magical beast, spoke to him and offered to take him to its kingdom under the sea. Intrigued, Taro accompanied the turtle under the waves. He had a great time, with feasts and parties and young women making much of him. But one day he decided to go home. Though the sea folk begged him to stay, he insisted he had to return. He was heaped with treasure and given a small box, which he was told he must not open. (They do that in fairy tales, all the time passing out boxes or locking doors that the hero/hero-

The dark brown spathes of *Arisaema thunbergii* have an unusual, threadlike extension to the spadix. Looking at this nice colony at BelleWood Garden, it is obvious that it is an easy species to cultivate. Photo by author.

ine is told never to open.) When Taro got back to the beach, everything had changed, and he recognized no one. Opening the box, time came rushing back to him, and suddenly aging into an old man, he died. I think it must have been the whiplike or fishing line appearance of the flagellum that provided the inceptive element of this story.

Other arisaema worth growing include *Arisaema serratum* (syn. *A. japonicum*), which has a tall pseudo-stem, spotted like a snake. A simple green ruff of leaflets crowds just below the flower. Somewhat tender, *A. kiushianum* is a diminutive species that makes me think of a little owl's face, as the spathe droops down over the spadix. Probably hardy only to Zone 7, I grew it as a container plant, wintering it over in a friend's alpine house. *Arisaema candidissimum* is another species I cherished in Connecticut but lost when we moved to Hunterdon County, New Jersey, with its heavier, colder, wetter clay soil. If I had it to do over, I would have kept them in pots for a couple of years until I had made soil improvements with compost and fine gravel. The spathe on this species is reminiscent of fine porcelain, delicately penciled pink on a white background. It makes a leisurely appearance, waiting until late spring/early summer to shoulder up out of the ground, sufficiently late to make a gardener nervous. *Arisaema fargesii* does the same thing, delaying growth until the same time. It, too, has a three-parted leaf with two attendant smaller leaflets and an outsize central portion. I raised it from seed sent to me by Carla Teune, curator of the Leiden Botanic Garden in the Netherlands. She had collected it while on an expedition to Mount Omei in China with Roy Lancaster. It first flowered for me in 1985, producing a hooded flower with striking white, green, and purplish black stripes. The spathe curved forward and downward at the tip, ending in a tail-like point.

Arisarum and *Pinellia*

The little mouse-tailed arum, *Arisarum proboscideum*, is a dainty charmer, surprisingly hardy for a tuber that originates in Italy and Spain. Medium-green with a dull finish, the leaves are shaped like arrowheads and make a dense mat, 4 to 6 inches (10 to 15 cm) high, in spring. The small, dark, chocolate-brown to maroon-black spathe is concealed beneath them, all except the slender, curling, upturned, tail-like tip that peeps out, indeed reminiscent of a group of mice burrowing beneath the leaves. It spreads nicely in humus-rich woodland soils, going dormant soon afterward. The small tubers can be lifted and divided as the leaves are turning yellow. This sweetling is for gardeners who crawl around on their hands and knees, as otherwise its somewhat hidden charm is easily overlooked.

The majority of the five or so species of *Pinellia* are deceptively attractive, looking rather like arisaema of modest size. Artfully beguiling the unwary gardener, once in the ground they are difficult to evict. Both the Scott Arboretum of Swarthmore College, Pennsylvania, and the T. H. Everett Rock Garden of The New York Botanical Garden have had problems with them, and in the Plant Delights Nursery catalog, Tony Avent once warned against planting *P. ternata*. These pretty plants are thugs with territorially acquisitive tendencies. *Pinellia pedatisecta* has seven to eleven leaf segments, neatly arranged (no surprise) in a *pedatisect* manner (palmately arranged with the basal lobes on each side lobed themselves). Native to northern and western China, it flowers in summer with a narrow, greenish hood around an upright spadix. *Pinellia ternata* has a simple leaf in young plants, becoming three-parted when mature. It is a common road-side plant in Japan, China, and Korea, growing 4 to 6 inches (10 to 15 cm) tall. Every stalk makes propagules just below the soil surface, so digging the tubers to discard them simply spreads these around. Rather similar in appearance, *P. tripartita* also has three leaflets, is native to southern Japan, and is also summer-blooming. Be cautious, and think twice about turning any of these three loose in your garden. The one that is truly a delight is a Chinese species, *P. cordata*, frequently cultivated in Japan. Narrow leaves, 2 inches (5 cm) long, are shaped like spearheads, narrowing to abrupt tails. Attractive as a summer foliage plant for shady places, the leaves are a medium to dark green, with the veins traced out in silver, and a strong beefsteak red color on the under-side. Plants are viviparous, and a small tubercle forms on the leaf where it joins the petiole. I have not found it invasive in my Zone 6 gardens. However, in milder climates one might want to be careful about planting it in the garden to run about. The green spathe, just over 1 inch (2.5 cm) long and strongly curling in on itself, wraps around the spadix that sticks out from the hood. The flowers have a very sweet and delicate per-fume, somewhat fruitlike. For this reason, my friend Nihei-san told me, in Japan it is often grown in containers, the more easily to lift it to your nose to enjoy the fragrance.

Woodlands are a special place, inviting a spring stroll down a path as early geo-phytes flower and ferns unroll their fiddlehead crosiers. On a hot summer day, the dappled light beneath the trees creates an inviting respite. And in autumn as leaves turn color and fall we are once again reminded of the turn of the seasons. Whether it is the earlier geophytes welcoming spring or the act of planting new ones in the fall, geophytes are part of the cycle of the seasons that welcomes us into the garden.

CHAPTER 4

Native North American Woodland Geophytes

Some of us tend to fall heir to this casual, automatic association: If plants are bulbs, they come from Holland and bloom in the spring. If they come from Holland and bloom in the spring, they must be bulbs such as tulips, daffodils, and hyacinths. Circular reasoning won't take us very far. Geophytes that happen to originate close to home are, for whatever reason, given the primary classification of "wildflower" or "native plant." It is not that wildflower and geophyte are mutually exclusive terms. Simply put, some wildflowers are geophytes. And given a suitable site, they can add grace and beauty to the woodland garden or, indeed, to any shaded garden. "Native" is another term with a somewhat ambiguous or tenuous definition. The dictionary applies it to animals or plants occurring naturally in a region or place. The puzzlement comes to me when I try to decide how big a region or what place. State boundaries are artificial constructs that fail to impress plants or animals. If a plant grows in one town but not the next community, is it native only to the first? When I add something to my garden that was not growing there but could have been found there historically, I suppose I could claim it is native. I don't really know the answer to the "What is a native?" question but will continue to rely on field guides and floras to provide an answer.

Defining Shade

Shade is a shady concept. It is not as easy to define as its antonym: a sunny garden receives a minimum of eight hours of sunshine per day—that's during the growing season, of course, as winter day length is much shorter than its summer counterpart. All sorts of expressive terms are used for shade: dappled, partial, moderate, and more. But they are descriptive rather than quantifying. Just keep in mind that a single small tree, such as a flowering dogwood, *Cornus florida*, planted in the middle of a lawn provides much lighter shade than a copse or grove of dogwoods. Majestic canopy trees such as oaks (*Quercus* species) and tulip poplar (*Liriodendron tulipifera*) contribute more shade, especially if understory trees such as dogwoods nestle beneath them. Certain deciduous trees such as Norway maple (*Acer platanoides*) and American beech (*Fagus grandifolia*) create conditions of Stygian gloom. As well, both of them have moisture-sucking roots that compound the problem. Evergreen conifers produce year-round shade and, again, dry soil conditions. Fortunately for gardeners, the spring-blooming geophytes are tolerant of shade. After all, their performance is in early spring before the leafy canopy closes in. Further, their life cycle naturally sends them down into dormancy while shade in summer is at its peak. These woodland-tolerant geophytes do not need the sunny summer baking that tulips and crocus from the steppes of Central Asia prefer. Our native woodland geophytes call the forest home. Only in northern climates, where temperatures are cooler and overcast weather more common, will sunny rather than shady conditions be acceptable.

In common with many other shade-tolerant geophytes, many of our "home-grown" spring-flowering genera are ephemeral. They emerge in early to mid-spring, quickly produce flowers, mature their seed, and return to dormancy until the next spring season arrives. Squirrel corn, *Dicentra canadensis*, is one such example. Such fugacious plants need to be partnered with others that provide interest when they are dormant. Additionally, by covering otherwise bare ground, these perennials and/or ground covers protect the dormant geophytes from inadvertent damage caused by an eager gardener digging around and looking to shoehorn in yet another plant. Other native geophytes, such as bloodroot, *Sanguinaria canadensis*, maintain their foliage through the summer. Since the majority of shade-tolerant plants flower early in the growing season, foliage is the more useful aspect. Their partnerships should focus on plant associations that provide an attractive contrast of foliage, with perhaps the bonus of fruiting effect for later interest. Bloodroot's broad leaf would pair nicely with a lacy-leaved plant such as astilbe, or a fern.

Dutchman's breeches and squirrel corn

Bleeding heart, *Dicentra spectabilis*, from Japan, is probably the most familiar species in many gardens. The perennial with husky, thonglike roots is popular with gardeners for its sprays of pink, heart-shaped flowers, dangling like a string of lockets from a chain. A big plant, growing 3½ feet (1 m) high and wide, it makes an untidy mess when its foliage weakens, turns yellow, and collapses as the plant goes dormant in early summer. This is quite a contrast to our two eastern woodland natives, which are far daintier in scale. Dutchman's breeches, *D. cucullaria*, grows from a cluster of small, white scales crowded together into a tiny bulb. Generally less than 1 foot (30 cm) tall, the slender stem supports 3 to 12 nodding white flowers, with twin spurs that provide the fanciful resemblance to pants hung out to dry. Clusters of lacy, glaucous leaves form an attractive mound. Making its appearance in early spring, plants make themselves at home in woodlands and along shady roadsides, on slopes under deciduous trees. Where happy, Dutchman's breeches can make a frothy blanket of white under the trees' still-bare branches. When they quietly fade away in late spring, it is without fuss or muss. Though happiest with shallow planting, bulbs should have a covering of humus-rich soil. If exposed to sunlight, they will "sunburn" and turn red. Propagation can easily be managed though division of the little scales, loose to begin with. Since they are so small, it is helpful to line them out in a flat and grow them on for a season or two before planting out in the garden.

Most gardeners find that Dutchman's breeches flower quite well under cultivation, but that often its cousin squirrel corn, *Dicentra canadensis*, does not. The bulbs of squirrel corn look like a loose collection of golden yellow grains of corn. They should not be buried deeply, but rather just lightly pushed into the surface of the soil. The "grains" are so loosely attached to each other that any disturbance leaves some that have separated. They can be pressed into the soil and new plants should develop. Squirrel corn has white, heart- or locket-shaped flowers with a touch of yellow at the tips of the nodding flowers. It, too, flowers in spring and then goes dormant soon afterward.

Squirrel corn, *Dicentra canadensis*, offers another ephemeral choice for the early spring woodland garden, with locket-shaped white flowers and ferny foliage. Photo by author.

Dog's tooth violet

Dog's tooth violets do indeed have a bulb that looks like a dog's canine tooth. The pendant, nodding flowers look more like little Turk's cap lilies, with recurved petals. Other common names run the gamut from fawn lily and trout lily to adder's tongue. Different species are found on the American east and west coasts, and even in between. One species is native to Europe and Asia— *Erythronium dens-canis*, with rose-pink to purple flowers, and occasionally with a white form. Several cultivars include rich violet 'Frans Hals' and self-descriptive 'Lilac Wonder', 'Pink Perfection', and 'Rose Queen'. Splitters allow *E. japonicum* its own species, while lumpers consider it merely a variety of *E. dens-canis*.

Erythronium americanum is the species found from New Brunswick to Florida, and from Ontario and Minnesota south to Arkansas and Oklahoma. This is the species commonly seen in Connecticut and New Jersey. Early in spring, it forms large patches of attractively mottled, shiny leaves, with here and there an occasional yellow flower, the petals strongly buff colored on the reverse. That is generally the way of it—patches in the garden increase each year, but generally only two or three flowers are produced.

Driving along one spring day, I noticed a rocky outcrop with a ledge positively yellow from the number of flowers in bloom. Quickly pulling to the side of the road, I hopped over the guardrail for a closer look. As best as I could figure out, the bulbs had become so wedged into the soil-filled hollow that they had nowhere else to go. A brief pause here for a botanical digression. Erythroniums, being true bulbs, make offsets. In the majority of species, the daughter bulbs cluster close to the original parent bulb, similar to narcissus, hyacinths, tulips, hippeastrum, and what have you. *Erythronium americanum*, on the other hand, sends out a long dropper root about the thickness of a strand of thin spaghetti that eventually produces a daughter bulb, but at some distance from the parent bulb. Look carefully at one of those sizable but sparse-flowering

An exceptionally well-flowered group of dog's tooth violet, *Erythronium americanum*, makes an attractive display of flowers and foliage that will shortly fade away at the native plant garden of The New York Botanical Garden. These early fugacious wildings need protection from eager gardeners digging around when the geophytes are dormant, such as appropriate perennials or a suitable ground cover. Photo by author.

patches of trout lily, and you'll realize that many of the plants are sending up only a single leaf. All the flowering plants, however, are sending up a pair of leaves. Clearly, the new bulbs need to bulk up. Only when they store sufficient reserves to produce a pair of leaves are they then also vigorous enough to produce a flower. Wedged into the outcrop's ledge, the bulbs could descend only so far before they hit an impenetrable barrier. Since they couldn't go down, they bulked up and flowered. The metaphorical cartoon sound bite with a light bulb flashing and "Eureka!" went off above my head. When planting trout lily bulbs, dig them a nice hole. Set a largish flat rock, a piece of slate, or some other sufficient barrier on a slant at the bottom of the hole. (The slant allows better drainage than flat.) Toss in some leafy soil, set your bulbs, and finish filling the hole; then water and mulch. Not the next year, but starting the year after that, the bulbs will flower better and better. Fortunately, the general run of other, readily available dog's tooth violets flower quite nicely without such heroic measures. I've seen mention of a similar situation in a woodland area a few miles from Columbus, Indiana, where large patches of *E. americanum* were absolutely covered with bloom. The assumption in this instance was that the dense mass of tree roots had inhibited increase and the plants had used their energy to produce flowers.

To compound the issue, the native plant garden at The New York Botanical Garden has several large patches of *Erythronium americanum* behaving as it generally does—lots of leaves, very few flowers. At the far end of the garden in some rather mucky soil are several clumps of yellow trout lilies that are much bigger in both leaf and flower than the usual ones. What's more, these make large clumps with lots of flowers. I have asked if perhaps these are *E. umbilicatum*, a different but still yellow-flowered native species, only to be assured that no, it is also *E. americanum*. When I grew *E. umbilicatum* in Connecticut, it freely made offsets that huddled close to mother, resulting in an attractive display each spring. One distinguishing characteristic taxonomists are apt to focus on is the seed capsule, which is not pointed, rounded, or beaked in *E. umbilicatum* as it is in *E. americanum*. Also, in *E. umbilicatum* the stem bends after flowering, depositing the seed capsule on the ground.

Other dog's tooth violets can be found across the United States. *Erythronium albidum* is a charming species native found in woodlands from southern Canada down to Texas. The narrower, lightly mottled leaves make a subtle background to the solitary white flowers lightly flushed with a hint of blue or pink on the outside. Yellow anthers are a color echo of the yellow center at the base. Yellow-flowered *E. tuolumnense* is rather localized, found in California's Tuolumne County. Large, pale green, unmarked leaves splay out beneath one to four bright yellow flowers. Increasing freely, this is perhaps the easiest to grow of the yellow-flowered dog's tooth violet species in cultivation. Another delightful West Coast species is *E. revolutum*, found in forests and in damp sites from California up to Canada's Vancouver Island. Attractively mottled leaves and ease of cultivation are two attributes that, coupled with its lovely, deep pink flowers, make this an excellent choice for the shady garden. 'White Beauty' is a selection of *E. revolutum* that has (as you would expect) white flowers, accented by brown spots at the base of the petals. Vigorous in growth, it has mottled leaves.

A certain amount of deliberate hybridization has given us several cultivars, some of relatively recent origin, that are popular with gardeners and often more available than their parent species. *Erythronium* 'Jeanette Brickell' is a cross between *E. tuolumnense* and *E. oregonum*, with lightly mottled leaves and as many as seven icy white flowers. Though selected in England in 1956, for some reason it took another 20 years before it was named, in 1978. 'Jeannine' was introduced by W. P. Van Eeden of the Netherlands in 1984. Sulfur-yellow petals with a brighter yellow interior give the flowers a bright, sunny appearance. 'Kondo' is an *E. tuolumnense* and *E. revolutum* cross, with lightly mottled leaves and sulfur-yellow flowers accented by a brown ring on the inside. 'Pagoda' has the same parentage, with a stronger yellow flower and somewhat stronger mottling on the leaves.

Given their early spring period of bloom, numerous choices are available for partnering perennials. Perhaps my favorite "marriage" matches dog's tooth violets with hellebores, particularly the Lenten rose, *Helleborus orientalis*, with its large, buttercup-shaped flowers in apple-green, white, and pale pink through deep rose to plum, the lighter colors sometimes speckled or freckled with darker spotting and other times clear of any markings. The earlier blooming, somewhat smaller flowered hellebores in the Early Purple Group with their deep plum-colored flowers and ivory stamens are also a pleasing choice.

Dog's tooth violets really dislike being out of the ground. They get soft and flabby very quickly, become moldy, and even if they consent to grow will often refuse to flower in the year following disturbance. When purchased, the dormant bulbs should be received packed in some protective wood shavings, both as cush-

The attractive Turk's cap flowers of *Erythronium revolutum* 'White Beauty' make an attractive combination with *Helleborus orientalis*, a pairing suitable for formal or informal shady gardens. Photo by author.

ioning and to reduce desiccation. If you are moving dog's tooth violets around in the garden, prepare the new site, dig and divide the healthy clump, and then sprint to deliver them to their new location. Deer sample but do not devour them. Often the tips of an emerging set of leaves are nipped off, after which they expand into an oddly squared-off appearance and will manage to flower.

Spring beauty

Widespread, from Newfoundland and Saskatchewan across to Minnesota, southward through New England to North Carolina, Georgia, Louisiana, and Texas, spring beauty, *Claytonia virginica*, is a good example of the "neglected native as geophyte" syndrome that today afflicts several of our wildflowers. Yet this was not always so. Louise Beebe Wilder was fond of spring beauty, and in her book *Adventures with Hardy Bulbs* (1936, reprinted in 1998), she referred to it as "this gay sprite of the early spring days." She suggests planting it as she did, intermingled with snowdrops, which would bloom in early spring. Then, as their foliage was yellowing, the spring beauties would "literally spring up all about them" and disguise the aging snowdrop leaves. She describes it well, as a plant of low woods and stream banks that is shaded by overhanging trees. There, from a small, deep-set tuber, a simple stem arises, bearing a pair of slender leaves and a cluster of dainty flowers, pale pink or white-veined with pink, fleeting and quick to wilt if picked. In the 1953 printing of *The Complete Book of Bulbs* by F. F. Rockwell and Esther C. Grayson, spring beauty is mentioned as "gay little wild flowers of the early spring woods." The authors suggest that once a colony is established, it will spread and increase. When I looked for a more contemporary reference, I found that The Royal Horticultural Society's *Manual of Bulbs* (1996) does not include spring beauty. Granted, it is not one with large, brightly colored flowers to flaunt in a blatantly obvious display. Yet each spring I find something sweet about spring beauty's dainty little flowers, as many as a dozen clustered in a raceme. It is their subtle beauty that spangles the woodland floor and then quickly vanishes away until the next spring season cycles back around. Where satisfied with a rich, moist soil in open woodland shade, spring beauty makes a wonderful, if transient, carpet.

Bloodroot

If garden space were apportioned out based on flowering display, then bloodroot, *Sanguinaria canadensis*, would be found not to pay its rent. The eight-petalled, daisylike, white flowers are charming from the time the shoots emerge clasped in a great webbed cloak of the rolled up leaf and as they expand in pristine whiteness. However, they are transient and last for only a few days, less if the spring sunshine heats up or breezes are more than gentle zephyrs. For weekend gardeners, their beauty might well come and go unnoticed. Then why am I so fond of bloodroot? More for the gray-green leaves than for the quickly passing flowers. The foliage of bloodroot provides excellent value right through the growing season, something that many geophytes do not do. The leaves are often as wide as my outspread fingers, and sometimes close to 12 inches (30 cm) across, and they're usually broadly rounded, though some are more kidney-shaped. There is great variation in the degree of scalloping, from nearly orbicular to others that have a few minor dents, while some are quite deeply lobed. Combine bloodroot with lacy-leaved plants such as ferns, astilbe, or dwarf *Aruncus aethusifolius*. Add in some strap-leaved plants such as liriope, and the reward is a sturdy, summer-long, no maintenance display.

Sanguinaria and *bloodroot* both refer to the orange-red sap that oozes from every wound, be it cut tuber, torn leaf, or broken flower stem. The underground rhizomes branch freely and can easily be separated. Just be sure that each new division has a growing point for the next season's leaf and flower production. Since in the wild I would find larger, more floriferous colonies along roadsides through woodland than in heavier shade, I try to emulate the dappled, light shade conditions when choosing where to plant bloodroot. When digging and dividing bloodroot, something I prefer to do as the leaves yellow at summer's end, consider dusting all cuts with a fungicide. Bloodroot also comes easily from seed, as long as it is sown fresh, as soon as it ripens. If the fleshy elaiosome on the brown seeds dries out, it seems to delay germination.

Since the flowers of bloodroot (*Sanguinaria canadensis*) last so briefly, it is fortunate that the foliage provides a good display from spring to early fall. Even rather casual observation shows interesting variation, from almost orbicular to deeply lobed. Photo by author.

Sanguinaria canadensis with lobed leaf. Photo by author.

Simply sow the seed where you want new plants to grow. Or sow the seed in a reasonably deep nursery flat. When I do this, the flat is set out in the garden, dug in so the rim is just above soil level. The advantage of this method is that the flat acts as a reminder that something is intended to happen here, while a dug-over patch of soil is not as clear a warning not to disturb. As well as the single-flowered form, with 8 to 12 petals, there is a handsome fully double form with flowers like miniature white peonies.

Sanguinaria canadensis 'Flore Pleno' (also sold as 'Multiplex') is a very vigorous, sterile form. The underground rhizomes fork and branch so freely that they quickly become congested and can rot. It is a good idea to lift and divide the double form every three or four years to prevent the plants from rotting out. Even so, one year in my Wilton, Connecticut, garden I experienced a great dying off of double bloodroot in every part of the garden where it was planted. I lost more than 95 percent of my plants. Interestingly enough, that same season Dick Redfield, a tremendously skilled and knowledgeable gardener of my acquaintance, lost nearly all the double bloodroot in his Scotland, Connecticut, garden. Since the double form is normally such a vigorous, easily grown cultivar, I am at a loss to explain what happened. A single-flowered form is handsomely flushed with lavender on the reverse of the petals, an attractive variation whose flowers also fade quickly.

The gorgeous flowers of double bloodroot, *Sanguinaria canadensis* 'Flore Pleno' (or 'Multiplex'), resemble little white peonies. The display is brief, however, lasting only about a week. Photo by author.

Trillium

Simple to identify, with several species easy to grow, you might be pardoned for thinking that trillium must surely be found in many shady gardens. The genus *Trillium* does offer us excellent plants for the shady garden. The various species are such an indicator of spring that desperate gardeners have been known to flee the snow-covered northeastern United States and head south to the Appalachian foothills in search of trilliums in bloom. British enthusiasts fly over for a three-day trip. Their goal: to see as many species of *Trillium* as can be crammed into that narrow time slot.

Such field observation is one thing, and garden cultivation is generally a simple matter. Ethical acquisition of the plants is frequently another story. The difficulty is that trillium grow very slowly from seed. To begin with, the seed must be fresh for the best germination rates. This is difficult unless you already have trillium in your garden or growing wild on your property (or you have an obliging friend). Sown promptly in autumn, the following spring it appears that nothing is happening as the seeds send down a radicle, with no above-ground action. It is only in the second spring that a small, spade-shaped leaf surfaces. The plant is not mature enough to flower in less than five years or so beyond that. And trillium does not bulk up like a hosta or daylily

In Dr. Barad's New Jersey garden, one of the sessile trilliums, *Trillium luteum*, is nicely paired with the coarse foliage of *Rodgersia podophylla* and a mass of the soft blue flowers of Jacob's ladder, *Polemonium caeruleum*. Photo by author.

for speedy increase by division. It is unfortunate that the majority of trillium offered for sale in the United States are wild-collected plants, as this puts pressure on populations already at risk from habitat destruction. A small ray of hope is offered for ethically responsible gardeners who wish to avoid the purchase of wild-collected trillium. *Trillium chloropetalum* 'Volcano' is a vigorous cultivar of a sessile species. Growing 18 to 24 inches (45 to 60 cm) tall with attractive mottled foliage and dark, maroon-red flowers, this selection from Barry Sligh of New Zealand is propagated by tissue culture and was introduced by an American wholesale nursery in 2001. But then, for whatever reason, they were not offered again. Chapter 2, "Geophyte Care and Cultivation," offers information on propagating trillium.

Trilliums have all their parts—leaves, petals, and sepals—in threes. The only other woodland plant with which you might possibly confuse it is Jack-in-the-pulpit, *Arisaema triphyllum*, whose leaflets are also in threes but with a very different flower. Also, trilliums' leaves are equidistant from one another, while our Jack-in-the-pulpit has its leaflets in a T. Trilliums come in two versions: either they are *pedicellate*, with a pedicel (a stemlike structure) between the flower and leaves, or they are *sessile*, and the flower sits down on the leaves. Other differences: Pedicellate trilliums have unmarked green leaves and open flowers. Sessile trilliums have mottled foliage and their flowers appear narrow, almost closed, even when mature. Approximately 40 species, including both types of trilliums, are native to the United States, while only five or six species, all pedicellate, are found in eastern Asia. And with names such as *Trillium smallii* and *T. apetalon*, the gardener is given a clue that these are not particularly showy.

While it is often said that picking trillium flowers (which, given the form of the plant, means taking the leaves as well) will promptly kill the plant, I have not found this to be so. Deer sometimes dine on trillium. An occasional browsing is not lethal, but it is definitely not good for the health of the plant. If they are eaten repeatedly, two or more years in a row, then, yes, that can be fatal. Trillium requires a chilling period before they come into growth. If foliage is damaged or removed during their growing period, they cannot produce another flush of leaves until the following spring. Of course, this weakens the plant but is not an automatic death sentence. A far greater threat is the loss of habitat, from shopping malls, highways, and houses built through the woodlands where these harbingers of spring reside. Collection from the wild for sale to the general public is another continuing problem and an environmental/ecological disgrace. In September 2003 my husband and I were shopping at a large home improvement center. While he looked for wall anchors, I checked out the bulbs. I found daffodils and tulips, hyacinths and crocus, and other assorted familiar geophytes. As well, a rack of wildflowers was offered, packed up in little peat moss–filled plastic bags, a flexible cardboard sleeve with a pretty picture on the outside and cultural information on the inside. Several ferns were available, May apple, Virginia bluebells, Jack-in-the-pulpit, dog's tooth violet, Dutchman's breeches, crested iris, and trilliums. These included catesby trillium (*Trillium catesbyi*), red trillium (*T. erectum*), white trillium (*T. grandiflorum*), and assorted trillium, with a picture of a sessile trillium on the sleeve. All of these plants— trilliums, ferns, and the rest—were uniformly priced at just $1.98 each. When the price is just too good to be true, there has to be a reason. There is just no way that trilliums, slow to reproduce as they are, can be sold for that absurd retail price and allow for any profit. Unless, that is, the plants are wild collected. A large sign attached to the stand mentioned that these plants are "nursery grown." It is legal to use such labeling for plants that are taken from the wild and then grown under cultivation for a matter of a few weeks or months—a very different situation from "nursery propagated."

Close to 50 species of *Trillium* emerge from fat, horizontal rhizomes that grow only 1 to 2 inches (2.5 to 5 cm) below the soil surface in humus-rich, moist woodland soils. Given suitable conditions, the plants are long-lived. All are spring-flowering. Each individual stem bears three leaves in a whorl and a solitary flower, with three petals and three sepals. Flower color varies from white to chartreuse and yellow, to maroon in the different species. They are easily recognizable to the rankest novice, and I can think of nothing with which they might be confused. Wake-robin, stinking Benjamin, wet-dog trillium, squawroot, and birth root are all common names for *T. erectum*, a familiar pedicellate species found from Quebec to Ontario into New England, to Ohio, Pennsyl-

Typically, *Trillium erectum* has rich maroon flowers. It is, however, a variable species and has both white and these deliciously ivory hued, pale yellow forms, as vigorous in growth as the type. Photo by author.

vania and Delaware, and southward in the mountains of North Carolina, Georgia, and Tennessee. In Fairfield County, Connecticut, I would find this species growing along the wooded roadsides in humus-rich, moderately moist soils, perhaps with a fast food wrapper blown in and caught against its stem. They would usually bloom in late April, but of course this will vary with the locale—later in Canada and earlier in Georgia. Wake-robin is a variable species growing anywhere from 6 to 24 inches (15 to 60 cm) tall, with plants from the northern portion of its range generally smaller than those from the southern regions. The typical form has deep, rich, maroon-red flowers, which may be held upright, somewhat nodding, or even drooping below the leaves. *Trillium erectum* var. *album* has white flowers, while the flowers of *T. erectum* f. *luteum* that I've observed were more of a rich cream than a true yellow. I've seen a bicolor form, with pale, nearly white color on the inside of the petals and dark red on the outside. Wake-robin is a grand plant for the shady garden, responding well to a modicum of care. It develops into sturdy clumps, producing several stems from each rhizome. Partner it with ferns, bloodroot, and violets in deference to its natural associations, or allow it to mingle with primroses and hellebores for a more singular combination.

White trillium and great white trillium are apt common names for *Trillium grandiflorum*, perhaps the most familiar species of this genus. Found from Quebec to Maine over to Minnesota, and southward to Pennsylvania, Ohio, Indiana, and Arkansas, it is also found in the Appalachian Mountains of Georgia, with cooler growing conditions. In Connecticut I would find modest groups of perhaps a dozen at most, and only as isolated aggregations rather than the more widespread, if scattered, wake-robin. The largest colony I have ever seen was in Ohio, extending from the boundary fence along Route 480 back into the woods farther than I could see. It was the 10th of May, and thousands of plants were magnificently in bloom, visible from the car as we sped down the highway. A brief stop, a scramble over the fence to take a few pictures, and then on our way again, with the promise of more time next year. That was not to be, for as we were taking our son to college the following year I discovered that the maple woodland was now a housing development, and any trillium that might have survived were nowhere to be seen.

Once pollinated, the white petals change to a drab rose-pink, turning flabby and collapsing. In a small portion of Virginia, within perhaps 100 miles of the Blue Ridge Mountains, is a strain with flowers that open up pink, in shades from light to dark. *Trillium grandiflorum* f. *roseum* is a showy plant, not necessarily better than the typically white form but simply different. The shade of pink that one of these plants exhibits is not necessarily consistent, as individual plants moved from one place to another at some distance will vary. Higher or cooler temperatures, more or less acid soils, even the mineral content of the soil could each have a role to play. Another variation is *T. grandiflorum* 'Flore Pleno', with all of the flower's reproductive parts transformed into petals, creating a fully double, sterile flower. Extremely showy, this outstanding form is coveted by gardeners willing to pay exorbitant prices when it infrequently becomes available. Since the true doubles are sterile, division is the only means of propagation, and this can be done only infrequently. When my mentor John Osborne gave me one, it lived for an additional year in his cold frame before he could actually bring himself to relinquish it and allow me to take it away. I like the cool effect

Trillium grandiflorum in a garden, arising through a carpet of sweet woodruff (*Galium odoratum*) with ferns, hosta, and a white-flowered azalea. Photo by author.

created by planting this trillium with the silver fronds of Japanese painted fern, *Athyrium niponicum* 'Pictum'.

Showy as the pedicellate trilliums are, I confess a certain fondness for the sessile species. The two with which I am most familiar are vigorous plants with attractive flowers and foliage. Purple toadshade or whippoorwill flower, *Trillium cuneatum* is found rambling around in southern and southeastern U.S. states, away from coastal areas. It is a stately plant growing as much as 18 inches (45 cm) tall, with broad leaves mottled in light and darker green. It flowers quite early and would often be in bloom by mid- to late March in my Connecticut garden, where it would tower over the white daisylike flowers of Grecian windflower, *Anemone blanda*. The upright petals may be richly colored maroon to maroon-purple or purple-brown, while other plants, *T. cuneatum* f. *luteum*, have green, chartreuse, or lemony yellow flowers. The flowers often have a faint, sweetly spicy odor. *Cuneatum* means wedge-shaped (think of cuneiform writing on Babylonian tablets) and refers to the tapering, somewhat wedge-shaped base of the petal. This is an important characteristic for distinguishing the yellow forms of *T. cuneatum* from the typically yellow-flowered *T. luteum*, since at a superficial glance they look much the same. In the latter, the petals are widest near the base, and the green-yellow to lemon-yellow flowers have a pleasant, strong scent of citrus. It flowers a month or so later, in mid- to late spring. Plant it with the soft blue flowers of wild sweet

Earliest of the sessile trilliums to bloom in spring, *Trillium cuneatum* flowers as early as Grecian windflower, *Anemone blanda*, whose small, daisylike flowers make it a pleasant partner for the late spring garden. Photo by author.

William, *Phlox divaricata*, for an elegant association. The smaller hostas with gold, golden-centered, or gold-edged leaves, such as *Hosta* 'Kabitan' and 'Wogon Gold', are also charming.

Jack-in-the-pulpit

Forty or so species of *Trillium* are native to the United States, with perhaps another five or six in eastern Asia. With arisaema, the numbers reverse themselves: two or three species are native to the United States, and the preponderance of species are found in Japan, China, and elsewhere in Asia. Our more familiar species, Jack-in-the-pulpit, *Arisaema triphyllum*, is another readily recognizable plant. Adaptable, this species is native from southern Canada to Louisiana and Kansas. The smooth-bottomed tuber produces one or two long-stemmed, three-parted leaves. At the top of a separate, some- what shorter, stem is a hoodlike spathe nodding protectively over a rod-shaped spadix. The spathe may be richly striped in deep brownish purple and white or more subtly col-

ored green and white. When the plant is too young to flower, it is, of course, neuter in the matter of sex. When it first reaches flowering size, the plant still has only a single leaf and produces only male flowers on the spadix. As the tuber increases in size and reaches reproductive maturity, it grows two leaves and actually changes its sex— now flowers will be female, and the plant is capable of bearing seed. This sex change is something botanists re- fer to as *paradioecious*. (This is differ- ent from hollies and bayberries, which are *dioecious*—a plant has either male or female flowers but not both on one plant, nor do they change from male to female, or vice versa.) If starved, grown in a sand bed with scanty nutri- ents, the tuber will reverse itself and produce only male flowers.

There's much to like about Jack-in- the-pulpit. I don't know that *beautiful* is the right adjective—perhaps unusu- al or bizarre might seem more appro-

In a damp, shady site a well-grown clump of *Arisaema triphyllum* subsp. *stewardsonii*, with its ribbed green and white spathes, associates well with a yellow vio- let—not only a good-looking pair, but also two plants that prefer constantly moist soil. Photo by author.

priate. In autumn, the fruiting effect of a female plant is quite showy, with a cluster of sealing wax–red berries. Often the leaves have yellowed and withered by the time the fruit is ripe. Easily satisfied, plants tolerate damp to average soil in full sun (if sufficiently moist) to moderate shade, and they are readily moved from one part of the garden to another at just about any time of year. New plants are easily raised from seed, which should be sown in autumn, either outdoors directly in the garden or indoors under grow lights. Be careful to wash your hands after cleaning the red skin and fleshy pulp away from the small, round tan seeds. The oxalic acid crystals are painful if accidentally ingested or if you rub your eyes. These same crystals make Jack-in-the-pulpit very pest-resistant, since all parts—tuber, leaves, spathe, and spadix—are laced with the sharp crystals, rendering the plant unpalatable to deer, rabbits, woodchucks, and voles. I like big ones (and a well-fed Jack in moist soil can easily reach 2 feet [60 cm] tall or more) rearing up out of a patch of Allegheny spurge (*Pachysandra procumbens*) or shoulder-to-shoulder with some evergreen Christmas fern (*Polystichum acrostichoides*).

Peggy French in Wilton, Connecticut, discovered a lovely variant, with the leaf veins thinly threaded with white. Shared among gardeners as "Mrs. French's Form," it does come true from seed. Some authorities recognize *Arisaema triphyllum* subsp. *stewardsonii*, which is found only in moist to wet sites, flowers somewhat later and has a ridged or fluted texture to its green and white spathe. Green dragon arisaema, *A. dracontium*, reminds me of an unruly child sticking out its tongue. A smooth, green spathe enfolds the elongated spadix, which protrudes as much as 7 inches (17.5 cm) from its wrapping, rearing upright above both spathe and leaf. Green dragon has a single pedatisect leaf, with 7 to 15 narrow, fingerlike segments in a horseshoe-shaped arrangement held horizontally out from the stem. Generally found on wet ground in woodlands, the fruits of green dragon are more of a warmer orange-red color.

Solomon's seal and false Solomon's seal

Solomon's seal and false Solomon's seal are two quietly attractive woodland plants. Both grow from a creeping, ivory-colored rhizome. Older rhizomes of *Polygonatum* (true Solomon's seal) have a curiously knotted appearance, residue of the previous years' stem scars, and in fact the very name means many-jointed. In spring a single arching stem arises, curving back over the branching rhizome. Native to the eastern half of the United States, great Solomon's seal, *P. biflorum*, grows as much as 4 feet (1.2 m) tall. *Polygonatum commutatum* is the name often used for especially tall forms, 6 feet (2 m) or more, and *P. pubescens* is native from eastern Canada to northern Georgia, with small hairs along the veins on the undersides of the leaves. It is somewhat smaller, reaching 3 feet (1 m) tall. Oval leaves alternate their way up the stem. In the axil of the leaves, from one to four nodding little bell-like white flowers droop down, each to be followed by a pea-sized blue-black seed. I enjoy Solomon's seal as an accent plant, adding some height to a carpet of Canada ginger (*Asarum canadense*). The branching rhizomes can be divided very early in the spring or, perhaps better, in autumn as the leaves yellow and the plants begin their dormant period. Make sure that each division has a pink growing tip, since the old rhizome can help nourish the plant but is unwilling to begin growing anew.

False Solomon's seal, *Smilacina racemosa* (also known as Solomon's plume), is a common woodland plant at BelleWood Garden. It grows under the trees, along the roadside, and under piles of grit scraped off the road by winter snowplows. Its other common name, Solomon's plume, is more descriptive of the feather effect created by the tiny white flowers massed on a panicle at the end of the stem. The arching stem, 3 feet (1 m) tall, takes a somewhat zigzag path from leaf to leaf, in contrast to the smooth curve of Solomon's seal. The fluffy white flowers are followed by tan berries that take on a red-speckled appearance, which develops into more of a mottling before becoming completely red. Play it off *Arisaema triphyllum*, which will also be in fruit at the same time. Happiest in moist woodland shade, Solomon's plume is excellent as a companion to hellebores, hostas, ferns, and other perennials that enjoy similar conditions. I like them best in moderate groups rather than as isolated individuals. Their autumn color, as the leaves turn straw gold, is accentuated by plants with evergreen foliage, such as *Euphorbia amygdaloides* var. *robbiae*, an evergreen carpet of *Phlox stolonifera*, or the fresh new growth of *Arum italicum* 'Pictum'. The skinny white rhizome is less convoluted than that of Solomon's seal.

I prefer a tapestry effect, where plants are allowed to interweave with one another. Here, ferns, the pale blue flowers of wild sweet William (*Phlox divaricata*), and the feathery flower plumes of *Smilacina stellata* blend foliage and flowers. Photo by author.

~~~~~~

CHAPTER 5

Geophytes for the Mediterranean Garden

Plants must adapt to survive difficult environmental factors. Only in tropical rain forests are conditions benign year-round, with adequate nutrients, ample moisture, and mild temperatures. Elsewhere, plants must make adjustments to survive. While we most often associate geophytes' adaptation of underground storage reserves of food and moisture with cold-hardiness—the ever-popular daffodils, hyacinths, and tulips of spring—the same strategy also works quite well to get a plant through dry times, or periods of drought. In fact, more geophytes are found growing wild in places with Mediterranean-type climates. The geophyte is, after all, an adaptation to hard times.

Geophytes, which grow when moisture is available and remain dormant when it is not, have found an excellent method of coping with environmental stress, such as a long period of drought. It is easy to understand why large numbers of geophytes are usually found in these hot, dry Mediterranean regions. In summer, these plants go dormant to conserve moisture, and they grow in the mild, rainy winter season.

Climate Parameters

Five areas fit the parameters we ascribe to "Mediterranean," and they all lie between 30 and 45 degrees of latitude. The Mediterranean Basin itself is in the Northern Hemisphere, as is California. In these regions, July is typically the hottest summer month, and the coolest month of winter is January. The Western Cape of South Africa, central Chile, and Southwest and South Australia are in the Southern Hemisphere. They also have hot, dry summers and mild, rainy winters, but with the months reversed—January is the Southern Hemisphere's hottest summer month and July the coolest winter month. Though not necessarily frost-free, Mediterranean regions have in common a relatively mild climate. All are characterized by arid, sunny summers, and moisture arrives in the winters. Average annual precipitation in regions with a Mediterranean climate varies from 10 to 40 inches (24 cm to 1 m) of rainfall, arriving mostly in winter. I specifically mention rainfall since snow is rare except in the higher elevations. Mountains also intercept moisture, and the rain shadow created by the Olympic and Cascade ranges of the western United States means their eastern slopes are drier. Another complicating factor for California's Mediterranean climate is that the major mountain ranges such as the Sierra Nevada get afternoon thunderstorms from about July on. Though not as predictable as the afternoon storms in the Rocky Mountains, they are frequent, so high mountain alpines and geophytes are not summer dry. One other factor influencing the amount of rainfall is proximity to the equator, with regions such as southern California receiving less precipitation than the northern parts of the state. Baja California is hotter and drier yet.

California's location on the continent's western coast affects its climate by more than just proximity to the ocean's heat sink that reduces variation between summer high and winter low temperatures. Cold offshore ocean currents have an additional moderating effect on summer temperatures. As well as influencing temperature, these cooling fogs provide moisture—consider San Francisco's foggy bay, for example. In Cape Town, South Africa, the mists that form around Table Mountain create cooler temperatures. This Mediterranean pattern disappears very quickly as you move to the northeast or east from Cape Town. Chile's Atacama Desert, 700 miles (1125 km) long, caught between the Pacific Ocean and the Andes, is exceptionally arid. In some places, rainfall has never been recorded—that is, there has been no rainfall at all. What vegetation survives does so by absorbing moisture provided by the fog. People also make use of the fog, collecting water with huge mist nets on which the moisture condenses, to drip into a collection trough and trickle into storage containers.

While California is recognized as Mediterranean, we tend to disregard other portions of the Pacific Northwest coast—Oregon, Washington, and British Columbia—as having Mediterranean conditions. True, a great deal of the Northwest is much colder in winter, and some of it is wetter. Also significant, some areas do get rain in summer. Keep in mind, however, the localized effects of microclimate. Washington's Olympic Peninsula and Canada's Vancouver Island mountains cast a rain shadow over the roughly triangular area surrounding Puget Sound and the Strait of Georgia. Port Townsend, Washington, receives a scant 18 inches (45 cm) of rain per year. Compare this with downtown Los Angeles and its annual rainfall of 15 inches (38 cm). Of course, not all places within the rain shadow are this dry. Bellingham, Washington, receives 34 inches (86 cm) of rain yearly, while the Seattle airport records an average 38 inches (97 cm) per year. Mediterranean plants expect dry summers, so the time of year that the rain arrives is also important. When the monthly rainfall averages are plotted over the entire year, a U-shaped outline appears as rainfall drops in summer, as little as 0.5 to 1.0 inch (1 to 2.5 cm) for the month of July. Thus, with dry summers and rainy winters, Victoria, British Columbia, with an annual precipitation of 27 inches (69 cm) and temperatures that place it into Zone 8, could easily be considered a Mediterranean climate, albeit on the cool side.

Let us begin with the Mediterranean Basin itself, which gives its name to this type of habitat. The lands that border the Mediterranean Sea experience hotter summers than comparable areas such as California, due to the fact that the water, surrounded by land as it is, warms up more than do oceans. While the region once sustained an open savanna of live oaks and grasses, the long history of human occupation has had a profound influence on the region. Millennia of wood harvesting for timber and firewood, and burning of woodlands to create pasturage, have reduced many areas to more open expanses. Cork oak, Aleppo pine, and olive trees have replaced the evergreen oaks. Today the dominant plant community is called *maquis* in France and *macchia* in Italy. It consists of dense, much-branched, thorny, aromatic, scrubby shrubs and small, stunted trees. These woody plants are often *sclerophytes*, with small, thick, evergreen leaves that exhibit various adaptations to drought, such as a heavily waxed cuticle, a reflective surface, or a coat of fine, pubescent hairs. Neither so tall nor as dense as *maquis* is the *garrigue*, a lower, more open plant community that is principally found in the south of France. These are really coastal habitats. Travel northwest or west from the French Riviera and quickly you will travel into areas that are not Mediterranean, not merely geographically in the sense of locale but in the mild winter with moisture, sunny-dry-summer-climate sense. One interesting variation is that the area between Rome, Italy, and Marseilles, France, has somewhat more summer moisture than elsewhere. The driest month occurs in July. Both have their peak maximum rainfall in the mid-autumn month of October rather than mid-winter.

Italy and the *Maquis*

Angelo Porcelli lives in southern Italy, near Bari. His garden is in the countryside, less than 500 feet (152 m) from the sea, in the region of Apulia. As might be expected, ecosystems change significantly as one goes from north to south and inland from the sea. This is the heart of the country for olive oil production, and the countryside is filled with fields of olive trees. The few remaining natural areas of Mediterranean *macchia* have Chios mastic (*Pistacia lentiscus*), whose shiny leaves reflect some of the intense summer sun, helping to control temperatures in the leafy canopy. Other woody shrubs and trees include mock privet (*Phillyrea latifolia* and *P. angustifolia*) and buckthorn (*Rhamnus*). *Macchia alta* is the community of taller shrubs, while *macchia bassa* includes low shrub vegetation such as sage-leaved cistus (*Cistus salviifolius*) and Phoenician juniper (*Juniperus phoenicea*), as well as the familiar Mediterranean shrubby herbs of lavender, thyme, and rosemary. Winters are rather mild, with a minimum temperature of 27° to 30°F (−3° to −1°C). Classic Mediterranean geophytes abound.

Narcissus tazetta

Where people live and plants grow, people grow plants. And where variation exists, gardeners select, cosset, and cultivate those that take their fancy. Angelo has assembled five heirloom varieties of *Narcissus tazetta*. They are found mostly in the old gardens, for new gardeners (perhaps not yet sufficiently experienced to appreciate the older cultivars) tend to grow modern cultivars. *Tazetta* is an Italian word meaning "small cup," appropriate for the dainty little corona of this species. The typical tazetta narcissus native to the region has a bright to deep yellow cup and white petals. These bloom for Angelo in late November or early December.

The common names of bunch-flowered narcissus or polyanthus narcissus refer to the several flowers (up to 15) that appear on each scape. *Narcissus tazetta* subsp. *italicus* is found in the area's old gardens and occasionally found in the wild, too, with 10 to 12 flowers per scape, each with a lemon-yellow cup surrounded by almost white petals, just hinting at yellow. Though native to Italy, it happily naturalizes in gardens on the French Riviera. The double form blooms in Angelo's garden in late December, to be followed by an old hybrid said to be a cross of *N. tazetta* and *N. poeticus* that blooms in February. *Narcissus* ×*medioluteus* (syn. *N.* ×*biflorus*) was first described from southern France in 1597 and is said to occur spontaneously where the two parent species grow in proximity. Imagine a yellow-cupped poeticus daffodil, with two fragrant flowers on each scape.

In March, the tazetta parade through Angelo's garden continues with *Narcissus* 'Grand Primo', a sterile form that happily reproduces freely through the production of numerous offsets. It is a charming variety, first mentioned in 1731, with 11 to 16 citron-yellow flowers on each scape. One variant form has a cup that fades on the third day, nearly to white. The form that does not fade is often (but incorrectly) called 'Grand Monarque'. The true cultivar, first mentioned in 1798, produces a nosegay of fragrant white flowers, each with soft, citron-yellow cup. It is frequently found growing in old gardens on the Riviera and in Algiers.

Angelo mentioned yet another of the tazetta daffodils that he grows: "I do grow *Narcissus tazetta* 'Early Pearl', another old tazetta hybrid (I can't remember all!) and this is really a carefree plant. It increases so quickly that I have to divide the clumps every three years or they will turn in a big mass of dark green long leaves with few flowers. A note on cultivation of the 'double flower' form of tazetta is that they require a not too rich soil (meaning low in nitrogen). Otherwise the heavy flowers will bend down at the first rain. I have grown them in a shallow, rocky soil and found they develop shorter but rigid stalks that don't bend. Concluding the seasons of daffodils is 'Geranium', a good grower which is in flower now (in mid-April) and is one of the latest." An heirloom variety dating back to the late 1930s, 'Geranium' has three to five sweetly scented flowers per stem, each with a rich orange cup and soft white petals.

One of Angelo's favorite companion plants for *Narcissus tazetta* is *Delosperma lydenburgense*, a charming ice plant from the Transvaal with purple-pink, daisylike flowers, which he finds much hardier than various *D. cooperi* cultivars and very successful for disguising the bare ground where his narcissus are dormant. It flowers continuously for him, from late spring through winter, and needs no supplemental watering (or, as Angelo refines his statement, "I don't water it at all!" leaving the narcissus dry, as they prefer). Dwarf, trailing, succulent plants that root down as they go, some ice plants, such as *D. dyeri* and *D. sphalmanthoides*, may offer interesting possibilities as perennials suitable for the arid U.S. West. Others have already become popular bedding plants, with cultivars such as *D. congestum* 'Gold Nugget' and 'White Nugget' readily available.

Tazetta daffodils thrive along both shores of the Mediterranean—the Iberian Peninsula, southern France, Italy, Corsica, Sardinia, Sicily, Greece, and the coastal areas of Syria, Lebanon, Iran, and Israel. As well, the species is found in North Africa to Libya, and India. As might be expected from its wide distribution, *Narcissus tazetta* is a variable species with regional subspecies. Where cold winters are common, as in much of the United States, many are too tender to be grown in the open garden.

Israel has become a major source for non-hardy tazettas, often known as paperwhites. These include *Narcissus* cultivars 'Galilee', 'Jerusalem', 'Nazareth', 'Omri', and 'Ziva'. Though found in China and Japan (even today you see them everywhere in the Japanese countryside), opinions differ as to whether they are native or naturalized, carried along the Silk Route as an incidental addition to the trade in silks and spices in the 13th century. Their European introduction was in Holland in 1557. Requiring little, if any, chilling, non-hardy tazetta daffodils are characterized by their early growth that begins in late autumn or early winter, with flowers opening from mid-winter into late winter/early spring. In the United States, consider planting them outdoors only in Gulf Coast and southern California gardens. Each stem carries four to eight very fragrant flowers, with a shallow little cup and petals that are often somewhat crinkled. Top-size bulbs often have two or even three flowering stems that grow 14 to 18 inches (35 to 45 cm) tall. These tazettas are less cold-hardy than other daffodils, and because they flower without any winter chilling, they are highly suitable for Mediterranean climate gardens in southern California, in the American Deep South, or in similar mild winter regions such as the coastal Pacific Northwest. Additionally, tazettas are great for coaxing into bloom indoors in as little as four weeks after potting up in a bowl of pebbles and water. Each flower of 'Soleil d'Or' (sometimes called 'Autumn Sol' or Chinese sacred lily), has a mandarin orange cup and clean, white petals, with a sweet, refreshing scent that is not as musky or cloying as such paperwhites as 'Ziva'. It will be in bloom by Thanksgiving in the Los Angeles area, even earlier in Santa Barbara.

When any daffodil cultivar sports from single to double, it is moved from its original classification, such as Division 8 for tazetta, into Division 4. That is the case for *Narcissus* 'Cheerfulness', which has creamy white petals and a well-filled yellow center. It is a sport of 'Elvira', a long-forgotten tazetta whose stamens developed a petaloid form. And 'Cheerfulness' itself changed to all yellow, giving us 'Yellow Cheerfulness'. Angelo includes these two as "modern" hybrids but notes that "they aren't so vigorous." Other daffodils of historical interest that he grows include 'Golden Harvest', an early hybrid yellow trumpet of Dutch introduction, and 'Armada', a large cup daffodil with yellow petals and an orange-red cup. Two small-cup daffodils he has in his garden include 'Ardour', once popular as a show flower (rather than for garden use), which has yellow petals and a deep orange-red cup, and 'La Riante', with white petals and a predominantly red-orange cup. These also are not as vigorous as the old tazettas.

Cape Region of South Africa and *Fynbos*

The *fynbos* region is the scrubby, shrubby, thorny, aromatic, arid habitat around the Cape of South Africa in the Southern Hemisphere. This is the mildest of the Mediterranean-type habitat regions. The average minimum temperature in Cape Town is 37°F (3°C), while the average maximum is 95°F (35°C). Annual precipitation averages around 25 inches (64 cm), and the region does receive a little summer moisture. Nearby Table Mountain provides summer mists that have a moderating effect, much as do the California coastal fogs near San Francisco. The winter months of May to August are the wettest, while the midsummer months of December and January are dry. *Fynbos* vegetation contains non-woody, grasslike *restioids*, shrubby protea and other *proteoids* with their larger, flattened, hairy or waxy-coated leaves. *Ericoids* are heathlike shrubs with small, narrow leaves. Just as with the *maquis*, *fynbos* soil is poor and infertile. And, again like *maquis* and chaparral, *fynbos* is adapted to fire and survives periodic burning. Indeed, fire is necessary for the survival of some of the plants. Geophytes thrive, especially members of the Iridaceae, or iris family, such as *Gladiolus*, *Freesia*, *Babiana*, *Sparaxis*, and *Watsonia*. Other Cape geophytes include such elegant favorites as *Amaryllis belladonna*, *Nerine sarniensis*, ×*Amarygia multifloria* (formerly *Amaryllis multiflora* and *Brunsvigia orientalis*), and *Lachenalia*. Those geophytes from Natal and the forests of the Eastern Cape are semitropical, well suited to Florida and adjacent southern states.

Australia

Southwestern and South Australia provide such suitable conditions that a number of Cape geophytes have gone walk-about—escaped the confines of the gardens where they were planted and struck out across the countryside. (See the appendix, "Bulbs Going Wild.") Southwestern Australia has a warmer summer climate, perhaps attributable to warm, southward-flowing offshore currents. The moderating maritime influence of most of these coastal climate areas gives them mild winter temperatures well above freezing even during the coldest month of the year. Rainfall is typically greater with increased elevation, especially on western slopes that face the ocean. For example, at 2400 feet (730 m) elevation, nearby Mount Lofty gets twice as much precipitation as Adelaide, the capital of South Australia. At near sea level, the city has an average annual precipitation of about 21 inches (53 cm). Also, the regions around Adelaide and Perth in Australia, and the Cape Town area of South Africa, have much wetter summers than other Mediterranean regions.

Southern California's Chaparral

Every year, wildfires sweep through the canyons of central and southern California. Unfortunately, in such areas our human desire to build in scenic places puts houses where they and their inhabitants are at risk. The *chaparral* (from a Spanish word meaning "where the scrub grows") is a plant community of semi-arid areas with average rainfall of 14 to 25 inches (35 to 63 cm) per year. Shrubs use branches, twigs, and leaves to sieve moisture out of fog-laden air. The dry summer conditions limit tree growth. Clothing the gravelly, rocky slopes and ridges of the coastal ranges—from Shasta County south to the western slopes of the Sierra Nevada mountains, and also the mountains of southern California—chaparral developed as a habitat dependent on fire ecology. The strong-scented shrubs grow, then burn, only to regenerate and grow again. Chamise (*Adenostoma fasciculatum*) has widely spreading branches clothed with evergreen, needle-like leaves that arise from a well-developed burl. Though its high resin content means chamise burns easily, it is also one of the first plants to resprout after a fire.

Fire is not always a bad thing, though. The Green Swamp along the North Carolina coast is a splendid habitat rich in plants, including many species of orchids and insectiverous plants such as sarracenia. Periodic burning removes competitive shrubs and trees, creating a grassy savannah under pine trees and allowing the noncompetitive orchids and insectiverous plants to thrive. Fire is an important part of the ecology of the chaparral and the *fynbos*. Diana Chapman of Telos Rare Bulbs offers the following observations: "You read and hear a lot of theories about why some bulbs will only bloom after fire (as in South Africa) or bloom much better after fire (as in California). The theories range from increased potassium and phosphorus released by the ash; removal of competing vegetation; raising of the soil temperature either by the fire or by exposing the soil surface to the sun from the removal of thatch; etc., etc. The first theory, release of potassium and phosphorus, is just silly. Neither could possibly be absorbed in time to make any difference to a bulb, especially phosphorus, which tends to get bound up in the soil. The removal of competing vegetation doesn't make much sense either, since the bulbs must have flower buds already formed from the year before (or even more than that—sometimes two or three years before) to enable them to flower after a fire. Again, it is almost certainly the release of gibberellin-like compounds that can penetrate the soil to reach the bulb. I tried a little experiment with *Lycoris*, which are notoriously difficult to flower in pots. I had a LOT of pots, so I divided them into several groups, treating each group differently. The two things that made them flower, and flower profusely, were smoke and ethylene."

California's Mediterranean climate can be said to have three subsets based on summer temperatures. The region with (relatively) hot summers includes Los Angeles and the Valley region of Sacramento, Stockton, and Fresno, where the highest monthly temperature averages above 72°F (22°C). The region with moderate to warm summers includes Santa Rosa, Santa Barbara, and Long Beach, with average temperatures below 72°F (22°C) for their highest monthly temperature; coastal areas with frequent fogs, like San Francisco, Santa Cruz, Monterey, and Eureka, have cooler summers.

Gardens and Geophytes in Southern California

Sue Haffner gardens in Clovis, in the central San Joaquin Valley of California, with very hot, arid summers and fairly mild, wet winters. Most areas of her garden are scorching hot in summer, and finding enough shade is a priority. She considers herself still a beginner, still learning, still experimenting. But then, aren't we all? There's always more to learn since gardening is truly the never-ending story. Geophytes that perform reliably for Sue include *Amaryllis belladonna* and that other amaryllis, as *Hippeastrum* hybrids are confusingly called. The beautiful naked lady from South Africa, *A. belladonna*, is a common sight in southern California. They appear in gardens, on grave sites in pioneer cemeteries, massed along driveways, and amid the tawny grasses of an empty lot. Bloom time is in late summer or early fall, when the bulbs produce sturdy stems crowned with pink lily-like flowers. They are called naked ladies since leaves do not emerge simultaneously with the flowers. (For more information on this growth pattern of some geophytes, see Chapter 10, "Geophytes for the Autumn Garden.") In common with several other geophytes that bloom from late summer into autumn, naked ladies do not take kindly to disturbance—not so much due to the time of bloom as much as the nature of the permanent fleshy roots at the base of the bulb. If they wither, dry out, or are trimmed away to fit into a package for shipping, the sizable bulb sulks and waits to bloom again until the roots have been restored.

Hippeastrum, commonly called amaryllis, are native to South America. They clutter the stores in early winter—big, fat bulbs primed to bloom. Their first flowering is guaranteed. Gardeners with deep pockets could even force them like a hyacinth, perching the hapless bulb on a suitably sturdy vase or jar filled with water. Depleted of nutrients after this exercise, the bulb is discarded after its performance. In chill winter regions they are better grown in pots, which at least admits the possibility of bloom in subsequent years. And gardeners in southern California, frost-free parts of Texas, and similar places can put them in the ground and watch them take off. Several years ago, when my daughter moved from Vermont to a community not far from Houston, Texas, several hippeastrum made the move along with the family, a dog, and their chattel goods. Once out of their pots and planted in the new garden, the bulbs happily grew, flowered, and multiplied.

Sue also grows several iridaceous geophytes, notably *Chasmanthe*, *Ixia*, *Sparaxis*, and *Watsonia*, all of which grow from corms. Their swordlike leaves resemble those of gladiolus, but their flowers are quite different from that familiar garden geophyte.

Chasmanthe

The three species of *Chasmanthe* are all recommended for the garden. Perhaps the most striking is *C. floribunda*, with stems 3 feet (1 m) tall, sometimes taller. The flower stem usually branches and carries numerous orange to scarlet flowers in a two-ranked progression. A yellow form, *C. floribunda* var. *duckittii*, is popular in gardens of the South African Cape. This is apparently a natural variation, genetically a simple recessive that inhibits formation of red anthocyanin pigment in the flower. Since in the wild chasmanthe are found in wetter sites, these easy-to-grow geophytes perform best when given a garden site with loamy soil, an occasional dose of fertilizer, and supplemental watering, which encourages vigorous growth. Quick from seed, plants can reach flowering size in their second year. Florists make use of *C. floribunda*, and it has become a popular specialty item in the cut flower industry. *Chasmanthe bicolor* is somewhat smaller growing, with attractive green-tipped orange flowers. The third species, *C. aethiopica*, is daintier yet, growing only 18 to 24 inches (45 to 60 cm) tall, with orange flowers on an unbranched spike.

At up to 48 inches (1.2 m) tall, the stately flowering stem of *Chasmanthe floribunda* displays orange-red flowers, neatly ascending the flower stalk in a precise, flattened manner. Photo courtesy of John Bryan.

A sunny grouping of the primrose-yellow flowers of *Chasmanthe floribunda* var. *duckittii* displays the softer coloration of this variety, rising nicely above the swordlike foliage. Photo courtesy of John Bryan.

Watsonia

Watsonia is a more diverse genus with different species ranging in size from small to tall, usually deciduous, but including a few that are evergreen. Flower color ranges from pink to orange or red, and occasionally cream-colored to pale yellow. Two-ranked, the scentless, rather tubular flowers that flare open at their mouth march along opposite sides of the flower stem in a tidy manner. Several species were introduced to Australia in the early 1900s, and work began both there and in California to develop cultivars with softer, more muted colors. They began appearing on the Australian market during World War I, and though never as popular as gladiolus, they had their heyday in the decades between 1920 and 1940. John Cronin, director of Melbourne's Royal Botanic Gardens from 1909 to 1923, worked with various species, including *W. borbonica*, *W. borbonica* subsp. *ardernei*, *W. aletroides*, *W. meriana* var. *meriana*, *W. coccinea*, and *W. versfeldii*, to produce several named cultivars. Cronin and other growers had as their objective not only to produce a wider range of colors but also to increase the size of the flowers. Additional branching of the inflorescence would produce a larger, more florif-

Watsonia borbonica subsp. *ardernei*. Photo by John Bryan.

erous bloom spike. Extending the flowering season to include early spring and adapting the plants to the hot, humid spring and summer conditions of Australia's east coast were also their aims. Most of these cultivars have been lost, and only brief, informal descriptions in catalogs and gardening magazines of the period remain to give us a clue as to what these cultivars were like. *Watsonia* 'Australia' was described as having large, old-rose to soft-pink flowers with frilly lobes; while 'Queenstown' had pale mauve, long-tubed flowers; and 'Ballarat' had broad-lobed, pale, blush-pink flowers. Today the few watsonias that are sold in Australia are either renamed or sold simply by flower color: 'Tivoli Pink', 'Lilac Towers', and 'Ivory Towers'. Watsonias are not very popular in Australia, given that these tough plants can establish themselves quite persistently around old homesteads and then spread. "Watsonia" as a derogatory epithet is perhaps best reserved for the voracious *W. meriana* var. *bulbillifera*, but all watsonia have become tarred with that brush.

In *The Color Encyclopedia of Cape Bulbs* (2002), authors John C. Manning, Peter Goldblatt, and Dee Snijman are quite enthusiastic about the garden value of watsonias, recommending that they be interplanted with *Agapanthus*, with the two plants providing consecutive waves of color for several months. Their other suggestion pairs watsonias with *Amaryllis*. In fact, they propose planting watsonias with other species of *Watsonia* to extend the flowering period, after which they can be mown down, to reappear and rebloom the following year. Though their native haunts are summer-dry, watsonias from the Cape Province tolerate summer rainfall and even mild winter frosts, provided they are of brief duration. Some popular species for garden use include *W. knysnana*, which has spikes 5 feet (1.5 m) tall of pink or orange flowers, and *W. pillansii*, 2 to 4 feet (0.6 to 1.2 m) tall, with scarlet to orange flowers. Both of these species are evergreen and bloom from November to January in Southern Africa. Very popular in gardens is *W. meriana*, especially the smaller growing selections 2 feet (0.6 m) tall rather than 6 feet (1.8 m) tall.

The tubular flowers of *Watsonia pillansii* open widely at the tip, offering a good display of soft, peachy orange flowers as they ascend the sturdy stem. Photo courtesy of John Bryan.

Flowers range in color from red to orange, pink, or mauve. Deciduous, the leaves die back after the plants finish their period of bloom, September to November in southern Africa. But beware of *W. meriana* var. *bulbillifera*. Not only is it sparse flowering, but clusters of cormlets are produced along the spike at each node. It is an invasive thug, causing problems in Australia and southern California. Dwarf and dainty *W. laccata* grows at most only 16 inches (40 cm) tall, with a short spike of pink to purple, orange, or white flowers. It, too, flowers from September to November in southern Africa. Variable in height, *W. borbonica* grows from less than 2 feet (0.6 m) to as much as 6½ feet (2 m) tall. In southern Africa, the purple-pink flowers appear in October to January. A brilliant white form is *W. borbonica* subsp. *ardernei*. Other lovely species that might be found in nurseries and garden centers include bright red *W. aletroides*, pink *W. amabilis*, and orange *W. coccinea*.

Ixia

All of the about 45 or 50 species of *Ixia* are deciduous. Its flowers come in a wide range of colors, from pink to mauve or violet, pale to deep blue, orange to yellow, or white. Sometimes a darker blotch marks the center of the upward facing, starry to cuplike, six-petalled flowers, and sometimes they are fragrant. Flower spikes are 8 to 16 inches (20 to 40 cm) tall. Some species have a few flowers closely clustered at the top of a stem, while others have more numerous flowers ascending the stem. In the southwestern Cape, where they are mostly found, bloom time is generally September to October,

Another choice for up-to-date gardeners, *Ixia* 'Hogarth' has well-filled spikes of creamy white flowers with purple centers. Photo courtesy of the Netherlands Flower Bulb Information Center.

with an occasional species flowering a month earlier or later. To find the Northern Hemisphere correlation, add six months. Flowers open wide in sunny weather but close when conditions become cloudy. Selected hybrids are popular cut flowers. 'Giant' has white flowers with a purple blotch at the base of the purple-tipped petals. 'Marquette' has warm, mimosa-yellow flowers with more of a purple-tinged red blotch and tip. 'Panorama' is a saucy blend of fuchsia-pink and purple. 'Rose Emperor' is earlier flowering, with a large spike of pale pink flowers flushed with a darker rose on the outside of the petals and at the center of each flower.

'Yellow Emperor' has bold yellow flowers, ringed with purple at the center and camouflaged brownish purple on the outside.

The corms are sufficiently inexpensive (in 2003, one well-known American mail-order source was offering 25 corms for $5 or $6) that they can be used for seasonal interest or container grown and discarded after flowering. Not only are they too tender for anything but a Zone 9 or milder winter, wet summer conditions quickly rot the dormant corms. Full sun, good drainage, adequate moisture while in growth, but dry conditions when dormant will best suit ixia. The species can be raised from seed, which should be sown in autumn under fluorescent grow lights or in a greenhouse. Sow thinly to allow seedlings to remain undisturbed in the seed pan until their second year. Some will flower in their third year. Offsets removed from the parent corm and grown on will usually flower in their second year.

We tend to think of plants we grow as being present-day, up-to-date components of our gardens. Two species of *Ixia*, the 8 to 20 inches (20 to 50 cm) tall *I. maculata* with dark-eyed orange flowers, and 6 to 16 inches (15 to 40 cm) tall *I. monadelpha* with its striking orange-eyed, icy blue flowers, were both popular in 18th and 19th century Europe. Pat Colville in Pasadena, California, (more about her garden later) grows several ixia hybrids, and three species have done well for her while others dwindled away. *Ixia dubia* has 4 to 15 orange to yellow flowers crowded onto the stem, often with a dark brown or purple center accenting the flowers. *Ixia flexuosa* has pale pink or mauve flowers, sometimes white with darker streaks, and purple veining. The flowers have a mild but noticeable musky odor. Finally, *I. rapunculoides* is a lovely and very variable species, with one to four flowers per spike. Its flower color ranges from cream to a pinkish mauve, pale blue or purple, and often with a yellow or green tube to the bell-shaped flowers.

Sparaxis

Sparaxis has about 15 species and can be grown much the same as ixia. Growing from a corm, these small, deciduous geophytes have large flowers relative to their dwarf stature. Several species have been cultivated for more than 200 years, and harlequin sparaxis, *S. tricolor*, perhaps the most popular currently in cultivation, was first described from specimens being grown in Holland in the late 18th century. Flower color in the different species varies from white to cream, sunny yellow to orange, to scarlet or pink, and some, such as *S. elegans*, with plump, rounded, peach-colored petals, are strikingly marked with sharply contrasting yellow and dark purple to black centers. *S. tricolor* has deep orange, call it brick red, flowers with a yellow center, and the two colors are separated by a black band.

Sparaxis hybrids flower well for Pat Colville, and even when the plants were virused, *S. elegans* flowered well, displaying its attractive salmon-pink flowers and a violet to

An assortment of *Sparaxis tricolor* provides a closer view of the mixed colors available in contemporary selections. Photo courtesy of the Netherlands Flower Bulb Information Center.

The terra cotta/coral flowers and yellow throat of this *Sparaxis tricolor* offer a warm Mediterranean option for the designing gardener. Photo courtesy of the Netherlands Flower Bulb Information Center.

purple band at the base of the petals, which is sometimes further accentuated with yellow. Sparaxis have a long history as garden plants. *Sparaxis grandiflora* was being cultivated prior to 1792 in Britain, Austria, and France, as well as in Holland.

Give sparaxis full sun and good drainage, and then enjoy their midsummer blossoms that are useful as cut flowers. While they prefer a Mediterranean climate, sparaxis will tolerate some summer rainfall. Bloom time can be manipulated through withholding water to force dormancy. For spring and summer flowers, plant in autumn. For flowers later in summer, plant in spring. Water sparingly in winter until the flower spike appears, and then water more freely. Keep watering until the leaves begin to die away, after which store dry and cool. Seedlings flower in their third or fourth year, while cormels flower their second year. Sparaxis would be charming in any Mediterranean climate garden, even tolerating summer rainfall—charming, that is, unless they take off and naturalize in the countryside, something that three species have done to the point of weediness in Australia.

Veltheimia

Veltheimia bracteata also does well in Sue Haffner's California garden, but with part shade rather than full sun. Not surprising since in South Africa where it grows wild, this veltheimia is found in the shelter of shrubs and trees. This is a bulb that I happen to adore, though my growing conditions in New Jersey require that I grow it in containers. Since it is winter-growing yet tender to frost, it has a home in my cool greenhouse.

Bulbs flowered just fine when they lived on the windowsill of a guest bedroom, where the heat was turned up only for overnight guests. Wavy-edged leaves form a rosette around the bloom spike in early winter; then it leisurely makes its way into flower in February. The upper two-thirds of the spike, 12 to 16 inches (30 to 45 cm) tall, is densely packed with up to 60 tubular, dusty rose flowers. Found in the coastal scrub of the Eastern Cape, *V. bracteata* prefers some light shade. It is more or less evergreen, and while it needs less water during its resting period, it should not be allowed to dry out completely to the point where it loses its foliage. *Veltheimia capensis* is a deciduous species, native to rocky slopes of the southwestern Cape, which needs full sun for better flowering and to keep the leaves from growing limp and flaccid.

Other Gardens, Other Geophytes

Eremurus, *Lachenalia*, ranunculus, tulips, and lilies are a few geophytes Sue Haffner has tried and lost. She mentioned that "What I want to try is *Ferraria crispa*, in the ground. Someone wrote that this was a thug in the ground, but that I would have to see to believe." Ferraria is an unusual South African iridaceous plant, which grows from a corm. It produces a few narrow, swordlike leaves at the base, with other, smaller ones ascending the stem. The curious and unusual six-parted flowers, mottled in dark purplish brown and olive green, have extraordinarily crisp and wavy margins. In common with many other geophytes from the Cape Province, ferraria wants an open, freely draining soil. In the wild, the corms often use contractile roots to pull themselves deep into the ground. They appreciate full sun, ample water while in active growth, and dry conditions when dormant. Though said to be malodorous, I did not find it so. Admittedly, I had to grow mine in a container since, while ferraria will withstand a kiss of frost, it does not tolerate cold winters.

Consider Shirley Meneice's garden in Pebble Beach, California, barely 100 yards (91 m) from the ocean on a southwest slope facing the sea. She notes, "I am in Zone 9, probably Zone 10, with temperatures around 30°F in winter (other than exceptional winters which occur about once a decade). Because we are on the coast there is considerable fog in the summer with resultant cool temperatures in the 60s. We may have a few days when it reaches 80° to 85°F. We seldom see temperatures above 90°F in summer. A prolonged 'hot spell' is three days. Every six to eight years we may get a few days in the 90°F range, at which point everyone complains, shops close, and most of us head for the beach. The bulbs seem more tolerant than we who plant them do. Our rain generally falls from November to 15 April and averages 18 inches per year. This rain year (1 July 2002 to 1 July 2003) we have had about 13 inches with not much more time to catch up. The summers are dry. My soil has been amended for over 20 years with compost, clippings, leaves and pine needles. The underlying soil is clay and partially decomposed granite. It drains poorly, thus the years of amending it."

Shirley is currently growing the following impressive list of geophytes from many different continents. From South Africa: *Agapanthus praecox* subsp. *orientalis*, *Amaryllis belladonna*, *Anomatheca laxa*, *Babiana rubrocyanea* and *B. stricta*, *Chasmanthe floribunda*, *Clivia miniata*, *Ferraria crispa*, *Gladiolus* ×*colvillei*, *Hesperantha*, *Homeria*, *Ixia maculata*, *Lachenalia mutabilis*, *Moraea*, *Schizostylis coccinea*, *Scilla peruviana* (which is also native to southwestern Europe), *Sparaxis*, and *Watsonia*. She grows geophytes from Europe, choosing those from the southern regions with a range into the Mediterranean that find her garden's climate a match for their native haunts: *Allium moly*, with a few golden bells dangling in a sparse-flowered umbel; and the exotic snake's head iris, or widow iris, *Hermodactylus tuberosus*, with its somber velvety brown-black falls and short, narrow, pale olive to apple-green standards from southern Europe into Greece, Turkey, and Israel. *Leucojum aestivum* is native from Europe to Iran, and *Cyclamen persicum* and *Dracunculus vulgaris* are from the Mediterranean. Shirley has welcomed several geophytes from South America into her garden: *Habranthus tubispathus* with its crocuslike, copper to orange, golden, or yellow flowers; *Rhodophiala advena* (syn. *Hippeastrum advenum*), with its flowers like a miniature trumpet lily, in red, pink, or yellow; and *Hippeastrum puniceum* (syn. *H. equestre*), with green-throated pink, scarlet, or bright red flowers. *Hymenocallis* ×*macrostephana*, that fragrant hybrid between

For the moonlight garden, wonderful, pure white flowers of *Babiana* 'White King' would shimmer as night spreads over the garden. Photo courtesy of the Netherlands Flower Bulb Information Center.

H. narcissiflora and *H. speciosa*, with white to pale green flowers, also graces her garden, as does *Ipheion uniflorum*, with its pale to violet-blue, starlike flowers, and *Tigridia pavonia*, from Mexico and Guatemala. Neither has Shirley forgotten native plants from the western United States: *Calochortus venustus*, *Triteleia ixioides*, and *Sisyrinchium californicum* and *S. angustifolium* from the southeastern states. She even grows plebian canna, native to the tropics and subtropics of the New World. Shirley finds that all of these geophytes—which are outdoors, planted in the ground rather than in containers—do well naturally, with some supplemental watering and absolutely no heavy shade. She does note, "I grow tulips but they are little better than annuals as far as bloom goes. The foliage appears for a number of years, but no bloom."

Though Shirley considers herself more of a plant lover than an expert, there's something revealing about a gardener with her patience. You don't just go out and buy plants like these at the garden center down the street or at a big box store, nor do they germinate immediately and pop into flower in a single season. She went on a University of California, Santa Cruz, Arboretum tour to see the "Flora of Namaqualand and the Cape." And that was where Shirley's collection of uncommon South African geophytes got its start—not as plants, mind you, but as seeds. "One of my first sources was seeds I purchased from Rachel at Silverhill. We heard about it from our tour guide, a nurseryman in George, S.A., and two of us found the location and paid them a visit. There was a TV crew there filming, but Rachel still took time to greet us, take down our orders, and put us on her mailing list." Other geophytes were acquired from specialty growers in the United States, often at one remove as a small, one- or two-person nursery would close due to age of the owners or other personal circumstances. She mentioned, "I have also purchased seeds and bulbs of native plants from Rana Creek Habitat Restoration here in Carmel Valley. Living in what is basically a Mediterranean climate, I find that the main requirement for me is patience in keeping pots of seeds several years before giving up on their growing. Our winter rains and dry summers are perfect for the geophytes I grow and, once established, they prosper if I can give them the conditions they prefer. They don't want to be killed with kindness for sure!"

On the northern California coast—with dry, mild summers; wet, mild winters; and an occasional frost—Mary Sue Ittner of the Pacific Bulb Society gardens mentioned, "We have haphazard rainfall in the fall. People start talking about how dry it is and how much rain is needed and worry about fires since there would be no rain from when it stopped, say sometime in April or May most years, until September or October or sometimes even November. Winter is when we get most of our rainfall, and then it tapers off in spring." Her garden is located in coastal Mendocino County, where she lives at about 840 feet (256 m) with a distant view of the Pacific Ocean. Her climate is a classic Mediterranean one, with rain starting in the fall, building in the winter, and tapering off in spring. Summers are completely dry. Temperatures in winter occasionally get below freezing, but not usually much below. Average rainfall is 64 inches (163 cm) but in *El Niño* years it has been much higher. Summer temperatures are moderate as well, with only occasional hot days in a row almost always followed by coastal fog that cools things off. Evenings are cool. It can be very windy, especially in spring and summer, which makes her part of the coast less foggy than areas north or south.

Mary Sue grows bulbs in containers, in raised beds (created just for bulbs that are not watered in summer), and in the ground. The geophytes in her garden are mostly native or South African, with a few others thrown in that have worked. She mentions,

"As I keep experimenting I'll probably find others that can survive. It's always a gamble when you live where there is so much rain and are passionate about flowers that don't bloom for very long. Since I grow so many things I am bound to get some of them to bloom on those sunny days between storms. My experience has been that you have to not only think genus, but species as well. Experimenting continues and I try to be philosophical about the deaths. I've run out of room long ago so I am always looking for a new place to plant. Perhaps those chasmanthes (*Chasmanthe bicolor*, *C. floribunda*, and *C. floribunda* var. *duckittii*) need to make room for something else. They have huge leaves and ever expanding corms, but no flowers."

Previously, Mary Sue had a garden in Stockton, California, where it was hotter in summer, slightly colder in winter, and certainly much dryer. Her garden had clay soil. The disparate conditions meant she could grow geophytes in Stockton that she cannot grow on the coast. For example, in Stockton, tigridia came back year after year, as did ranunculus. She brought tigridia with her to the new garden, where it bloomed the first year and has never been seen since. The same holds true for ranunculus, which she occasionally sees in gardens around town in her part of coastal Mendocino, but never the second year. "So maybe," she speculates, "it is our excessively wet winters. My father-in-law grew wonderful ranunculus in his San Francisco pure sand garden. Temperatures were similar to mine, but rainfall significantly less." She notes that "his biggest weeds there were *Ornithogalum umbellatum* and *Oxalis pes-caprae*."

Many different narcissus were also reliable repeat performers in Stockton but not where she gardens now. Mary Sue thinks it is not so much temperature and rainfall as it is a matter of sunshine: "There are a few narcissus that bloom for me here, but I suspect my garden just isn't sunny enough. Many watsonias are weedy in my area. We joke about it because the community to the south, The Sea Ranch, only allows native plants. There are watsonias, narcissus, *Amaryllis belladonna*, and *Zantedeschia aethiopica* that are survivors that can be seen in common areas where they aren't supposed to be. I have planted a lot of *Watsonia coccinea* in the ground. One lasted three years before disappearing, but mostly they don't come back. *Watsonia pillansii* was a reliable bloomer for a friend in San Diego, but bloomed only every five or six years here so I took it out. However, I have a number of some of the shorter species that may be too happy in one of my raised beds."

Mary Sue has tried some geophytes with no luck. They either die, vanish, or (perhaps even more frustrating) grow but do not flower. "I never saw *Habranthus tubispathus* again after it went in the ground. Many crocus have lasted zero to one season. I planted *Gloriosa superba* in the ground when Rachel (of Silverhill again) said she could grow it in Cape Town but it never came up. Neither did *Rhodophiala bifida*, the only colchicum I ever tried, or *Bulbinella nutans* with its bottlebrush spike of white flowers. Now I didn't realize when I planted the latter that it was going to be in the path the dog took to chase the neighbor's cat that used to tantalize the dog since it was safely protected by the deer fence. So that could be the explanation for that one. The alliums and calochortus I have tried are not successful, with the exception of *Allium unifolium* and *Calochortus vestae*.

"Summer rainfall species of kniphofias aren't very happy, and some of the *Ixia* species I have tried have not returned. However ixia hybrids are weedy, so score one for hybrid vigor. I have nerines in the ground and most have never bloomed. I planted out a number of *Leucocoryne*s once, and they were beautiful but never came back. *Moraea comptonii* and *M. minor* were short-lived, showing that not all *Homeria* types are weeds. Muscari grew and returned for me in Stockton, but mostly has dwindled here. *Ornithogalum arabicum* both here and in Stockton lasted only a year or two. *Rhodohypoxis* was short lived in the ground. Either it was too wet in winter or too dry in summer, or maybe both.

"One Peruvian lily, *Alstroemeria* cultivar, that I had in a very large wooden container eventually expanded to such a degree that the boards were coming apart. I emptied it out, found an old issue of *Herbertia* that told how to divide them, and repotted it. Some of the leftovers I just dumped on the ground and left. Eventually I disposed of them on the other side of my fence, which is land that belongs to the water company. I was making a brush pile there and one day saw on the very top of this tall pile that there were alstroemeria blooms. The tubers had survived and a stalk had made its way through the pile. It bloomed well until the deer eventually found it. Now at least three years and maybe more later I have an ever-increasing clump of alstroemeria where I dumped those tubers I didn't want on my side of the fence. I made a bed there and added soil and I don't remember leaving any tubers there. No sign of life for years and then. . . . So my experience with alstroemeria has been that if I try to grow it in the ground I can't, but if I mistreat it I can."

Pat Colville thinks that alstroemeria must taste bad because it has been seeding itself in the ground from pot plants and spreading. She lives in Pasadena, California, around 20 miles (32 kilometers) inland from the ocean and in the foothills of the San Gabriel Mountains, with peaks to 10,000 feet (3050 m) or more. She described her locale as having "an average annual rainfall of 19 inches. Then there was last year (2002) when we got less than 5 inches. That's comparable to the Mojave Desert. Temperatures are cool at night, with warm days going to hot, 90° to 100°F in the summer. Freezing is rare. The soil I have is terrible decomposed sandstone, the yard a little too shady. There are mean gophers or moles that eat anything tasty, so I assume only poisonous bulbs are surviving. Other animals, probably possums and skunks, take labels and turn over pots so names get lost. There are plants in the raised beds that are thriving, too, and some of those could probably be successful in the ground. Plants go in the ground if I think they will do better there, if I have extras I want to test, and if they are not blooming anyway. Some in the latter category then bloom and others are never seen again. We are fenced from the deer and don't have gophers, but we do have moles and other critters that dig holes. The squirrels seem fixated on the pine cones in the pine trees, but some day they may figure out that nirvana is awaiting them and I'll be in trouble. We water occasionally in summer, but the tree roots soak that up and when you dig down in the soil it is completely dry."

Pat has an astonishingly wide range of geophytes growing in pots, raised beds, and in the ground. "In the ground, in order of abundance, there are lots of agapanthus, daylilies, narcissus, veltheimia, *Amaryllis belladonna*, and clivia. There are *Hippeastrum papilio*, who especially like the shade. One oxalis, a pink *Oxalis purpurea*, was probably introduced as a hitchhiker. If this doesn't seed, how is it that it can appear everywhere? It only blooms with good sun and has spread way too much, but looks nice with the yellow naturalized freesia that is spreading wildly. Less abundant are hymenocallis, rain lilies (yes they bloom lots and are in semi shade), *Scilla peruviana*, canna, brunsvigia, dietes, ginger, ixia, and chasmanthe. I have some iris: *Iris douglasiana* is a real survivor, gophers eat the showy hybrids, and *I. wattii* likes the shade. (Well, maybe it isn't *wattii* since it came from a not always reliable source, so I have to check that out.) Then there are daffodils, hyacinths, watsonia, kniphofia, and zantedeschia. Easter

The irislike leaves and violet-purple to intense fuchsia-pink flowers of this well-grown group of *Babiana stricta* would reward any gardener (in this case Mother Nature, who tends this colony growing in the wild outside Cape Town). Photo courtesy of John Bryan.

lilies—I just dump them in the ground rather than throw them out after blooming, and they like shade, too. In the ground they bloom in June. *Crinum moorei* also likes the shade, and reproduces."

Objective about what geophytes she is growing, Pat takes note of how they perform and what she might do to improve things or if, perhaps, it is time to discard them. Some of the bulbs that are growing directly in the ground and blooming reliably are "the usual suspects" one expects to find in California gardens. At least a few of the *Amaryllis belladonna* bloom every year, but not all them. Babianas, some of which are hybrids, are doing well. Iridaceous, deciduous, with a deep-seated corm, the cup-shaped flowers come in a modest range of colors, from blue to mauve or white, and some species have red or yellow flowers. What's more, the flowers can be a single color or marked with white blotches or darker ones, and they can be fragrant or have no scent. *Babiana rubrocyanea* is a show-stopper, with deep blue-violet flowers, each petal

The diversity of colors found in *Babiana stricta*, with its pale cream, dark purple, blue, or mauvish blue petals, is remarkable. Photo courtesy of the Netherlands Flower Bulb Information Center.

marked with an attention-getting red blotch. Not bad for something 6 inches (15 cm) tall, or less. Mauve to pink or dark red *B. villosa* is also doing well, and Pat is sure some other species are also in her garden. *Chasmanthe aethiopica* has to be watched for weediness, while the others she has tried increase rapidly but don't bloom.

Moraea

A goodly selection of geophytes that Pat obtained as *Homeria* have now been reclassified as *Moraea*. They are all over her garden and bloom for a long time. Some of the 120 species of *Moraea* are called peacock iris for their large, spreading outer petals marked with a bold, even iridescent, central blotch. Others, perhaps less spectacular yet still garden-worthy, are more or less irislike. Still other moraea have cup-shaped flowers. Some species have flowers that last for three days while others last just a few hours. Some are sweetly fragrant, others unpleasantly scented. Nearly all are deciduous. The winter-growing species from the southwestern Cape flower in early spring to spring. Their deeply buried small corms are covered with a fibrous tunic that may be either black or very pale and can quickly dry out while out of the ground—prompt replanting is important when digging to divide a crowded clump. Moraea can follow fire, blooming after it has swept through the *fynbos*. In the garden, they prefer a heavy to sandy soil, but good drainage and a site with ample moisture when they are growing are essential. Moisture when they are dormant soon leads to rotten corms. Fertilizing during the growing season is beneficial. For the enthusiastic gardener, raising morarea from seed is one way to obtain a wide range of healthy corms. The smaller species will perhaps flower their second year, with good flowering to be expected from three-year-old corms.

Pat grows several species: *Moraea collina* with lightly scented yellow or salmon flowers, and *M. flaccida*, which has salmon-colored flowers with a yellow center, and some are entirely yellow. *Moraea ochroleuca* has cup-shaped yellow to orange, sometimes bicolored flowers, and their shape is suggestive of a small tulip. Unfortunately, they have an unpleasant, fetid odor. This is another species that blooms soon after a fire. She also grows hybrids of these same species.

Mary Sue Ittner in northern California also grows moraea, but different species than Pat grows. Mary Sue has *Moraea aristata*, a gorgeous aristocrat with three broad, white tepals marked with a violet halo around a royal blue or emerald green blotch as bee guide at the base, and the three inner tepals are icy blue. *Moraea atropunctata* is more subdued, with grayish white outer tepals darkly speckled at the center, and brownish on the reverse; *M. bipartita* has blue flowers with yellow nectar guides; while *M. tripetala* has blue to violet flowers with cream-colored nectar guides. Variable, a few infrequent plants may be white or yellowish. And *M. vegetata* has buff to dull purple-brown flowers with yellow bee guides on the inner three tepals. Some of Mary Sue's moraea are in the ground and others are in raised beds with better drainage, but all bloom simultaneously.

Veltheimia bracteata is a good performer in Pat's garden, and *Watsonia humilis* and *W. marginata* also thrive. *Freesia alba* is very invasive but since it is long-blooming and fragrant, it remains. *Freesia laxa* is less weedy, does bloom, and would probably like more summer water.

Brodiaea, Dichelostemma, and *Triteleia*

There has been some confusion (some people think confusion reigns) when it comes to the taxonomic sorting out of *Brodiaea*, *Dichelostemma*, and *Triteleia*. They all started off in brodiaea, and then this one was split away to a different genus while that one was left for yet another one. I'm not stepping into that discussion and intend to follow the lead of current trends in nomenclature.

Pat Colville grows a few California native geophytes, such as *Brodiaea californica*, with from 2 to 12 bluish purple, lilac to violet or pink, funnel-shaped flowers with dark midveins accenting the petals. Reaching up to 30 inches (0.8 m) tall, it is a robust plant that grows in grassland and chaparral. The dark brown corm is so fibrous coated as to appear shaggy. *Brodiaea elegans* has violet-purple flowers, sometimes with a rosy tint, which makes it look mauve. Both of these are hardy to Zone 8. *Brodiaea minor* is smaller, growing only 10 inches (25 cm) tall, often less. While it is hardier than the two preceding species (down to 0°F, or 32°C, in western Oregon, in free-draining gravelly soil kept dry in summer), it isn't very attractive since the tepals are very narrow and linear—what a friend of mine in Connecticut used to refer to as "B.I.O."—shorthand for "botanical interest only." Pat mentions, "Interestingly, I haven't had luck with *B. terrestris* when I have planted it out, and it grows where I live."

A striking color pairing of two complementary hues matches the violet-blue flowers of *Triteleia laxa* 'Queen Fabiola' with the hot-orange blossoms of *Asclepias tuberosa*, creating an out-of-the-ordinary display for the sunny summer garden. Photo courtesy of Brent Heath/Brent and Becky's Bulbs.

In this species, the scape varies from barely an inch (2.5 cm) to 8 inches (20 cm) tall, with numerous, showy, mauve-pink to blue-violet flowers. Found in grassland and oak woodland along the California coast from San Diego to Humboldt County, it seems to prefer a sandy soil. Some dappled shade or afternoon shade is helpful in hot climates, and water is not needed in summer.

Grass nuts, *Dichelostemma capitatum*, is a small species, ranging far and wide from northern Mexico up into Douglas County, Oregon, and eastward to Utah and New Mexico. It is found in a wide range of habitats as well, from open woodland to scrub, grassland into desert areas. In common with other species in the *Brodiaea/Dichelostemma/Triteleia* cohort, the important cultural advice seems to be "keep it dry in summer." Growing from 4 to 16 inches (10 to 40 cm) tall, *D. capitatum* has a tight head of blue-purple, occasionally pink in various shades, or white flowers. Wild hyacinth, *D. multiflorum*, differs from the previous species, and from brodiaea, in its preference for clay soils in grassland and scrub thickets, where it may be found from around San Francisco Bay to southern Oregon. The umbel of 10 to 35 rosy to bluish purple flowers forms a dense sphere. Pat also grows firecracker flower, *D. ida-maia* (formerly *Brodiaea ida-maia*), which gardeners are likely to find available, since corms are raised from seed in Holland. Pollinated by hummingbirds, the bright red, tubular flowers, tipped with pale green, dangle from the top of a stalk 12 to 24 inches (30 to 60 cm) tall. Leaves begin to wither and fade as flowering begins in early summer. It is easily raised from seed and may also be propagated through the new corms that form on short stolons. Propagation may also be accomplished by scoring the corm's basal plate to encourage the production of additional offsets. Said to be hardy down to 15°F (−9°C), I think that to be successful, firecracker flower requires complex conditions that include sharp drainage, deep planting, and dry conditions in summer while it is dormant. *Dichelostemma congestum* 'Pink Diamond' is a cultivar available from Dutch bulb growers, which may be a cross between *D. congestum* and *D. ida-maia*.

Then there is *Triteleia ixioides* (formerly *Brodiaea ixioides*), which is found in coastal California and northward, barely making it over the line into southern Oregon, growing in gravelly or sandy soil among scrub and at forest margins. Four subspecies have dull yellow, bright golden-yellow, pale yellow, or white to pale yellow flowers. In the 1990s, Wim de Goede, a Dutch grower, selected a good buttercup-yellow form with a green stripe on the outside of each petal and began propagating it. With up to 60 flowers on each stem of 20 to 24 inches (30 to 60 cm) tall that open in succession, *T. ixioides* 'Starlight' offers a long period of bloom in early summer. Triplet lily, *T. laxa*, has blue to violet, sometimes white flowers. Adaptable, in the wild it may be found in grassland, open woodland, or brushy slopes, growing on slopes or on flat ground that can be rather moist in spring. What gardeners will readily find in catalogs is *T. laxa* 'Koningin Fabiola', sometimes known as 'Queen Fabiola', with as many as 25 large, dark blue, upward-facing, bell-like flowers at the top of stems 20 to 24 inches (30 to 60 cm) tall in early summer. Pat grows both of these triteleia species and also *T. hyacinthina*, with bowl-shaped, elegantly white flowers, neatly marked with a thin dark line down the center of the petal on the outside. Occasionally plants are found with blue or lilac flowers. Height varies from 4 to 16 inches (10 to 40 cm). Though it, too, requires a dry summer, in spring *T. hyacinthina* prefers moist conditions and may often be found growing in swales. Native from British Columbia southward to California and eastward into Idaho, this attractive plant is also the hardiest, reputedly reliable to Zone 4.

A final few

Pat is experimenting with a handful of other geophytes. Calochortus have not been successful when planted in the garden (as opposed to container cultivation), but in the last two years *Calochortus vestae* has bloomed. She planted a lot of crocus and many are gone, but *Crocus imperati* is better each year, *C. chrysanthus* hybrids survive, and *C. vernus* also persist. Fisherman's wand, *Dierama pulcherrimum*, which should need more summer water and does not like wet winters, is doing fine. Summer snowflake, *Leucojum aestivum*, is long-blooming and very satisfactory, rather surprising when I consider how well it does in New Jersey, where it is wet all year long and significantly colder in winter.

Altogether softer in appearance, the umbel of greenish yellow flowers of *Triteleia ixiodes* 'Starlight' offers a more subtle option for garden design. Whether partnered with blue or with orange, the effect will be more restrained. Photo courtesy of Brent Heath/Brent and Becky's Bulbs.

I have seen it suggested that certain of these dry summer geophytes will do better when given some water in summer. In the wild, many of these geophytes are buried deep in the soil or nestled up next to rocks, situations where some residual moisture will remain year-round. If they are growing under shrubs, the soil is shaded and at least minimally cooler than a site in the open. Recall how when you turn over a rock the soil beneath feels cooler, even on a hot summer day after a dry spell. It was shaded, and just a trace of moisture makes it feel cooler. Keep in mind that cultivation in a garden and survival in the wild are two quite different situations. If one or some or most of a population of geophytes in a garden-sized area out in the wild fail to thrive in a given year, no one minds except their pollinators and any creature that might dine on the seeds. Gardeners, however, prefer a pleasant, if not lavish display of flowers every year. Once I read a "recipe" for making martinis: "Carry the bottle of vermouth past the liquor cabinet every now and again." Summer watering of dry summer geophytes is something like that: once every three or four weeks give the area a bare minimum of a sprinkle to keep a modicum of moisture in the soil. But don't get carried away—just a smidgen of water is all that's needed in summer. As one California gardener points out, virtually any bulb from mild areas around the Mediterranean, the Western Cape of South Africa, south and western Australia, and central Chile can be easily grown in California—that is, so long as they are given a mild, moist winter and a warm (even hot), dry summer. The biggest reason California gardeners fail with these bulbs is their insistence on watering in the summer, thus rotting the bulbs. Select geophytes suited to your garden habitat. Tulips want a dry summer, and they have that in southern California. What's missing is the cold winter that tulips also require. No tulips, then, unless you intend to dig and refrigerate them, and then replant on a yearly basis. How much happier the situation when you choose geophytes that thrive with the dry summers and winter rain that comes to the Mediterranean garden. As Pat Colville says, "Experimenting continues."

CHAPTER 6

Geophytes for Texas Gardens

Climate, Conditions, Gardens, and Geophytes

"Where does central Texas fit into the Mediterranean climate scenario?" asked Cynthia Mueller of College Station, Texas. "We have summer days usually always 90° to 100°F, with nights not dropping below 80° or 82°F most of the time (which curtails the survival of plants such as pelargoniums). Rainfall in the summer is scattered, but sometimes there will be periods of drizzle/rain for a week or more, which is very rough on rosemary, lavender, lemon verbena, succulents, aloes, and yuccas, which can rot under these circumstances. Species gladiolus are also vulnerable to these irregular wet spells. When this does not occur, and watering can be done on a controlled basis, everything is fine. Another 'climactic change' has occurred in my area, because almost every home has an irrigation system, which sometimes are too thoroughly wetting flower beds on a continual basis. Rain lilies, *Zephyranthes* in particular, are not triggered to have 'bursts' of bloom under these conditions. It appears that bulbs such as *Scilla peruviana* have to be lifted in June and not replanted until late fall. The extreme heat of summer must blast the developing flower buds. *Hippeastrum* can live outdoors successfully in all but the worst winters (dropping to 8°F on one occasion, which killed everything in above-ground containers and froze bulbs that were in the ground down to the basal plate. Who could let me know if central Texas can be included in the concept of 'Mediterranean gardens'?"

If Cynthia lived in California, such questions could be readily answered through recourse to the Sunset garden guide. Developed by *Sunset* magazine, it divides the Pacific Northwest, California, and adjacent western states into numerous zones based on temperature, duration of hot/cold weather, rainfall, coastal fogs, elevation, and more. Gardeners elsewhere in the country are stuck using the USDA zone map, which makes do with significantly fewer zones. Based on minimum winter temperature alone, the duration of that low temperature is not considered as a factor. So a place that dips below freezing at night yet warms above 32°F (0°C) each day is considered to be in the same zone as regions that go below freezing and stay there for a week or more. Recent revisions to the previous zone map do nothing to improve things; it now shows Wilmington, North Carolina, in the same zone as Washington, DC.

The answer for Cynthia's question, I think, would be to take the USDA zone map only as a starting point and then examine the weather patterns and climatic conditions as she has already done. Pragmatically, if plants that are known to thrive in Mediterranean conditions also do well in central Texas, then, yes, the concept of "Mediterranean gardens" does hold sway. And the determination cannot be made from observations over just one or two years but must be taken over a sufficiently long period as to even out fluctuations of temperature and rainfall. Cynthia does know that Roman hyacinths have been around at least since 1900, having endured in the gardens around old houses in her area, and she thinks they very rarely come from seed. I remember these being used for forcing when I was a child, their deliciously fragrant flowers all the more special for blooming while it was still winter outside. After they were finished flowering, the bulbs were discarded. Today they are difficult to obtain and expensive when they can be found.

Schoolhouse lily, *Rhodophiala bifida*, is another bulb that Cynthia says is frequently seen in many older yards and abandoned gardens. The common grape hyacinth (often inhabiting drier lawns or open places) and summer snowflake, *Leucojum aestivum*, are even older inhabitants of gardens in central Texas, but ornamental garden hyacinths and tulips do not last. On her "to try" list are *Moraea* in the *Homeria* group; pretty pink to rose *Romulea bulbocodium* var. *clusiana*, with purple blotches around its yellow throat; and *Gladiolus tristis*, a little, pale yellow gladiolus with two to five flowers that are sweetly fragrant in the evening.

Cynthia points out that the Texas gardener must consider a juggling act of climate, temperature, rainfall, and other factors as well. For example, much of central Texas has alkaline soil. She claims that "one characteristic of Texas weather is that it has no reliable structure on which to plan." Temperatures may range from 8°F (−13°C) in very severe winters to a few degrees of frost, and then only for one or two days at a time in mild winters. Gardeners become encouraged after several mild winters and start experimenting with various subtropical or tender plants, only to have their hopes dashed during more severe weather. Rains, drizzle, or dampness may come for one to three weeks at a time in winter or in summer, or perhaps it might not rain at all for six weeks during the summer. Under these harsh and frequently irregular conditions, some geophytes are capable of long-term survival. Heirlooms that she mentions as growing around College Station since the early 1800s include "amaryllis" *Hippeastrum* ×*johnsonii*; Roman hyacinths with their small, starlike blue flowers widely spaced along the stem, and a fragrance that rightly should come from a larger flower; *Leucojum aestivum*;

and schoolhouse lilies, *Rhodophiala bifida*. *Crinum bulbispermum* and its many hybrids, especially milk-and-wine lilies, are also reliable. Many of the ornamental onions don't succeed, but heirloom leeks, garlic, and Neapolitan onion or Naples garlic, *Allium neapolitanum*, can.

The Peruvian lily or alstroemeria commonly found around College Station is the early variety *Alstroemeria pulchella*, a variable summer-flowering species from Brazil with green flowers overlaid with dark wine-red, spotted and streaked with red or maroon. The single Mexican tuberose, *Polianthes tuberosa*, succeeds better than *P. tuberosa* 'The Pearl', which is a double form. Parrot gladiolus, *Gladiolus dalenii* (syn. *G. natalensis*) and *G. psittacinus*, and the Byzantine gladiolus, *G. communis* subsp. *byzantinus*, have survived as heirlooms. There don't seem to be any long-lasting crocus or *Sternbergia* growing there. The tubers of four o'clock, *Mirabilis jalapa*, have no trouble surviving without attention. Dahlias usually go belly-up in the summer months, but calla lilies will thrive in a suitable setting. The old strain of the Easter lily, *Lilium longiflorum*, is still found in central Texas, and Philippine lilies, *L. philippinense* var. *formosanum*, have no trouble recurring annually from seed or from bulbs. Both of these are native to subtropical regions. The latter is found on Taiwan, as is the Easter lily, which also grows in southern Japan. In addition, cannas grow taller than eastern catalogs claim they are capable of. (Must be that Texas influence, Cynthia adds.)

She notes that Dr. Bill Welch of Texas A&M University lists the following narcissi and daffodils as candidates for naturalization: *Narcissus jonquilla* and the Campernelle jonquil, *N.* ×*odorus* (a cross between *N. pseudonarcissus* and *N. jonquilla*), with two or three pleasingly sweet-scented, yellow flowers with a bell-like cup surrounded by six rounded petals. (I expect the double Campernelle jonquil would also be suitable for Texas.) 'Trevithian' is another jonquilla hybrid on the list, fragrant and with a couple of golden yellow flowers on each stem. Of the heat-tolerant tazettas, Dr. Welch recommends *N. papyraceus* (sometimes called *N. tazetta* subsp. *papyraceus*), and several *N. tazetta* cultivars: 'Constantinople'; 'Silver Chimes', a *N. tazetta* × *N. triandrus* cross with rounded, white and pale cream flowers; 'Pearl'; and white and creamy yellow *N. tazetta* subsp. *lacticolor* 'Grand Monarque'. 'Erlicheer' is a popular favorite, with as many as 16 highly fragrant double flowers to a stem, milk white with small, creamy yellow segments filling out their center. Two other daffodil cultivars are frequently suggested for Texas and other hot climates. 'Carlton' has deep yellow petals and a darker yellow long cup that gives a pleasing two-tone effect, and 'Tahiti' is a double with a sturdy stem that supports its soft, butter-yellow flower accented with some orange-red petals mixed into its ruffled center.

Theresa Massey of Austin (currently Zone 9 and previously Zone 8b) finds that the biggest challenge to gardening in Texas is the ferocious summer heat. Forty-plus days of temperatures above 100°F (38°C) have been typical, especially in the past decade. This is not like desert heat, where things cool off at night. During these heat spells, her nighttime temperatures lower to the 80s (high 20s to low 30s C), sometimes only to the mid or upper 80s. Spring and fall are generally her best growing seasons, although mild winters mean that early narcissus bloom in November and December. *Crinum* 'Hanibal's Dwarf' and 'Elsie' will also bloom in December or January if no hard freezes occur. Long droughts, at any time of year, are also typical. For example, in 2003 the only significant rain in her immediate area between 20 February and mid-May was a scanty ½ inch (1 cm). Other bulbs, corms, and rhizomes that Theresa finds adapt well to these growing conditions include *Hymenocallis*, several *Lycoris* (especially *L. radiata* and *L. squamigera*), rain lilies of course, many of the crinums (some, such as *Crinum asiaticum*, *C. ×powellii*, and others even naturalize), and lily of the Nile (*Agapanthus*).

Now living in Chicago, where he is employed at the Chicago Botanic Garden, Boyce Tankersley remembers growing up in Texas in the 1950s and 1960s and then returning there for graduate school and work during the 1980s. He points out that the heat and length of the Texas summers were the doom of many of the bulbs traditionally supplied from Holland (not to discount the occasional summer floods). When he left Texas, the heirloom bulb boom was in its infancy and he was just beginning to see the reintroduction of some well-adapted "easy keepers." Since then, Boyce has learned

Displaying the vigor that hybrids often possess, the fragrant, pink flowers of *Crinum ×powellii* and its elegant white counterpart, *C. ×powellii* 'Album', have been around since the mid- to late 19th century, a good indication of their popularity with gardeners. Photo courtesy of Brent Heath/Brent and Becky's Bulbs.

more about the wealth of bulbs just south of the border and hopes that they will make their way into Texas landscapes. And he thinks that geophytes from Argentina suggest exciting possibilities for the Texas climate. In addition to the weather, Boyce recalls a number of pests, of which perhaps the most visibly destructive were armadillos; they love to eat bulbs, corms, and tubers.

His parents leased ranches for a number of years between San Angelo and Midland, Texas, which varies from short-grass prairie to high-elevation desert. People do water their gardens, and Boyce notes that, "I'm not sure much would survive with just what nature provides." He can recall only one native geophyte, *Zephyranthes drummondii*, on the ranches—nicely fragrant and, if memory serves, primarily in crevasses in limestone. After getting amaryllis, *Hippeastrum* hybrids, for Christmas presents, a lot of people plant them out and they come back to bloom every year, even though Boyce thinks it should be too cold.

Boyce remembers that reliable bloom from many tulip cultivars was problematic. While working commercial landscapes in Fort Worth, he found the multiflowered, peach-colored 'Georgette', double-pink 'Peach Blossom', and red 'Kingsblood' reliably gave a good show. "The only tulip to perform well in Galveston was 'Kingsblood', typically flowering around Valentine's Day on the University of Texas Medical Branch campus on Galveston Island. The campus displays were frequently harvested by 'want-to-be-docs' trying to impress their true loves on a student's budget." He recalls other traditional geophytes being planted in Fort Worth, of which some did well and others poorly. *Narcissus* 'Unsurpassable', a yellow large trumpet, was planted in quantity but slowly declined over time. *Muscari* held on and crocus declined, usually fairly rapidly. Pot lilies such as *Lilium* 'Enchantment' were reliable perennials as were gladiolus. *Hippeastrum* hybrids, if planted deeply, came back and flowered every spring. *Lycoris radiata* grew and flowered well. Rhizomatous iris were "easy keepers," and cannas grew like weeds. He said cannas also grew like weeds on Galveston Island, but the foliage was seriously disfigured by the larvae of a moth. Crinums were much better adapted to this warm, subtropical climate. *Heliconia*, bananas, *Hedychium*, *Costus*, and other members of the Zingiberaceae grew luxuriantly until the two weeks of winter arrived and they turned to black mush overnight. *Hymenocallis caribaea* were to be found in the thousands around the older buildings on campus.

During one of the few weekends he did not spend on graduate studies at TAMU, Boyce and a group of friends discovered *Hymenocallis galvestonensis* in sandy soils above the flood plain of the Brazos River outside Bryan/College Station, Texas. This is an uncommon species with a very different habit of growth than other native spider lilies. Gray-green leaves appear in spring, at which time the plant appreciates an ample supply of water. The leaves then wither away and during its resting period dryer conditions are preferred. In coordination with the summer thunderstorms of July, up come the white flowers on naked stems, in just the same manner as all the other naked lady or surprise lily geophytes.

Giddings, Texas, is in central Texas, with *Rhodophiala bifida* and *Hippeastrum* ×*johnsonii* in many abandoned yards in the area. Geophytes such as these can be plants of remembrance, connecting people and places and providing memories that join the different generations. Joyce Carleston remembers digging schoolhouse lilies, *Rhodophiala bifida*, from her grandmother's house in Giddings and taking them to Pearland, where she and her husband were living at the time. When they moved back to Giddings, some of the schoolhouse lilies came with her. The soil there is often just a thin layer over rock, and Joyce planted the bulbs in the best pocket she could find. They have pulled themselves quite deeply into the ground, too deep to try and dig again from that hard Texas earth. And early each fall, like some enchanted clockwork the flowers reappear, right on schedule. Joyce enjoys the rain lilies—*Habranthus, Zephyranthes,* and *Cooperia*—with crocuslike flowers that magically appear after a rainstorm. Magic lilies, *Lycoris radiata*, are another delight, with their crown of bright red flowers at the top of a stalk. The narrow petals curl backward, and the stamens stick out like the antennae of some strange shrimp. Spider lilies (*Hymenocallis*) and crinums (*Crinum*) are other familiar geophytes Joyce frequently sees around Giddings and in other nearby towns. And in spring Joyce loves to see the patch of blue flowers as grape hyacinths bloom in the cemetery where her great-grandmother is buried.

Even though Lee Poulsen doesn't live in Texas anymore, he has fond memories, especially of when he was an undergraduate there in the 1980s. He recalls that, compared to places like the East Coast or California, a lot less is known about what geophytes can successfully be grown in Texas, something Lee attributes to the agricultural service agents and Texas A&M, who were very conservative about growing any kind of plant. And, he adds, horticulture in Texas, with a very few exceptions, takes the basic attitude and follows the philosophy that "anything that hasn't been tried and true for the past 100 years or so probably won't grow well so why bother." Perhaps this is attributable to the difficulties gardeners face in coping with the climate. As Lee says, the Texas climate is "not really Mediterranean. It is too humid, and there are summer thundershowers that make it not an equivalent for that climate type. Also, the summer nights are way too warm. The rest of the year it does match up a lot with the typical Mediterranean-type climatology, especially the further west you go. I'm excluding the eastern third of Texas, which is definitely your typical Deep South type climate, much like Louisiana. However, since in-between those occasional thunderstorms it is so dry during the summer, some Mediterranean things survive quite well, especially if planted in very well-draining soil. Austin is Zone 8b with mostly mild, lightly rainy winters with the occasional Arctic cold front, and very hot, somewhat humid summers with occasional thunderstorms, but usually mostly dry."

As he was growing up in Austin, Lee remembers huge beds of *Hippeastrum ×johnsonii*. "Because they were large and bright red, at the time I thought they were the Dutch 'Amaryllis' [*Hippeastrum* cultivars] that were sold every Christmas. So I planted some *Hippeastrum*, and although they don't grow as well as the *H. ×johnsonii* they did survive. They all easily made it through the winters, and the *H. ×johnsonii* easily made it through the two super-freezes of the 1980s. The key thing for bulbs that go dormant in the winter is that the ground *never* freezes in Austin. So anything that can survive cool, wet soil while dormant will almost certainly grow in central and south Texas. Standard hybrid gladioli

Hippeastrum ×johnsonii close-up. Photo by author.

At Natchez-Under-the-Hill in Mississippi, a front yard is edged with a line of *Hippeastrum ×johnsonii*, no doubt the result of regular division. The strong, glossy leaves and clear red flowers, accentuated by a crisp white stripe down the center of each petal, are a popular bulb in gardens in the U.S. South. Photo by author.

all survive easily in the ground and flower year after year. But most people don't know that—even though one [Agricultural Extension] agent would write about it every year in the spring because he was a gladiolus hobbyist. One that won't survive is caladium. They absolutely thrive in the hot, humid summers but rot away if the soil temperature doesn't stay above about 50°F or so during the winter while dormant. So the tubers either have to be dug or new ones planted each year. On the other hand, almost any edible banana corm easily survives. And whenever there is an occasional winter where it basically never freezes and the top consequently doesn't get killed, that second year there will be banana fruit ripening all over Austin. It makes it into the paper, since this is fairly rare and happens only once or twice a decade.

"*Rhodophiala bifida* grow fantastically well, since the triploid type that most people grow was first introduced in the Austin area. Sadly, almost no 'typical' gardener grows it, because they don't know about it. You also don't find *Hippeastrum* ×*johnsonii* being grown by the current crop of new gardeners, mainly because it isn't offered for sale anywhere they might be shopping, just through a very few specialty bulb catalogs. And the old beds seem to be disappearing as old homes are bought by upscale people who rip out the beds to put in their own 'modern' upscale landscaping. Our neighbor had a bunch of *Lycoris radiata* that would spring up each year in late summer to early fall, like clockwork, out of the bare ground. And when we first moved to that house when I was digging up a spot for my vegetable garden as a kid, I threw away a bunch of rain lily bulbs. My mom really liked them after a rain, but they were so ephemeral, only seeming to show up after the occasional summer thunderstorm in the fields behind our house."

Lee says his mother still grows the solid white and the solid purple tall, bearded German irises "that were handed around the neighborhoods as pass-along plants. They always spread and have to be yanked out and thinned every few years after they get too crowded to bloom well. Back in the early 1980s, one autumn I planted a number of Dutch iris I got at the local nursery. They're in a big flower bed in the front yard, in mostly full sun. Not only do they come back each year, the clumps have continued to grow in size. They continue to be one of my mother's favorite springtime flowers since there are so many of them and they bloom for a few weeks. The foliage doesn't start to appear until late winter/early spring. These are the common blue, white, and yellow types." Lee wants to test a bunch of geophytes at his parents' place in Austin, but he has been seriously interested in geophytes for only the past five years or so. He's been building his collection and the knowledge of how they grow where he now resides, in California's truly Mediterranean climate.

"We also discovered that the standard Easter lily, *Lilium longiflorum*, naturalizes and spreads very well. Standard oriental and Asiatic lilies don't do well at all. The summers are too hot, I think. Or perhaps the winters don't provide enough chilling. That's the problem with so many of the usual spring blooming bulbs. Way too many people did and do the 'put the tulips, hyacinths, and daffodils in the fridge for 60 days bit,' and then plant them. And they do it every year! The newspapers and the Ag agents all pushed it, and everyone, including businesses and gardens did/do it, too. It's considered the norm. Then the bulbs would die during the hot summers. Now I know better. The same was true of anemones and ranunculus but in reverse. They always survived the winters and flowered beautifully in the late winter and spring, but would die out in the moist summers."

Lee says crinums do grow around town, "but mostly just the old, drooping, light pink flowered version on huge plants that neither my mom nor I really thought was that impressive or beautiful. So we never planted them. However, my mom did like spider lilies that were all over the place—some kind of *Hymenocallis*—and she planted some of those. They did really well and always came back from bad freezes. We grew a few other things that came back every year, such as dahlias. Louisiana irises thrive near the outside water spigots. Oh, and I almost forgot about canna. It's so common and easy, another weed growing everywhere in Austin, that I forgot it was a 'bulb.' If you are trying to get rid of them and leave even a little piece of the rhizome behind, you'll have a clump again in a few years."

Rhodophiala bifida

Schoolhouse lily, oxblood lily, and hurricane lily are all common names given to *Rhodophiala bifida*, a delightful little bulb that blooms at summer's end. The first name memorializes its sturdy ability to thrive around long-abandoned one-room schoolhouses and sagging old frame farmhouses. The next common name describes its color, a deep crimson red. Interestingly enough, the dark red form common in Texas and other southern states grows only in a single location in Argentina, in the province of Entre Rios. Elsewhere in Argentina and Uruguay, the flowers are brighter red, occasionally an orange-red or pink. And the third name reflects its time of bloom, as the hurricane season begins to peak two-thirds of the way through August. The deep, oxblood-red strain is, for all

At first glance, oxblood lily is a more obvious name than schoolhouse lily for *Rhodophiala bifida*. A good survivor in neglected gardens, the cluster of flowers (like miniature trumpet lilies) provides a strong note of color accented by golden pollen. Photo courtesy of Brent Heath/Brent and Becky's Bulbs.

practical purposes, sterile. It sets very few, if any, seeds. In common with other sterile bulbs, *Lilium lancifolium* for one, it is very vigorous. My supposition is that this is a direct relationship to the fact that all food production is sent directly to the bulb rather than diverting a goodly portion into seed production. Instead of seeding about, the oxblood lilies produce lots of offsets, an ideal means for gardeners to share pass-along plants such as this—if, that is, you can dig them up. Strong contractile roots may pull the long-necked little bulbs as much as 18 inches (45 cm) deep. That is surely more than any gardener would dig to plant them, but it is a depth that helps to shelter the bulbs against the torrid Texas summer heat.

Often the first step after getting something new is to divide or otherwise propagate it. Not only is this a security measure (should something happen to one plant, you have a fallback) but it provides "trade goods." Gardeners pass plants along, something with a long and honorable history, from Olgier Ghiselin de Busbecq and the tulip seed he sent to Carolus Clusius in the mid-16th century right up to today. The story of how oxblood lilies made it to Texas is an interesting one. In the 1840s, Peter Henry Oberwetter was one of many immigrants from southern and western Germany who moved to Texas. Just as gardeners today share their plants, he sent rain lilies, such as *Zephyranthes drummondii* that grew wild in the hills around his farm in the town of Comfort, to gardeners around the world. When the War Between the States began to heat up in the fledgling United States, Oberwetter and many other German colonists, some of whom sided with the North and others who were pacifists, moved elsewhere to avoid persecution. He went to Mexico, still continuing to collect and export bulbs while he was there. After the war he moved back to Austin, Texas, where he still collected and shipped bulbs. While oxblood lilies are found throughout the U.S. South, they are especially common in the old Germanic communities of central Texas.

Taxonomists have bounced the genus around. Several species were placed in *Habranthus*, then all of them were classified as *Hippeastrum*, for a while as *Amaryllis*, and even given a new genus of their own, *Rhodolirion*. Currently they are *Rhodophiala*, and let us hope they stay there. Native to the southern portion of South America, *Rhodophiala* is in the family Amaryllidaceae. That is good news for gardeners, as it means the flowers are deer-resistant, and the long-necked bulbs are unpalatable to mice, chipmunks, and other rodents. While the deep oxblood-red schoolhouse lily is the one found growing in Texas (and adaptable in the South and Southeast, such as the Raleigh-Durham area of North Carolina), it is not the only species of this charming genus. *Rhodophiala bifida* is an autumn-, winter-, and spring-growing species that is summer dormant. Although long, hot summers are common in its indigenous South American habitat, in its native haunts schoolhouse lily does receive rain year-round. A complete summer drought that would cause the loss of schoolhouse lily's permanent fleshy basal roots would be harmful. I give my bulbs, perforce grown in pots here in New Jersey, a little trickle of water every three or four weeks in the summer. Flowers appear in early fall before the narrow, straplike leaves appear, and their color ranges from the typical bright red to orange in subspecies *granataflora*. This color form is very rare, found only in a few sunny, rocky hillsides in Uruguay, with very large flowers on a taller scape, larger leaves, and a bigger bulb. A pink form is named subspecies *spathaceae*. In the wild, generally, each colony or isolated population has flowers of only a single color with few (if any) variation. The bulbs are always to be found growing in full sun.

As well as the notable deep oxblood color of its flowers, the dark red form produces no seed and propagates via numerous offsets. When repotting bulbs I have found as many as a dozen little bulblets clustering snugly around the mother bulb, cloaked beneath her dark brown outer tunic. Even the littlest offsets have long, skinny necks that cluster with that of the original bulb and find their way up to the surface. Bulbs of *Rhodophiala bifida* growing in the wild are often found at an astonishing depth, as much as 3 feet (1 m) or even a bit more. They'll move themselves down in cultivation. This can be a problem if you are growing them in small pots. The bulbs expend their energy trying to get deeper and deeper and do not flower. I find that a "long Tom" (a flower pot much deeper than it is wide, rarely seen in today's world of plastic pots) is much more suitable. And even then it is better to place the bulb near the bottom of the pot.

As far as gardeners are concerned, the other species of *Rhodophiala* (mostly grown

In common with several other autumn-blooming geophytes, *Rhodophiala bifida* flowers "naked," without any leaves. Where stems are tightly clustered, it is a good indication of bulbs that have made numerous offsets underground. Photo courtesy of Brent Heath/Brent and Becky's Bulbs.

by serious geophyte fanciers) may be separated into different groups based on their habit of growth. Several species from Chile require a dry summer dormancy and grow in autumn and winter and on into spring. Although some of them can tolerate cool conditions, they are all best grown where they can be protected from frost. Among these is red-, pink-, or yellow-flowered *R. advena*, which is perhaps the most cold-tolerant (to 23°F, or −5°C) in situations where it can be given perfect drainage and a dry, airy winter mulch. In the wild it is always found in full sun and always as single bulbs without offsets. Another group includes spring- and summer-growing species from the Andes Mountains of both Chile and Argentina, where they spend a long, very dry winter under snow. Spring-blooming *R. rhodolirion* has bright red to pink flowers, the latter with darker veins. White-flowered forms with a yellow throat are also found. As might be expected, it needs cool summer weather.

Hymenocallis

Hymenocallis is a genus of summer-blooming bulbs variously called summer daffodil, Peruvian daffodil, and spider lily. The last common name may easily lead you to confuse it with the red-flowered *Lycoris radiata*, also known as spider lily. And Peruvian daffodil is a misnomer for all except the four species that are found in Peru. The other 35 or so species are native to the southeastern United States, Mexico, Guatemala, Ecuador, Brazil, and the West Indies. With various revisions to the Latin name, some may still be found in catalogs as *Ismene*. In the Amaryllidaceae, amaryllis family, they are unpalatable to deer and other pests that might dine on geophytes. Their bulbs are large, rather fleshy, and have a papery tunic. Leaves are long, thick, straplike, and vary in number from four, to six, to eight or more, depending on the species. Some species are deciduous, and their leaves appear in spring, remaining through the growing season. Species from the tropics and subtropics are usually evergreen. A few white, ivory, or creamy yellow, fragrant flowers are grouped at the top of a stout stem. Peruvian daffodils grow well in full sun or light shade, preferring a rich, well-drained soil with ample moisture during their summer growing season.

A native of the southeastern United States, *Hymenocallis caroliniana* (syn. *H. occidentalis*) displays the interesting flower form that gave this species the common name of spider lily. Photo courtesy of Gene Bush/Munchkin Nursery.

Sweetly fragrant at dusk and early in the morning, *Hymenocallis narcissiflora* has two to five white flowers on a stalk 18 inches (45 cm) tall. Each funnel-like flower is embellished with six narrow, elegantly curling outer segments at the perimeter. It is deciduous, and the six to eight leaves yellow and dry off at the end of the growing season. Native to the Peruvian Andes at altitudes as high as 8000 feet (2450 m), this is perhaps the most cold-tolerant species, able to withstand temperatures close to the freezing point. The bulbs quickly multiply by offsets. I remember a small wooden bungalow near Giddings, Texas, one summer, where the footings of the front porch were all but concealed by a bed of Peruvian daffodils in full bloom. Though the homeowner offered me bulbs, we could not find a handy shovel, and the bulbs were so well rooted that pulling one out was not an option. (Goes to show you, even when away from home, I should always have a folding trenching shovel and a supply of plastic bags in the car's trunk.) Peruvian daffodils are usually propagated by division, when bulbs are going dormant for the deciduous species, either in fall or in early spring for the evergreen specious. When seed is set, collect as the pod ripens but before it *dehisces*, or drops the seed. Sow fresh seed promptly before it has a chance to dry out, in a flat of sandy soil, kept moist and lightly covered. Germination will be scattered and irregular. You may find this listed in catalogs as *Ismene calathina*.

Amancaes is the Peruvian name for their native summer daffodil, used as its species name, *Hymenocallis amancaes*. My brother, Ben Orlove, remembers a song, a *vals criollo* that mentions the flowers. Written and composed by Chabuca Granda, this kind of waltz used to be popular on the coast of Peru. The lyrics go something like this: "Elegantly dressed in traditional style, wearing a poncho of white linen, Jose Antonio is an accomplished horseman, showing fine mastery riding his horse. Why, asks the woman, why did he leave her, hoping that when he returns to see the amancay in bloom, he will sweep her up on his horse."

This "lily of the Incas" has three deep yellow, very fragrant flowers. On 19 July 1835 Charles Darwin made a note in his journal about fields of amancaes flowering on the desert coastal hills of Peru: "On the hills near Lima . . . the ground is carpeted with moss, and beds of beautiful yellow lilies, called Amancaes. This indicates a

Hymenocallis narcissiflora is a popular bulb for the summer garden, adaptable to container cultivation and prized for its attractive, fragrant flowers. Photo by author.

very much greater degree of humidity, than at a corresponding height at Iquique." Official emblem of the city of Lima, amancaes used to be found growing wild on the banks of the Rimac River that flows through the city. Though a district of Lima is still known as Pampas of Amancaes, the places where this flower was once so numerous are now nothing but buildings and city streets. Club Floralíes de Lima is dedicated to bringing it back and has created a preserve called Pachacámac on land outside the city of Lima, where this and other native plants are being reintroduced.

In the desert around Lima, it is not so much humidity as coastal fog that provides the necessary moisture. Summer humidity in Texas and the Deep South is more than amancaes can cope with. However, when crossed with *Hymenocallis narcissiflora*, the popular hybrid offspring *H. amancaes* 'Sulphur Queen' demonstrates much more tolerance of these conditions and is valued for its six lightly fragrant, primrose-yellow flowers, each with a green star in its throat, flowering in an umbel and appearing in midsummer. Hybridizing with *H. speciosa*, an evergreen, autumn- to winter-flowering species from the West Indies, with five to seven fragrant, white to greenish white flowers, gave us *H.* 'Advance', an early summer–blooming cultivar introduced in 1932, with intensely fragrant, large, pure-white flowers.

Hymenocallis ×*festalis* (sometimes offered as *H.* 'Festalis') is a cross of *H. narcissiflora* and *H. longipetala*, another Peruvian species with greenish white flowers. Bred by Arthington Worsley, a British horticulturist who lived in the last half of the 19th and first half of the 20th century, it was introduced by the Dutch bulb firm of Tubergen in 1910. *Hymenocallis* ×*festalis* is a freely increasing bulb, and this tendency to make offset bulbs is somewhat at the expense of flowering. *Hymenocallis* ×*festalis* 'Zwanenburg' was selected as a cultivar, favored for its larger, fuller, ivory-white fragrant flowers that Tubergen introduced just two years later.

The unusual shape of the elegant, fragrant white flowers of *Hymenocallis liriosome* make it one of the more remarkable native bulbs of the southeastern United States. Photo by author.

Native to the West Indies, *Hymenocallis caribaea* (the species name means of the Caribbean) is the species Boyce Tankersley recalls as thriving at the University of Texas Medical Branch campus on Galveston Island. Numerous glossy, evergreen leaves nearly 2 feet (60 cm) long form a dense mound, enhanced with 8 to 10 or more flowers on a scape 2 feet (60 cm) high. Elizabeth Lawrence, who gardened in Piedmont, North Carolina, and wrote so very evocatively and informatively about plants, people, and gardens, discusses hymeno-callis in her charming book, *A Southern Garden*, which was first published in 1942. She mentions that this species and also *H. galvestonensis*, from Texas, "are among the hardier species but neither has proved hardy in my garden."

Mirabilis jalapa

When I was a small child living in Chicago, my neighborhood consisted of single and small multifamily dwellings, tiny back yards, garages, alleys, and mirror-image sets of garages, back yards, and houses on the next street. Greenery was scarce, but what I do remember are the four o'clocks (also called marvel of Peru), *Mirabilis jalapa*, that made a hedge between our four-family apartment house and the tiny plot of grass. Every year, the bushlike plants with bright fuchsia flowers opened in the afternoon and closed the next morning. Now that I have more garden expertise than I did as an eight-year-old, I know that the thick, tuberous roots would be marginally hardy at best, perhaps helped along by warmth seeping though the foundation from the coal-fired furnace in the basement. If the plants did not survive Chicago's weather from one year to the next, they came back as self-sowing volunteers. Four o'clocks produce lots of black seeds, each the size of a kernel of corn.

Mirabilis jalapa is an obliging, adaptable plant with a diversity of flower colors that can perform as an annual in colder climates while functioning as a perennial in mild winter areas. Photo by author.

Recently I found four o'clocks growing in the high, weedy grass up against the Baptisttown, New Jersey, post office, a small operation that closes from noon to 1 p.m. so the postmistress can have her lunch. Most are a clear, sunny yellow, with a small branch of white to pink-streaked white flowers on one plant. When I inquired, someone told me that they were probably planted by Marie Buck, the former postmaster's wife, who passed away in 1985.

Four o'clocks thrive in Texas, where some find them invasive and unwelcome and other folks like them. Boyce Tankersley recalls a friend living on a ranch just south of San Angelo, who always looked forward to their summer flowering. And even though Lee Poulsen's mother finds them weedy, she so enjoys their nocturnal fragrance that some are allowed to volunteer in her Austin garden.

With species native to the southwestern United States and South America, *Mirabilis* is an oddball genus in the family Nyctaginaceae, which includes an assortment of familiar and much less well-known genera: bougainvillea, sand verbena (*Abronia*), scarlet musk flower (*Nyctaginia*), and bird-catcher tree (*Pisonia*). The marvel of Peru—or four o'clock as it is more frequently named—has elongated, tuberous roots; it blooms in summer and is indeed native to Peru. It is a garden escapee in North America, meaning it has naturalized north of the border. The fragrant flowers open in late afternoon and can be purple, crimson, apricot, yellow, or white. One plant can display several different shades, and the flowers may be mottled or striped. *Mirabilis jalapa* 'Kaleidoscope' has flowers of solid fuchsia-pink, yellow streaked and blotched with fuchsia, and white streaked and blotched with fuchsia, all on the same plant. 'Broken Colors' has similarly blotched and patterned multicolored flowers on individual plants. Four o'clock will flower the same year from seed, interesting in a plant with tuberous storage roots, since normally such plants are more leisurely about reaching maturity. If the growing season is very short, they can be started indoors six weeks before frost-free conditions arrive in the garden. Since they are bushy plants and reach 2 to 3 feet (0.6 to 1.0 m) tall, four o'clocks can be planted as a temporary hedge. While the

Mirabilis jalapa close-up. Photo by author.

plants are tolerant of heat, humidity, drought, and neglect, a better display comes with a modicum of care, regular watering, and a monthly fertilization. Their long, black roots can be dug and easily stored through the winter, much as you would a dahlia.

The Book of Annuals, written by Alfred Hottes and published in 1928, mentions that they "were favorites with our grandmothers, just as they are admired by us today." He suggests that they are useful since "a few plants will fill the bare spaces found, in so many cases, between the house foundations and the walk leading to the backyard." He continues, "In beds by themselves they are also attractive, but the range of colors is peculiar and difficult to combine with some other annuals." One rather new cultivar, *Mirabilis jalapa* 'Baywatch', could be used more as a screening plant than a hedge. In average soil it grows 5 to 6 feet (1.5 to 2.0 m) tall and has been known to reach 9 feet (3 m) on a well-prepared site. Pale, champagne-yellow flowers contrast well with the dark green foliage, opening somewhat later in the day than four o'clocks. The fragrant flowers attract hummingbirds on their last swoop through the garden and night-flying moths. Plant bloom from midsummer until cut down by frost.

I've had one plant of *Mirabilis longiflora* for years, raised from seed that came to me from Monticello, Thomas Jefferson's estate. (Now *there* was a president. How can you improve on someone who said that the best service one could do for one's country is discover a new plant of value? But I digress.) Of course, in my New Jersey climate this American native from west Texas, Arizona, and Mexico must be protected in winter. It has thick, substantial tuberous roots covered with rough "bark." It is woody in texture, which I know from the year it got accidentally sliced as it was being dug up. This umbrellawort, its common name, prefers good drainage, sunshine, and not too much water. Its climbing stems seem equally happy when they can scramble up an adjacent shrub or simply sprawl on the ground. After it accidentally got the chop that autumn, I decided to grow it in a pot and provide a supporting framework of twigs as scaffolding. Softly downy, heart-shaped, medium-green leaves make a modest covering, standing out from the stems on long petioles. In late summer, the long-tubed, small, white flowers appear, accented with violet stamens. Night-blooming, it has a sweet fragrance. Winter storage is in my unheated, attached garage, where temperatures can drop to 38°F (3°C) during cold spells. I used to dig it up in late autumn (when it was planted out) and pack it in a box, surrounded with dry peat moss. Now I just take it out of its pot and box it up with no packing material. My plant is at least ten years old, perhaps a year or two more. A hybrid of *M. longiflora* and *M. jalapa*, *M. ×hybrida* is said to carry white flowers, sometimes flushed or marked with crimson or yellow in dense inflorescence.

Dutch iris

Iris, goddess of the rainbow, bestowed her name to an incredibly showy range of perennials for herbaceous borders and a few for shady gardens. The genus includes an assortment of geophyte forms as well as fibrous-rooted perennials. Lacking the hairy tuft that is characteristic of the bearded iris flowers, these are all beardless irises. Some are best grown in the rock garden, and others are better for the flower garden. The latter group includes the somewhat confusing medley of the so-called English, Spanish, and Dutch iris, so popular as the florists' cut flower.

Spanish iris, *Iris xiphium* var. *lusitanica*, grows in western Europe and North Africa. Its narrow leaves make an autumn appearance, and the flowers, one to a stem in shades of blue or violet, wait until late spring or early summer to make their display. Once named *I. lusitanica*, yellow forms are found principally in Portugal. Native to scrubby grasslands in rocky or sandy soil, its bulbs have a dormant period after blooming and prefer a hot, dry rest. The usual recommendation is to plant in autumn and protect in winter with a mulch of evergreen boughs after the ground freezes.

Iris latifolia (syn. *I. xiphioides*) is native to damp meadows in the Pyrenees and northern Spain. Somehow, in the 16th century it acquired the moniker of English iris, a name it has kept. The leaves are somewhat larger and coarser that those of the Spanish iris and wait until spring to make their appearance. English iris usually has two bluish purple to violet, or occasionally white, flowers on a stem 16 to 24 inches (40 to 60 cm). Jane McGary, who gardens in northwestern Oregon, finds it a good perennial, flowering in late June. As the Spanish iris likes moisture, especially while in growth, and the English iris prefers a dry summer, you would think that one or the other would find a niche in just about any garden with conditions to its liking.

Dutch iris, popular as cut flowers and also as garden plants, are the result of crossing *Iris xiphium* with *I. tingitana*, a North African species. Native to Morocco, its name means "of Tangiers." Dutch iris are so lovely and their bulbs so inexpensive that even in gardens where they do not persist they can be worth growing. James Waddick has difficulty keeping them beyond the first year in his Kansas City, Missouri, garden. He asks, "The Dutch must grow them literally by the ton as they are cheap and widely available. What's an Iberian bulb doing flourishing in Holland?" Same as every other geophyte the Dutch grow. They begin with a sandy soil and control of the water table. Then the bulbs, corms, and tubers can be dug and stored in temperature- and humidity-controlled warehouses if winters are not to the geophytes' liking. And with 100 mixed Dutch iris priced at U.S. $13.50 (as listed in one fall 2003 catalog), *cheap* is the right word. Dutch iris have three upright petals called *standards* and three trailing, drooping petals called *falls*. A yellow blotch on the falls, called a *bee guide*, shows the insects the way to pollen and nectar. The colors and combinations range from many shades of blue—from soft flax and wisteria blue to rich gentian, violet-blue, and bright plum-purple—to pretty pastels, white, yellow, striking shades of yellow tinted or greeny bronze, and bicolor flowers.

Resembling its Spanish parent, the Dutch iris flowers somewhat earlier, in mid-to late spring. The first cultivars were introduced by Tubergen around 1891. *Iris* 'Blue Magic' has bluish violet standards and deep blue falls, accented with a yellow blotch. 'Carmen' (occasionally offered as 'Carmen Beauty') has pale lavender standards and white falls lightly veined in dark blue, accented with a yellow blotch. 'Ideal' has lobelia-blue standards with yellow-blotched, bluebird-blue falls. 'White Wedgwood' has creamy white standards with just a hint of blue, greenish white falls, and a buttercup-yellow blotch. The Beauty series offers attractive cultivars in a range of colors. These include strong yellow 'Amber Beauty' with darker falls and a still darker blotch, and glowing 'Rusty Beauty' has warm, brownish buttercup-yellow standards and bronzy, brownish yellow falls. Dark mahogany-bronze standards on 'Bronze Beauty' contrast well with amber-bronze falls accented with a yellow blotch. 'Cream Beauty' has ivory-white standards and white falls that age to a primrose-yellow, accentuated with a darker saffron-orange blotch. Bicolor 'Gipsy Beauty' has blue-violet standards and red-violet falls, penciled with darker veins and set off by a yellow blotch. 'Silvery Beauty' has pale, sky-blue standards and creamy white falls, marked with a narrow yellow blotch. Wisteria blue 'Oriental Beauty' has yellow to bronze-green falls with a dark yellow blotch. Violet-blue standards and bluebird-blue falls, set off by a narrow yellow stripe, make 'Sapphire Beauty' a dark and elegant flower.

In Cologne, Germany, Jamie Vande finds that Dutch iris do rather well in his Zone 8 garden, and a few are even reliable repeat bloomers for him. They are planted in deep, humus-rich soil wet in winter when they start growing, that becomes a bit dryer as the ground warms. Summers tend to get a bit dry toward the end and then the autumn rains come. Jamie notes, "I can't say they increase well, but they do increase. They may well require more sun to truly prosper. Being stately and firm, they make excellent cut flowers, although they hold only a few days. As they are so cheap to buy, I pay little attention to them and consider them decoration more than charges. I have always assumed them to be quite hardy, but perhaps Zone 6 or 7 is their limit. I planted them deep, a good 6 inches down, which they apparently liked. The xiphium iris are very satisfactory between other perennials." Since he buys mixed lots (because that is what is most available), Jamie is unsure of the names. He does have a number of blues and a glowing yellow, and 'Oriental Beauty', and sometimes 'Bronze Queen' and 'Professor Blaauw', an early-flowering cultivar with gentian-blue flowers and a narrow, yellow bee guide, plus occasionally others, but they are the exceptions. As we discussed his experiences, Jamie sent me a mid-September e-mail that happily mentions, "Interestingly, I picked up some more xiphiums yesterday, as I found them as single bulbs. So another 15 of 'Imperator' [raised in Denmark and introduced by Tubergen prior to 1915, with indigo-blue flowers and an orange blotch], 'White Perfection' [introduced in 1944 by De Graff Brothers of Noordwijk, the Netherlands, with white standards and ivory white falls] and 'Symphony' [a relatively modern introduction by Nijssen and Sons, in 1968, with yellow-veined, ivory standards and canary-yellow falls] will be added to my garden.

"We enjoy a mild climate, rarely reaching 14°F in winter or broaching 95°F in summer. Generally speaking, the continent is much warmer than most people expect, even Moscow can reach 86°F or somewhat higher. I would say our average summer day is just about 85°F, with nights around 65°F, but it does vary and 95°F days are not that unusual. In many ways, we resemble the Pacific Northwest in the U.S.A. Due to the relatively crowded nature of older European cities, large gardens are seldom found and I am indeed lucky to have about 600 square meters to cultivate. In comparison with the space my American gardening friends have, a veritable postage stamp! Such restrictions force me to concentrate my efforts and make every square centimetre count. I'm always amazed at just how much one can cram in!"

Jamie mentioned that he is "always fascinated by geophytes, finding that they are nature's amazing surprise packages, tangible promises, as it were. Having adapted to an extreme in growing conditions, even the easiest provide a bit of a gamble for the gardener. Being larger than most seeds, geophytes provide a challenge one can physically grasp and, again differing from seeds, these have been grown by someone else beforehand, so the gardener becomes the next steward. A sense of responsibility, a connecting link, is imbued, which I find makes them special."

Lee Poulsen finds Dutch iris easy, a perennial, permanent addition that he planted in his parents' Austin garden in the 1980s. "Not only did they come back each year, the clumps have continued to grow in size and they continue to be one of my mother's favorite springtime flowers since there are so many of them and they bloom for a few weeks. The foliage doesn't start to appear until late winter or early spring. These are the common blue, white, and yellow types."

And Boyce Tankersley relates similar success with Dutch iris: "For years during the 1970s a yellow and at least one of the blue-flowered cultivars of Dutch iris grew and flowered well at my parents' garden in southern New Mexico, climatic Zone 7. They eventually declined, but I assumed it was because the bulbs were not divided. The foliage still comes up. . . . The bulbs are in among other bulbs and perennials and so get supplemental irrigation in summer. They don't really spread at all but it is obvious there are daughter bulbs produced. Other colors, bronze and white, did not perform well. I don't even recall them coming up to flower the first year. Could be they are not as hardy?"

Tigridia

El tigre refers not to the great striped tiger of the Indian subcontinent, but rather that chunky yet lithe spotted cat that we call jaguar, native to Central American forests. It is easy to see how the cat's roseate black spots bestowed both the common name of tiger flower and Latin name of *Tigridia* to this splashy and colorful bulb that is native to

Mexico and Guatemala. The most readily available species, *T. pavonia* was cultivated by the Aztecs more than a millennium ago. They called it *cacomitl*, very close to *cacomit*, the name used for it today in Mexico.

Tigridia, also known as peacock flower, was introduced to European gardens well over two centuries ago, in 1785. It is definitely not a flower for gardeners with refined and subtle taste. It is blatant, conspicuous, ostentatious, perhaps even vulgar, but definitely not subdued. Visualize a large, cuplike flower, 4 to 6 inches (10 to 15 cm) across. The three outermost petals, which are the largest, have a clear, solid color that may be white, gold, rose or red, pink, or even purplish. It is the smaller central petals that are strongly, heavily spotted and blotched in a contrasting color. (I find the markings somewhat like the brown mottling on an overripe banana.) Nan Sterman of Encinitas, California, in the San Diego area, has some tigridia growing in her garden. She describes them quite well: "I am never quite sure whether they are exquisite or horrendous or a combination of both. . . . Perhaps that is the definition of gaudy." For those gardeners who insist on genteel flowers, *Tigridia pavonia* 'Rosalind' has a more subdued phlox-pink flower, with phlox-pink markings on the white inner petals. Sunny yellow 'Lutea Immaculata' and pink 'Rose Giant' are two cultivars with unmarked flowers.

In August 2002 I was entranced by the field of tigridia down the road from Hotel De Nachtegaal in Lisse, The Netherlands, as brilliant as a Mexican fiesta. The Floriade, that once-every-10-years extravagant horticultural show, also had tigridia on display. The Dutch seem to manage quite nicely, assisted by their well-drained soils and lifting bulbs to store them dry over the winter. Tender to frost, you would think that that this summer-blooming bulb would be popular with gardeners in Texas, southern California, Arizona, and other regions with mild winters. The one caution—since peacock flower (also called Mexican shell flower) is summer-growing and winter-dormant, wet conditions during its resting period are detrimental. It is easy to work around this. Plant the inexpensive bulbs (25 for $7 in mixed colors, 25 for $10 if you prefer 'Canariensis', whose flowers are a sunny yellow with carmine-red blotches) in late spring, and they'll bloom with other summer flowers. Upright swordlike leaves grow

Tigridia aurea has tropical-looking flowers, each lasting just one day. The three larger petals are clear and unmarked, while the center is commonly streaked and spotted with a contrasting color. Photo by author.

12 to 18 inches (30 to 45 cm) tall, a nice visual support for the flower stalk 18 to 24 inches (45 to 60 cm) tall. Needing full sun, tolerating heat, and accepting of dry conditions, tigridia offers brilliant-colored flowers that are at their peak in the midday sun. Each flower lasts only one day, but ample buds keep them blooming for quite literally weeks on end. If we accept a daylily's flowers as a here this morning, gone tomorrow affair, that cannot be a drawback. But tigridia just don't seem to make it into many gardens. Boyce Tankersley tried tigridia in Fort Worth, Texas, but found that they seemed to get spider mites to the extent that the flower display was affected. Somewhat surprisingly, they were not ground-hardy and never matched the displays that he saw in the Las Cruces Tropical Botanic Garden (now the Robert and Catherine Wilson Botanical Garden) among the cloud forests of southern Costa Rica. Nor can he recall seeing them in any of the landscapes on Galveston Island.

Every spring, Lee Poulsen says, tigridia is offered in the "regular" nurseries around Austin, along with the familiar "Dutch" bulbs. He has tried it several times at his parents' garden, and in his experience the bulbs would flower the same year they were planted but then always disappeared. He tried tigridia in the ground and in pots in southern California where he now lives, but he gets the same response—spring-planted bulbs flower, and then they fail to reappear in subsequent years. Tony Avent, of Plant Delights Nursery at Juniper Level Botanic Garden in Raleigh, North Carolina, has a similar experience: "I have ordered and grown tigridias from Dutch sources and never had any overwinter here in North Carolina." Interestingly, Tony then went on to say that "conversely, those that we grew from wild collected seed from Yucca Do have grown and multiplied each year. These are all growing in the very same part of our rock garden." That precisely matches Lee Poulsen's experiences: "Then one year Yucca Do offered a variety that they said they found at low elevation in northern Mexico. Yucca Do said that the bulbs offered by all the Dutch companies were from varieties found at high elevation in central Mexico. For that reason they do quite well in Holland and in more northern U.S. climates (or milder ones further south), but they don't like or can't take the summer heat that occurs in the South or in Texas. And Yucca Do claimed that the ones they've collected do just fine in Texas.

"It does very well; comes back every year. It is blooming right now [September] and has enormous flowers that have a very intense reddish hue. I think they are completely eye-catching. I've never understood why some of the professional types (landscapers, garden writers, etc.) always worry about or never seem to like what they consider 'gaudy' flowers."

It is easy to underestimate just how tough tigridia can be. Some plants just prefer the spartan life. Theresa Massey gardens in Austin, Texas, where the temperatures range wildly in summer and the annual rainfall arrives as flash floods punctuating long droughts. Afraid that full sun in the harsh summer would be too much for tigridia, last spring Theresa planted several that she got either from Yucca Du or Plant Delights. The site had rich, loamy soil at the sloping base of a live oak tree, with bright, filtered light all day. She watered them well every five to seven days. Two of the three plants put up some scraggly, sparse foliage and the other did nothing, never even the hint of a blossom; it was indigestion from an overwatered, too-rich diet. Nan Stearman, a garden writer and horticulturist well-known to southern California gardeners, grows her tigridia in hot, full sun, poor soil, and little water. She has a colorful, bold, and daring half-acre garden used as a testing ground for mostly low-water plants from Mediterranean and arid regions around the world. The garden's backbone may comprise trees, shrubs, and herbaceous perennials, but it is the bulbs and rhizomatous plants, Nan finds, that "provide the zing, the punctuation that elevates the garden from ordinary to extraordinary." Nan recalls that her tigridia bulbs came from a home improvement center, rather than from a high-end catalog or other specialty resource.

Carolyn Craft was very successful growing tigridia in Saratoga, California (near San Jose, about 45 minutes southeast of San Francisco and 30 minutes from the coast, in USDA Zone 9). Carolyn planted them in morning sun and afternoon shade and gave them some water (but not much) in summertime. And they were beautiful. Things are different now that she lives in nearby Los Gatos, and she adds, "Wish I had dug them up and moved them with me." Mary Sue Ittner did move her tigridia, but with less than successful results. She also had them in Stockton, California, growing them for years in a raised bed, together with perennials. The tigridia bloomed without fail every summer, and Mary Sue said, "Even though it was gaudy, I loved it." When they moved to the north coast she brought some with her. They bloomed the first year but then departed. In an attempt to assess why they perished, Mary Sue came up with lots of choices: "I assumed it was either that they hated our extreme winter rainfall or they didn't get enough sun or heat or summer water in my garden here." She's trying some in a large pot, thinking that she could shelter them from the winter rain that way, but they are not doing well, producing only a couple of flowers. Someone told her that tigridia don't like life in a pot and

Flowers of mixed tigridia display the diversity of available colors. Photo courtesy of the Netherlands Flower Bulb Information Center.

prefer to be in the ground. But then, plants don't read the books and sometimes do what they want, rather than what it is said they want.

Liz (who wants a certain level of anonymity) is one gardener who finds *Tigridia pavonia* grows readily for her. Claiming not to be an expert—just someone who grows a few easy bulbs for her area—she thinks they are uncomplicated bulbs for coastal southern California. The difference, she believes, between other parts of the country and conditions around San Francisco/Oakland and southward are low humidity and no summer rain for about six months. Even if it is not raining, Liz points out, hot and muggy weather can be hard on some plants. As long as the drainage is excellent and they don't get too wet, tigridia grow for her in sun or shade. Those that she has in the ground are in full sun on a dry hill. Some are growing in a container with tuberous begonia in the shade, and other tigridia are in a different container in partial shade. Concerned that too much moisture would likely rot the bulbs, she is careful that none of them gets a lot of water but neither do they go completely dry. Given the variations of sun and shade, they bloom at different times.

Jamie Vande in Cologne, Germany, has grown purchased bulbs and raised *Tigridia pavonia* from seed. They are hardy in his Zone 8 continental climate, if given some winter protection. Those he grows in pots are less attractive since the leaves are inclined to be floppy and each flower lasts only one day. (Lots of deadheading, and pots of flowers are more blatantly obvious about poor grooming than might be apparent in a garden.) When Jamie transplanted the bulbs into the garden, he became aware of the fleshy roots that you don't see on the dried bulb. Now he thinks that these are important (just like the fleshy permanent roots on lilies, lycoris, hippeastrum, cardiocrinum, and certain other bulbs) and should not be removed. "This winter," Jamie sadly mentions, "I lost most of the tigridia in the garden. We had six weeks frozen solid at around 17°F, which was just too much for them."

The authors of older books mention tigridia with enthusiasm. In *Bulbs for Summer Bloom* (1970), John Philip Baumgardt talks about growing tigridia in his Kansas garden with no special protection, siting them above a garden wall (but they rotted away when planted below the wall). In 1930's *Bulbs for American Gardens*, John C. Wister says the "brilliant garden plants . . . of the easiest culture, should be planted in earliest spring" and recommends lifting and storing them over the winter in a warm, dry room. Allen H. Wood Jr., in his 1936 book *Bulbs for Your Garden*, also calls tigridia "brilliant garden plants . . . noted for their spotted, tawny flowers." He mentions that the flowers are *fugacious* (lovely word, meaning "fleeting") and continues, "yet there is a succession of bloom; it is not unusual for a tigridia to blossom steadily for a month." He also suggests lifting and storing them with the foliage still attached and warns against mice, for "they are especially fond of tigridia bulbs." In *Adventures with Hardy Bulbs*, also published in 1936, Louise Beebe Wilder provides her usual thorough background. Tigridia have been grown in gardens since the mid-1800s. A Spanish physician sent to Mexico by Spanish King Philip II reported it growing wild about much of Mexico and also cultivated it "because of its excessive beauty, and for the medicinal virtues of the roots." Wilder, while keeping in mind that she lived in Rockland County, New York, writes that tigridia are "often cherished by rural women, procured . . . from itinerant peddlers of horticultural wares." And she describes seeing some tigridia in bloom "in the mountains of Rockland County. Its bedfellows were dusty-cheeked Bouncing Bet and round-eyed periwinkle. It looked strangely exotic and out of place—but it was flourishing." In rural Hunterdon County, New Jersey, where I live, though the crop fields of hay, soybeans, and corn around here are being replaced by housing developments, it is still an agricultural area. And heedless of traffic, I would bring my car to a screeching halt should I see as exotic a sight as tigridias blooming in a dooryard.

~~~~~~

CHAPTER 7

Geophytes for the South and Southeastern United States

We Americans live in such a big, broad, diverse nation that horticulturally it might just as well be several different countries. Consider this situation: It is toward the end of March and we're just beyond the vernal equinox. Here in New Jersey the snow lingers in shady places. I do have flowers in my woodland garden but only the very earliest to bloom—snowdrops (*Galanthus*), snowflakes (*Leucojum vernum*), winter aconites (*Eranthis hyemalis*), *Crocus tommasinianus*, and the first *Scilla mischtschenkoana*, along with hellebores and *Adonis amurensis*. *Narcissus* 'Rijnveld's Early Sensation' is still in tight bud. Compare this with late March in Raleigh, North Carolina, where Jim Sherwood is happily reporting, "You know, we wait and wait all winter (which, in this climate, ain't such a long wait!) for blossoms, and then all of a sudden they begin and there's such a breathless headlong rush you can't get around to seeing everything you want to see before they finish and the next crop comes on! We're at the midseason point in daffodils here, and I've already found a couple of really old things I've never seen before except in books. Glorious clear, breezy days; magnolias and corylopsis full bloom; bloodroot and erythroniums abloom; and the early-iris trio coming on." These would be *Iris albicans*, native to Saudi Arabia and Yemen, with gray-green leaves and scented white or blue flowers, the shaft of both the standards and the falls greenish yellow, and a white beard. Either native to the Mediterranean or a fertile heirloom hybrid that has become widely naturalized, *I. germanica* also has gray-green leaves and flowers in shades of blue to violet and white, the falls accented by a yellow beard. *Iris kochii*, native to northern Italy, is similar but smaller, with deep bluish purple flowers, the shaft on the falls veined with brownish purple. Same year, same month, same time of month, different places, disparate flowers.

Alabama

Jim Sherwood is an enthusiastic gardener, despite the fact that he's moved from here to there and back again, and, as a tenant rather than a homeowner, he currently has his plants in pots. He grew up in hot and humid Tuscaloosa, Alabama. Jim's father was a doctor and had a patient who raised bearded irises. He shared these with the physician, and the iris beds were Jim's responsibility from the time he was fairly young. That was his introduction to gardening and his first step on an ongoing journey down the garden path. Some of his efforts, as with the bearded iris, were more successful than others. Jim remembers that he made a "rock garden" when he was about nine: "Unfortunately, it was in shade and the soil was red clay: not too successful, but *very* artistic!" Jim's earliest recollections of how he first learned about plants and gardening come, in fact, mainly from his grandmother. He has memories of her taking the grandchildren to the forest to see *Magnolia macrophylla* and telling them how she and her siblings used to visit *her* grandmother. As a little girl, Jim's grandmother would run to the woods, take off all her clothes, and tie on the big magnolia leaves as play clothes.

Jim has, indeed, moved around more than a bit. He became seriously interested in gardening while living in Brooklyn, New York, in his early 30s. As an antidote to all the masonry and pavement in the city, he volunteered at the Brooklyn Botanic Garden to gain access to greenness, mainly working in the Local Flora section, which increased his early interest in native plants.

This makes me smile, because when I was very young, my grandmother lived on St. Marks Place in Brooklyn. And when I became too restless (make that rambunctious), I'd be taken to the Brooklyn Botanic Garden to run off some of that energy. Jim's experiences as a volunteer convinced him to move home to make a garden in north Tuscaloosa County, on some forest land that his family owns. "It came down," Jim relates, "like my gardening, through a female line in my grandmother's family."

In addition to his childhood endeavors and adult efforts at garden-making in Alabama, Jim has experience in Athens, Georgia, and currently in Raleigh-Durham, North Carolina. While less extreme than Tuscaloosa, "the Triangle" can also be challenging, weather-wise. As Jim mentioned to me in late February 2004, "You may have heard of our recent, all-too-typical weather. Last Friday we had 2 inches of snow, and by Monday the highs were up to the mid 70s to low 80s, where they've been ever since. Crocuses are drying up in the heat, camellias (of which there've been none for weeks and weeks—I'm from further south, so I'm not used to that!) are opening and dropping off in two days. It's 'way too hot!' I feel like my favorite part of the year is running by in very-fast motion." Even so, he emphatically commented that "I hope—*hope*!!!—I'll never leave the Triangle. Gardeners need to be still! And it's due to all the moving that

I keep so many things in pots—they have no real home yet! Mostly bulbs, and then some special woody things I'm afraid will go out of commerce. Bulbs, because many of them are satisfied for a while with pots, and because I can move them with me."

Daffodils

Jim got interested in bulbs mainly through narcissus. His fascination began especially while looking for varieties that would naturalize in the Deep South. "If," as he notes, "daffodils can be said to do that. And that's how I got obsessed with the Edwardian daffodil varieties—biding time until I can really have a garden! The older varieties often take our climate better than the more heavily hybridized ones, and they are often smaller, less 'perfect,' and 'starry' (the opposite of the correct 'show' daffodil)—that is, more graceful, and fitting better into a naturalistic garden than the overdeveloped modern varieties. That's how I came to love the old things that do very well down here such as campernelles, the best daffodil, in my estimation. 'Grand Primo' types, species jonquils, Lent lilies, *Narcissus ×intermedius* (which my grandmother and I dug from an old homestead about 40 years ago, but I couldn't identify them until Scott Ogden's book *Garden Bulbs for the South* was published in 1994). Daffodils in the first three divisions (trumpet, long-cup, and short-cup) are not great this far south. Usually they bloom for a year or two or four, say, but then stop flowering. I find that the older clones (those hybridized, generally, before World War I, and closer to the species) are more vigorous in the heat than modern cultivars.

"In Tuscaloosa, the much-encountered daffodils include the following. They're in no particular order, just as they come to mind: Lent lilies, campernelles (the most common daffodil to be found as you go from Tuscaloosa further south), and the several and diverse plants that we usually call 'Grand Primo.' True tazettas are not common aside from Grand Primo types. Several different varieties of paperwhites such as 'Geranium' and 'Erlicheer' turn up in old gardens. Paperwhites, which bloom earlier and are often caught by the cold, have stem damage below about 25°F, the flowers at about 20°F. However, Poetaz daffodils are quite at home above the coastal south and take the red clay well. Then there are *Narcissus jonquilla*, 'Trevithian', *N. ×intermedius*, *N. ×incomparabilis*, and the old doubles. The doubles usually don't open well, but in the occasional year do make a show to remind us just how *many* of these reside in old gardens. Common, but less so than above: Some of the older Barrii and Leedsii types such as Barrii Conspicuus, 'Queen of the North', and 'Mrs. Langtry' have been blooming for decades without division in old gardens, and I also see 'Sir Watkin'. Poets [slang for poeticus] are quite uncommon, but 'Actaea' can succeed on better soil, and occasionally you find a clump of the old wild *N. poeticus* var. *recurvus* or *N. radiiflorus* var. *poetarum*. Jonquils—*N. jonquilla* and its hybrids—of course love us and are among the most persistent forms we can grow.

"I found much the same varieties in Athens, Georgia, with the following exceptions: More paperwhites in the older gardens, significantly fewer campernelles, and a good old tazetta-poet cross called 'Martha Washington' turns up here, blooming late with 'Queen of the North'. 'Twin Sisters' (*Narcissus* ×*biflorus*) [now *N.* ×*medioluteus* 'Twin Sister'] is very common here, but uncommon in Tuscaloosa. As you get to the warmer climes (south Georgia and Alabama), the list diminishes, with only jonquils and tazettas and their hybrids being common. For example, in South Georgia I find 'Soleil d'Or' outside, but it declines quickly in 'chilly' Tuscaloosa. At Sisters' Bulb Farm in Louisiana, *N. bulbocodium* is as happy as *N. jonquilla*, naturalizing there on sandy soil, which we do not have in Tuscaloosa. I think sand is the key factor with the hoop-petticoats."

Miscellaneous geophytes

Jim also mentions that "aside from the daffodils (and remembering that most of my experience is in Tuscaloosa and Athens), we see lots of what folks call 'snowdrops,' but are really summer snowflake, *Leucojum aestivum*. There aren't many true snowdrops, *Galanthus*, and no spring snowflakes, *L. vernum*. Assorted other bulbs include *Ipheion*, *Oxalis crassipes* and *O. brasiliensis*, *Ornithogalum nutans* and *O. umbellatum* (a weed), and Spanish bluebells, *Hyacinthoides hispanica*. Of course there are the 'Southern bulbs' like surprise lilies and crinums. Red spider lily, *Lycoris radiata*, is common, and pink *L. squamigera* grows as far south as Tuscaloosa, but it needs dividing more than it does further north to keep it blooming. Crinums, especially 'Ellen Bosanquet'; *Hymenocallis*, especially 'Tropical Giant'; *Gladiolus communis*. Occasionally, but only rarely, I'll see *Tulipa clusiana* and *T. undulatifolia*."

Georgia

An amateur gardening for pleasure, Nell Jean Campbell is used to conditions in the humid lower South of Zone 8b. Her

The large, deep pink flowers of *Crinum* 'Ellen Bosanquet' are familiar occupants of many American southern gardens, here seen in combination with pineapple lily, *Eucomis bicolor*. Photo courtesy of Brent Heath/ Brent and Becky's Bulbs.

mother, Audrey Jones, gardened in northwestern Georgia, Zone 7a, and Nell gardened in the metropolitan Atlanta area for 30 years. Now she gardens in Colquitt, Georgia (50 miles north of Tallahassee, Florida), on property that belonged to her husband's family. Her mother-in-law, Alberta Campbell, had cultivated a garden here since 1939, but the property became somewhat neglected later on. For a span between about 1973 and 1986, Nell was not gardening there, and things may have been removed or just died. The grass was mown, but that was about it as far as maintenance went. Still, huge camellias managed to thrive without any attention. 'Butter and Eggs' daffodils were there, along with other daffodils, a few tiny jonquils, and lots of *Lycoris radiata*, the red spider lily that blooms in early autumn. Dozens of amaryllis survived up until the 1970s, when they disappeared. "Whether from freezing, neglect, or constant mowing, I'm not sure," notes Nell. "And small surprises still turn up." She and her husband took over the property in 1985, and it was their second home until 1994, when they moved there permanently. The differences between Zones 7a and 8b are enough to affect what plants her mother could grow well and Nell must often struggle with. She mentions, "I know not to plant lilacs and peonies, two more that grew well at home. And I know that some of the bulbs don't belong here, but I enjoy the small successes that I have."

Nell describes Foxes Earth (as she named the property) as follows: "My yard is on what I consider 'high ground' for southern Georgia, well-drained except that once in a while when a 4 inch rain falls in less than an hour, parts of it flood, but soaks in or runs off in a short time. There are no naturally boggy areas in my garden at all." The property includes both forested woodland habitat and open grassland meadow areas. The natural part of the garden has native plants such as sassafras (*Sassafrass albidum*), scrub oak (*Quercus ilicifolia*), old-field cedar (*Juniperus virginiana*), and sumac. Any neglected area is quickly taken over by pines and wild cherry trees. Vines, both native and invasive exotics, swarm everywhere: Virginia creeper (*Parthenocissus quinquefolia*), wisteria, smilax, poison ivy (*Toxicodendron radicans*), cypress vine (*Ipomoea quamoclit*), wild grapes, Halls honeysuckle (*Lonicera japonica* 'Hall's Prolific'), and passion vine (*Passiflora incarnata*), or maypops as they are called locally.

The region typically experiences a winter low of about 20°F (−7°C), but as Nell mentions, "We usually don't have a hard freeze before Christmas. This past winter, on 24 January 2003, the low was 15.6°F. A previous low of 19°F had killed back most everything. In 2002, February was unseasonably warm and wet and March was freezing. The tulips bloomed at the wrong time and had to be picked for bouquets. 2003 was perfect for bulbs. I picked tulips to share the beauty." Nell grows tulips as annuals—but more about that later. Often in southern gardens it is not winter cold that is the limiting factor but rather summer heat. "Sometimes, in June, we have several consecutive days with temps above 100°F. July and August usually have many days hovering at 100°F or higher. The humidity is a killer." Also, just as elsewhere in the country, rainfall patterns have been disrupted. "The past few years," Nell remarked, "have been unusually dry. This year (2003) is unusually wet. This spring and summer we've had only two occasions on which I felt compelled to drag hoses and soak the gardens. Usually we're watering frequently.

"Like Topsy," she explained to me, "this garden 'just growed' and I like it that way." And the geophytes thrive. "There are numerous *Lycoris radiata* that have been here for many, many years. Huge clumps of green in the spring, hit-or-miss blooms in September because many are mowed too early. I keep moving the boundaries."

Daffodils

Daffodils were a big event where Nell grew up in northwestern Georgia. Nostalgically she remembers, "We had thousands blooming in the spring, most planted in the 1920s and '30s. I carried great armloads to school, wrapped in newspaper. My mother continued to plant daffodils (and tulips, she planted red and white Emperor with great success) for years. I remember when she planted a 'pink' daffodil in the '50s and was annoyed when it bloomed because it was only kind of apricot." One of Nell's favorite daffodil stories was about the farm equipment salesman whom her father invited to lunch. "All the gasoline truck delivery men, fertilizer salesmen, and other visitors to the farm would show up near noon because my father always invited them to eat. This particular gentleman stayed for lunch, and my mother picked a large handful of daffodils, offering them to him to take home to his spouse. He replied, 'Oh, lady, I can't take these home to my wife. She would be convinced that I'd been up to something if I brought home these flowers!'

"My experience has been that daffodils listed as 'heirloom' are more reliable than newer cultivars." Vintage daffodils were planted by her mother-in-law. "Some Tazetta type [is] scattered about along the fence, under the shrubbery, probably in five locations, huge clumps that bloom sporadically. They have numerous small, white blossoms with a pale yellow cup. I suspect they've been here for more than 50 years. There are dozens of 'Butter and Eggs' type daffodils that I moved that are still recovering from the shock." 'Butter and Eggs' (also known as 'Eggs and Bacon' or 'Codlins & Cream') appeared before 1900. A double daffodil, it is a mutation of large cup daffodil *Narcissus* ×*incomparabilis*, a *N. poeticus* and *N. pseudonarcissus* cross from the 17th century. All were given the family name of Phoenix, with descriptive names referring to their color, such as 'Yellow Phoenix', 'Primrose Phoenix', 'Apricot Phoenix', 'Golden Phoenix', 'Orange Phoenix', and 'Sulphur Phoenix'. While these may not have the show bench appeal that suits modern fancy, they exemplify the vigorous cultivars that thrive as plants exchanged by gardeners over the garden gate. (And if a southerner offers you any plants, remember that you must not say, "Thank you." As the saying goes, if you thank for plants, they won't grow.)

Nell mentions that "about a dozen 'King Alfred' type daffodils were planted in front of the house about 1965 that were kept beaten down by lawn mowers for years. I moved some of them, which were not happy about the move. The original location has flourished again since the mower has been banished from that spot and they are happily multiplying once again." But not all daffodils are happy in Georgia. "A few dozen 'Ice Follies' daffodils have been here for the past 15 or so years. They wax and wane. About 1996 I planted 100 'Carlton' in several locations. Not a one persisted after the first year when they bloomed nicely. Because they were in more than one location, I think the fault may not be entirely my own. The same year, I planted 25 'Saint Patrick's Day', from another distributor. They also did not persist. Eventually, the source of these bulbs mentioned virus in 'Saint Patrick's Day'. These did have yellow streaks in the leaves well before time for them to die down." And there are always other daffodils to try: "There's a double-white that I believe to be [*Narcissus*] *albus plenus odoratus* [now *N. poeticus* 'Plenus'] that has returned nicely. 'Tête-a-tête' is a reliable daffodil, 'Sweetness' is reliable, 'Jack Snipe' blooms some years, skips a year when he chooses. 'February Gold' is good. 'Thalia' has bloomed for me in a bed with daylilies surrounded by liriope under a deciduous oak for some years. 'Petrel' is as pretty as 'Thalia', but pricier. Love 'Hawera' in the shade of a live oak. 'Baby Moon', the last to bloom, so pretty snuggled up to an oak. I planted a number of new to my garden daffodils last season (that would be in the fall of 2002), including 'Fortune', 'Fortissimo', 'Hillstar', 'Gigantic Star', and 'Topolino', in numbers ranging from handfuls to dozens. They all flowered well. 'Jetfire' was spectacular the year before but failed to rebloom. Two Tazettas that did not perform for me were 'Grand Soleil d'Or' (bloomed poorly, did not return) and 'Minnow', which has been a sulker: one or two unhappy little blossoms from a handful of bulbs.

"I am mostly planting in drifts in fairly open spaces. 'Ice Follies' . . . is under pecan trees. Some 'Ice Follies', which were under high shade pines, finally gave up because of competition from the pines and ancient liriope. Last year I planted several dozen daffodils and a few tulips between some young edible pear trees because 1) there was space there and 2) white pear blossoms look good above blooming bulbs."

Nell lets the daffodil foliage dry off with no mowing until they're brown. She plants daffodils in wide swathes, leaving room for the mower to make paths through the area. So, as flowers fade and foliage needs to mature, there isn't just one big weed patch but a series of little "meadows." It looks shabby but eventually becomes a grassy plain when the foliage dies back. Nell comments that she is "afraid weeding is a fact of life if your garden isn't so full there's no room for weeds, or the mulch so deep the weeds can't grow. I was just thinking this morning about the weeds I let grow, things like bluets, Venus looking glass, *Legousia speculum-veneris*, erigeron, oxalis. When they look tired, I pull or mow like any other weed."

Hyacinths

Hyacinths are another favorite of Nell's because of their fragrance. She remembers as a child that she had "the old-fashioned kind, I think they're called Roman hyacinths, with drooping single blooms." I remember them, too, as French Roman hyacinths, very popular for forcing. They are difficult, if not impossible, to find today. Nell grows hyacinths with reasonable success, noting "Early oriental hyacinths come back for me. (I buy those that say 'early forcing.') Purple tends to persist well for me. There are some *Hyacinthus orientalis* 'Top Hit' that came from Brent and Becky's Bulbs about five years ago that have been wonderful, earlier than the other hyacinths, blooming before the others are hardly out of the ground. They are a pale lavender and I think they're beautiful. I tried 30 bulbs of 'Blue Jacket' and 25 of 'Gipsy Queen' last season. 'Gipsy Queen' was pinker than the photos, but it's a strong beauty. I forced several of the 'Blue Jacket' in water for gifts. They aren't as spectacular as those in the garden, but they sure amazed the recipients. It was also my first time for 'City of Haarlem'. They turned almost pure white in the sun here, but I think they are great. The pinks, 'Pink Pearl' and 'Jan Bos', came back, except for the ones that were in water the previous year, which had only foliage, but strong foliage and I am hopeful for the next season. Hyacinths have exceeded my expectations from what I had read about them."

Tulips

Tulips hold a fascination for Nell, even though she realizes they're not suitable to her climate. Her mother, who gardened in northwestern Georgia, Zone 7a, used to overplant her tulips with Shirley poppies, *Papaver rhoeas*. Like the Michigan gardeners who try to grow familiar plants in south Florida sand, Nell longs for "home." When the bulbs appear in fall, she craves to see them bloom. When she first moved to Colquitt, a couple just over the Decatur County line in Bainbridge planted thousands of tulips each fall and the local paper would publish photos in the spring. Since he died, his widow doesn't have tulips any more, but it was a novelty that was appreciated by many. Nell is more modest in her efforts and is satisfied with 50 here and a handful there.

"Every year, I plant more tulips despite the fact that every year is different. I am ever hopeful. Year before last, I made a note to myself: '*No more tulips*.' Later I went back and amended it to 'if you *must* plant tulips, only plant purple.' In 1996 I planted Emperor tulips. 'Solva' was the only one to bloom well. The others had sick appearing foliage and I pulled most of them up when it was obvious that the blooms were not going to be attractive. The 50 'Lavender Lady' from the 'big box store' were outstanding. I sent an e-mail to the distributor and they said they were Triumph type. 'Queen of Night' (about 25) bloomed well, too. 'Jan Reus', of which I had only a handful, were too, too pretty.

I prechill for at least 8 weeks, which seems to be about right, and plant after Christmas. I've had the occasional purple (single late) to return and bloom the second year.

"Species tulips have not done well for me. *Tulipa dasystemon* last season failed to come up. I don't think I prechilled them. I planted some lilac tulips that made good foliage the first year, no bloom, better foliage the second year, no bloom. They are in a dry, west-facing spot on a kind of little hillside."

Miscellaneous geophytes

Nell continued, "Knowing that the tulips are only good as annuals here, I conduct little experiments on the remaining bulbs. Grape hyacinths, *Muscari armeniacum*, persists, while not wildly reseeding and multiplying. 'Blue Spike' has not persisted. The recommended *M. neglectum* bloomed the first year (2002), was poor to return the next. Because of the sheer numbers of muscari that it would take to make a stunning show in a large area, I have decided not to plant more, but the occasional clumps of blue blossoms are a fun addition to the garden. Spanish bluebells, *Hyacinthoides non-scripta*, were one that I tried last season. I planted 50, starting with mixed colors despite reading that they should be all of a color to persist well. They made good foliage, in the shade under the edge of a live oak, but only a couple of pink blooms showed up. I dug into them recently and there are little white bulbs persisting and multiplying. If they multiply, they will not be a problem in this location. *Brodiaea* 'Queen Fabiola' are still to be evaluated. They made good foliage and bloomed beautifully late this spring. I read that the foliage might die down ahead of the blossoms, but it persisted until they bloomed. I dug into the edge of that bed, too, just to see, and there are long white roots with no rhizome that I could determine and that white root appears to be drying up as well.

"In the late spring and summer, I enjoy many lilies: Longiflorum Asiatic hybrids, Asiatics and orientals." *Lilium longiflorum* is the white trumpet lily so popular as an Easter flower. It is native to the mild winter region of southern Japan. Asiatic lilies are hybrids of Japanese and Chinese species of lilies, excluding *Lilium speciosum* and *L. auratum*. The Oriental hybrids were developed primarily from those two species. Nell mentions that she "started out about five years ago with some Orientals from a discount store, probably mislabeled, but pretty. I've added 25 mixed Asiatics, usually about 5 at a time." The Asiatics have increased well, and the orientals were spectacular in 2003. Trumpet lily 'African Queen' was beautiful, but Nell found the fragrance unpleasant. Preferring bold blossoms that can be seen from a long way off, Nell has not planted any species lilies. She's begun propagating her lilies, digging and replanting the little bulbs, and has even tried scaling on about five, 2-year-old plants.

Nell feels that the best companions she's tried for lilies are the perennial salvias. They are small when the lilies bloom and spread out to cover the fading lilies' ankles and most of the dying stalks by fall. Pineapple sage (*Salvia elegans*) and Mexican bush sage (*S. leucantha*) are her favorites. She's thinking of planting some lilies closer to the vitex plants (chaste tree, *Vitex agnus-castus*) to see how those might look together, since the vitex are just coming into bloom as the lilies start to fade. The vitex are fairly airy. One serendipitous combo she has paired are Stargazer lilies with *Clerodendrum bungei* (known, says Nell, as "Cashmere Bouquet" in most quarters, because of the similarity in fragrance, or Mexicali rose). This suckering shrub is a thug in her estimation, but after watching butterflies nectaring on it one morning she decided it is one of the nicer thugs—nicer, that is, if you have a sharp spade and plenty of room. She mentioned that the leaves and stems have a really unpleasant odor when crushed. (An earlier name, now invalid, was *C. foetidum.*) But the clustered, rosy-pink blossoms are fragrant and look good near the lilies. And speaking of fragrance, true lilies grow beautifully well.

One geophyte that I must dig and store through New Jersey winters is a proper, in-the-ground-the-year-around perennial for Nell, who says, "It's really hot here, but cannas are very forgiving. These have survived uncultivated for decades. I dug up every one from under an oak tree three or four years ago. The tiny roots left behind have sprouted back into the original circle. They've been plowed up, mowed down, and covered over with Virginia creeper, Confederate jasmine, and wild grape vines. They still come back. They are shy bloomers in part sun, never bloom under the oak tree, but the will to persist is there. I checked this morning, there's not yet a bud anywhere. In the wet weather we've been having this year I need to tell you that these cannas have rust. . . . They will survive and I won't spray, but [I will] just clip and destroy debris and wait for next year. I thought maybe the ones over under the tree are okay. At first glance they looked pretty good, but it's there, too. Some had been cut down by the mower and came back clean, but it's creeping up again, leaf by leaf. These are survivors, but they are probably the 'Typhoid Mary' of the canna world. Did I forget to say I've planted five-dozen caladiums this year? Some are planted with the cannas, which is not particularly outstanding because the grass is encroaching. The pink cannas and white caladiums in front of a bank in the next county were beautiful last year.

"*Crinum zeylanicum* have been here for 50 or more years. They bloom without care, have been making huge seed pods this year and new plants come up in unlikely places. When I was digging some, some were so big and the pine roots growing over them so big, I had to leave them in the path where I have to step over them. There's another crinum here that has not bloomed since I planted it three or four years ago. I forgot the source and I believe it must be planted too shallowly as it has not bloomed but has increased. There's a beautiful *C. americanum* that blooms along the creek about a mile from here, but I am not of a mind to try to dig and transplant this native to my drier garden. And there's another native, *Zephyranthes* (atamasco lily), which grow along roadsides in swampy areas. People here call them 'Easter lilies' because that's when they bloom. The rainier years bring out more 'Easter lilies.'"

Some *Lycoris squamigera* in a bed at Foxes Earth have been growing there for years. Nell has never seen a blossom since she planted them. When the foliage appears every spring, she intends perhaps to move them; then, hopeful of a miracle, she forgets about them until they've died back.

When her mother-in-law was alive, *Hippeastrum* grew everywhere at Foxes Earth, bright red trumpets of bloom. Nell suspects that they died both from neglect and a hard freeze in 1984. Some gardeners in town have great borders and beds of them, calling them "amaryllis." Nell says, "There is a particularly spectacular bed of white amaryllis about 12 or 14 feet in diameter around a pine tree.... Many bulb dealers promote amaryllis as 'tulips for the South.' I don't think of them as substitutes for tulips at all, and they bloom later. It's similar to the suggestion that crape myrtles are 'lilacs for the South.' There were once *Hedychium coronarium* growing here. Beautiful, fragrant 'butterfly lilies,' which I guess went the same way as the Amaryllis."

Tulbaghia violacea, with its sweet-scented, violet flowers and broad, flat leaves strongly smelling of onions, is popular around Colquitt, with the most spectacular display Nell's seen growing in front of the electric utility in the next county. (In California, I've heard it called society garlic.) Other geophytes come and go in Nell's estimation and plans for the future. *Oxalis crassipes* persists for her, though it is less hardy than *O. rubra*. It waxes and wanes, gets rust, and melts in the humidity; then it pops up in a new spot, sometimes along an edge where it looks really pretty and she forgives its vagaries.

Zantedeschia aethiopica has done well for Nell. She never thought to try them until seeing them described as 'pig lilies' in their native habitat. They seem happy by the birdbath where a faucet drips continuously. They usually die back in the hot summer but return for more bloom in the fall before going truly dormant for winter. Nell notes, "Mama used to grow *Neomarica gracilis* as a pot plant. I mean to try it as a garden plant here." Attractive, irislike, white to yellow flowers more than 2 inches (5 cm) across are carried on stems 2 feet (60 cm) tall, which nod

Growing in a ditch in Giddings, Texas, this husky specimen of *Crinum zeylanicum* is clearly one of those unfussy bulbs that thrives on neglect. Photo by author.

over from the weight of new plantlets that form on the flowering stem, giving rise to the common name of walking iris. Bulbous irises simply do not persist in southern Georgia. The rhizomatous Louisiana irises are well adapted to their climate, though. Nell grows only the "blue flag" iris that have been at Foxes Earth forever. She has noticed "yellow flags" in the next county that are spectacular around (in) a pond in the city park. And although *Cyclamen coum* has been recommended, she has not tried it but thinks it might persist in the dry shade close to the trunks of the oaks.

Starch hyacinth

Found in old gardens in the American South, starch hyacinth were used in laundries, where starch extracted from the bulbs gave shirts a nice, crisp finish after they were ironed. In Texas, Cynthia Muller finds starch hyacinth growing in waste places, where it often coexists nicely with grass. She gives starch hyacinth the academic name of *Muscari racemosum* and says that sometimes it is locally referred to as grape hyacinth. My contemporary/current reference books say that this muscari is now to be called *M. neglectum* and mention that it is a very variable species native to Europe, North Africa, and southwestern Asia, with a deep blue to blackish blue flower and a thin white line around the opening of each. In *Daffodils, Tulips, and Other Hardy Bulbs*, published in 1966, Michael Jefferson-Brown says that *M. neglectum* is a free-flowering plant with very dark, almost black, blue flowers with a white ring at the mouth, and the sterile topmost flowers are a lighter shade. He dismisses *M. racemosum* as a dark-blue, small-flowered species with invasive tendencies that "can soon make a nuisance of itself."

Rain lilies

Two different genera are commonly called "rain lilies." Both are in the family Amaryllidaceae, have crocuslike flowers, are frost-tender, and grow from long-necked bulbs. The speed with which rain lilies come into flower after a summer storm is phenomenal, often taking only a few days. Empty ground, a cloudburst, and suddenly up come the flowers. Interestingly, a heavy hand with the watering can or a good soaking with a hose does not always seem to do the trick—rain lilies they are named, and rain is what they prefer. Perhaps some less obvious connection, such as a shift in the barometric pressure, causes their growth. While they'll produce a couple of flowers now and again in midsummer, rain lilies are really waiting for drenching rains that come with a late summer thunderstorm. Compare this irregular burst of activity with the more precise scheduling habits of all those large and small spring-blooming geophytes such as daffodils and snowdrops. The timing may shift a week or two this way or that depending on the weather. But when a given daffodil cultivar flowers, all daffodils do so together—not like the rain lilies that flush and then fade, only to flower again. The sequence of rain and flowers must be preceded by a dry spell, for if the soil is constantly moist, rain lilies won't flower. As Cynthia Muller pointed out, almost every home in her part of Texas has a sprinkler system for irrigating lawns and gardens. The flower beds are kept continually moist. And under those conditions the rain lilies, in particular, do not get the proper signals to stimulate them into a spurt of bloom, and they produce only leaves.

Telling apart the two different genera of rain lilies is relatively easy, once you know how. *Zephyranthes* have six stamens. Either they are all of the same length, or three of them are longer than the other three. In *Habranthus*, the six stamens are of four different lengths. Fairy flower, flower of the west wind, and rain lily are all common names for the various species of *Zephyranthes*. Indigenous to the Western Hemisphere, the various species are found from the southeastern United States southward to Argentina and Uruguay. In general, it is the deciduous species that do better in Texas, while those that prefer some summer moisture are found in the American South and Southeast. Generally speaking, they are hardy to an occasional frost of brief duration; extended cold weather quickly does them in. Some are more tender than others, and with reluctance I list the USDA hardiness zone ratings usually given for the rain lilies. But experimentation is part of the gardening game. Soil type—sandy and free-draining versus water-retentive clay—is just one variable that can change things around. Jane McGary grows a wide range of geophytes 1000 feet up a mountain in northwestern Oregon. She likes to emphasize that with geophytes it is important to look at when they make their growth. What's going on below ground when are they are rooting or resting is as important a consideration as when they produce leaves and flowers; also important, for those that grow in summer, are their summer heat requirements. Jane claims "the best gardening advice I ever got was 'try everything,' and that's the best advice I can give."

Atamasco lily, *Zephyranthes atamasca*, is a spring-blooming species found in the light shade of deciduous woodlands, with pure white flowers, sometimes flushed with purple on the outside. They are native from Virginia to Florida and Alabama, and Nell Jean Campbell sees them in Georgia, growing in swampy areas along roadsides. The local name for them is Easter lilies, since that is when they flower, most profusely in rainier years. The short-necked bulb is only 1 inch (2.5 cm) in diameter, producing four to six light green, glossy leaves about a foot (30 cm) long, arching toward the ground, and a fragrant flower 3 inches (7.5 cm) tall. Hardy to Zone 8 or perhaps 7, it is an elegant, practical alternative to crocus for southern gardeners. *Zephyranthes candida*, another white-flowered species, is described in Chapter 8, "Geophytes for Damp to Wet Places."

Zephyranthes citrina is a lovely yellowed-flowered species that Elizabeth Lawrence grew in Raleigh, North Carolina. Native to Mexico, it is somewhat hardier than its tropical American origins might suggest and grows well in USDA Zone 7. Adaptable, it also often does well in drier Texas gardens around San Antonio and elsewhere. Summer sees a scattering of its bright-yellow flowers, but the big display is in late summer

A grassy field in Hertford County, North Carolina, is spangled with atamasco lilies, *Zephyranthes atamasca*, as Mike Chelednik enjoys the floral richness of this natural habitat. While the field may be difficult to replicate at home, a potful of rain lilies is, fortunately, easy to cultivate. Photo by Bobby Ward.

into early fall. The bulbs are about $1^1/_2$ inches (4 cm) in diameter, with a tidy brown tunic. Three or four bright green leaves make a spruce backdrop to the late-summer flowers. 'Ajax' is a charming hybrid of *Z. citrina* and *Z. candida*, with dark cream to yellow flowers. Crossing 'Ajax' back onto *Z. candida* resulted in 'Aquarius', with luscious midsummer flowers the color of clotted cream, accented by bright golden stamens. Vegetatively quite vigorous, the production of offsets means that 'Aquarius' quickly develops into a mound of foliage. It is hardy in USDA Zone 8.

A close-up of their pristine white flowers reveals the elegant beauty and delicate contrast of this form of *Zephyranthes atamasca*, with its wide petals and six golden stamens. Photo by Bobby Ward.

The inch (2.5 cm) wide, deep rose-pink flowers of *Zephyranthes rosea* open in hurricane season. Native to Guatemala and the West Indies, the round little bulb, practically neckless and not much more than a half-inch (1 cm) in diameter, prefers shallow planting. This late summer to early autumn flowering species is happier in Florida, where its narrow and linear evergreen leaves are not subject to drying out as would happen in the arid reaches of central Texas. Grand, indeed, *Z. grandiflora* has vivid red buds that open into bright pink flowers with a white throat. They may appear in late spring, more usually in midsummer, and they manage a repeat performance in late summer or early autumn. Neutral to slightly acid soil rich in organic matter suits it best. Native to Mexico, it is popular throughout the Gulf Coast, from Virginia and Kentucky to southern Florida. Inland, in the middle and upper South, a mulch of pine straw will help bring the somewhat tender bulbs through winter. The pass-along clone found naturalized and in gardens is a sterile strain that sets no seed, instead multiplying freely from offsets.

It is easy to become confused when the nursery trade offers *Habranthus robustus* under the name of *Zephyranthes robusta*. With large, lavender-tinted pink flowers in summer, it looks very much like *Z. grandiflora*. The flower's white center slowly turns green as the flower ages. Keep in mind that while zephyranthes hold their symmetrical flowers upright, the flowers of habranthus nod outward from the stem, rather like a miniature hippeastrum. If still in doubt, look at the stamens. If they are of assorted lengths, it's a habranthus. Native to Argentina and southern Brazil, and because it prefers shallow planting, *H. robustus* is plant-and-forget hardy only in the lower American South, where it grows equally well in shady, moist woodlands or drier sunny areas. In inland gardens this robust rain lily will need a pine needle mulch for winter protection in some years. A fertile species, it multiplies both by seeds and from offsets. It has a respectable garden history, being introduced into England in 1827.

Yellow is the brightest color we perceive at midday out in the sunlight, and this little flower just glows. Golden rain lily, *Zephyranthes citrina*, offers a rich yellow cup and stamens dusted with orange pollen. Photo by Bobby Ward.

Of course it is not hardy for me in New Jersey, so I grow the bulbs in a large, shallow bowl from a hanging basket without its hangers. The bulbs were originally obtained from a big box store of one flavor or another—and I remember that the original package did not bother to mention that a Zone 6 winter would be lethal for them, since they are hardy only in USDA Zone 8 or higher. They are so reliable. They spend the winter on the floor under a bench in my cool greenhouse, kept dry while things heat up in early summer, and then parked outside when a good rainstorm is in the forecast: rain equals flowers. The pan of bulbs will take a break now and again, and then the plants will flush with a goodly show of pink flowers when a dry spell is followed by rain. I usually top dress the little bulbs grown in pots rather than repot, since disturbance is not something they enjoy. All that means is at the end of a dry resting period, I scrape away the soil in the upper part of the pot and replace is with some fresh, gritty potting mix before watering to wake them up.

Brian Whyer, a friend in England, sent me some bulbs of *Habranthus martinezii* a couple of years ago, back when this sort of thing was not only easy, it was also legal. In 2003 their pot was ignored and overlooked in my greenhouse in the summer, after all the other "stuff" got moved outdoors. In late July I dribbled some water on the soil in the bare, empty pot and within five days the bulbs were in flower. It started off with three lovely little bluish white flowers with a darker eye and worked its way up to eight. When Brian heard how they were doing, on 29 July he responded, "Good to see your rain lilies are doing okay. Mine have been in flower for some time. It seems I have had

This pot of rosy pink *Habranthus robustus*, the most readily available of the rain lilies, clearly shows why it is so popular. The generous number of buds that accompany the open flowers are a good indication of the sort of display it presents in return for modest attention to its needs. Photo by Bobby Ward.

several flushes of flower with very irregular watering, although I guess it is different bulbs that flower each time." In his book, *The Smaller Bulbs* (1987), Brian Mathew mentions that "it is very easy to grow if the bulbs are dried out in summer." I've seen mention of a nameless cross between *H. robustus* and *H. martinezii* that flowers in late spring with clear pink flowers 2 inches (5 cm) across, accentuated with a faint greenish eye. It sounds charming.

Another species frequently seen in Texas is the native copper lily, *Habranthus tubispathus* var. *texanus*, which produces its dainty, thimble-size orange to golden yellow flowers at irregular intervals in mid- to late summer. The inch (2.5 cm) wide flowers flaunt themselves on a stalk 7 inches (17.5 cm) tall. Darker copper, bronze, or brown streaks on the outside create an elegant effect when late day sun shines through the petals. Native to central Texas, it dislikes attempts to cosset it with extra moisture or richer soil, preferring instead to naturalize itself in rough, dry fields, where its flowers display themselves against tawny dry grass, lasting just for a couple of days before they wither away. A disjunct population appears a huge leap away, to northern Argentina, southern Brazil, Uruguay, and southern Chile. As well as duplicating the coppery bronze flowers found in the Lone Star State, the South American population includes in addition a soft rosy pink form, *H. tubispathus* var. *roseus*. Stubborn and intolerant of the lush life to be led in a tended, well-watered garden, *H. tubispathus* is content to seed itself about, reaching flowering size rather quickly.

A rain lily I once had and have since lost is *Cooperia pedunculata*, now known as *Zephyranthes drummondii*. Tom Peace was kind enough to dig me some bulbs from a gunky, muddy Texas ditch. The books say the bulbs are deeply seated in the ground. When I opened the box, the gray caliche clay that still adhered to the large bulbs, 2 to 3 inches (5.0 to 7.5 cm) in diameter, and the bulbs' long necks made it clear that Tom's gift had required some serious excavation. They were wonderful when they bloomed—clean, white, gobletlike flowers, opening at night, and fragrant too, as so many other night-blooming white flowers tend to

Summer rainstorms bring copper rain lily (*Habranthus tubispathus*), which is native to dry grassy fields, into rapid bloom. After a downpour we're presented with flowers modest in size and rich in color, from the paler yellow interior to the nearly metallic copper tracery on the outside of its petals. Photo by Bobby Ward.

be. In the throes of the move from Connecticut to New Jersey, they got overlooked, and one cold night they froze. I sure would love to have them back again. Native to the hill country of central Texas and northern Mexico, it can flower from late spring to early autumn. It is quite possibly a parent of *Z.* 'La Buffa Rose', which titillates the viewer with a few flowers in midsummer but waits for late summer thunderstorms to produce its main display. Variable in color from pure, clean white to deep, rosy pink, and everything between, each of the flowers, nearly 3 inches (7.5 cm) wide, stands up on a stem 8 inches (20 cm) tall.

North Carolina

Bobby Ward thinks of himself as an amateur when it comes to gardening, one who grows plants for the pleasure of working in the soil, learning about new plants, and the pass-along pleasure of sharing plants with others. His Zone 7 Piedmont garden is in Raleigh, North Carolina, with only occasional snow in mild winters, and hot, wet summer weather. July and August are the hottest and wettest months, helped along by hurricanes and tropical storms that contribute to the annual precipitation of 40 to 45 inches (102 to 114 cm) per year. Summer rainfall is a problem for many South African bulbs, geared as they are to a Mediterranean cycle of winter wet and summer dry, which is no doubt why they fail to thrive in the Raleigh area. These two months also have the highest nighttime temperatures, difficult for plants as they continue to respire at high rates, using up the sugars made during the day. About half of Bobby's garden is in medium shade and the rest is in full sun only about eight hours maximum in midsummer. The bulk of the garden soil is red clay, but one area (about 25 percent) is sand, having been deposited by an ancient creek that still runs through the middle of the property. As well as mulching, Bobby adds amendments to the clay areas when he is planting bulbs, working them into the soil to loosen it and provide drainage. Fertilizer usage is only moderate. He applies a bulb fertilizer when planting bulbs and then scatters some about in the bulb areas each winter, usually in early January, as narcissus begin poking up. Alternatively, he occasionally uses an all-purpose 5-10-10 granular fertilizer.

Squirrels are generally not a problem in the rest of the year, but in autumn they are a real nuisance as they look for places to bury acorns and nuts. "When I plant new bulbs," Bobby points out, "they know where the 'turned' soil is, so I try to disguise it by covering the area lightly with leaves. I have some voles (pine vole) but I can't be sure they are damaging bulbs. And chipmunks have undermined some bulb areas."

With a location in Zone 7, Bobby can grow a wide range of bulbs, from *Lycoris* to other even more tender genera: several *Crinum, Hymenocallis, Rhodophiala bifida,* *Sprekelia, Hippeastrum,* and a couple of *Nerine.* Cyclamen straddle the mild-to-colder dividing line, with *Cyclamen coum* and *C. hederifolium* suitable for Zones 5 and 6, and other more tender species such *C. graecum*, *C. trochopteranthum*, and *C. purpurascens*.

He is also able to grow bulbs that would be found in colder regions and fail to thrive in the Deep South. No tulips, but Bobby is fond of daffodils, and for good reason. "How is it possible," he e-mailed me in January, "that *Narcissus* 'Rijnveld's Early Sensation' is in bloom today, even with snow all around it? It can't possibly have had the requisite physiological chilling that folks say that daffs need to blossom—at least not here in North Carolina. I probably have 20 in bloom today (and the temperature was 17°F last night) and they are gleaming in the brilliant sun and snow (from Friday) now." When I thought about this, it seemed obvious that different daffodils can have dissimilar requirements. Otherwise, how to explain the tender *N. tazetta* subspecies and cultivars, some of which can flower with less than a week of temperatures at or below 48°F (9°C), which is practically no chilling period at all. And since 'Rijnveld's Early Sensation' lives up to its name by always flowering ahead of the other daffodils, even in my New Jersey garden, no doubt its need for cold is minimal compared to others. (Tulips are a very different story and need an extended chilling period if they are to flower well.) Along with the precocious daffodils come the first galanthus. *Iris reticulata* soon follows, and when spring has more definitely arrived, a diversity of crocus add lots of color. Other little bulbs such as *Scilla siberica* add to the display. A few alliums show in late spring, and colchicum in fall.

Bobby is especially fond of several species *Zephyranthes*, which he grows both in pots and in the ground. (Squirrels investigate the pots, finding them choice pantries for acorns.) The hardiest ones are *Z. atamasca*, which is native in the area, and *Z. candida*. The species that are not fully hardy are grown in pots, which Bobby moves to the south side of his house during the winter, after mulching the pots lightly with leaves.

Why grow bulbs? That's an easy question for Bobby to answer: "I like bulbs because they are easy to manage, easily shipped when dormant, have few diseases (for me at least), and take up little space. Bulbs are above ground for only a short time, thereby allowing space for other plants during the rest of the year. Generally bulbs are planted in the fall, and they reward me with blossoms with minimal care in a short time. Spring bulbs emerge when the rest of the garden is bare."

Struggling with "traditional" bulbs unsuited to a region is a source of gardening frustration and disappointment. Instead, growing the right bulbs in the right place is a source of pleasure for Mike Chelednik. His garden is in the coastal South, near Greenville, North Carolina. The hot, humid summer weather is accompanied by warm nights. Winters are mild, with minimum temperatures generally in the mid-teens, placing his garden in USDA Zone 8. Rainfall, with a total accumulation of approximately 50 inches (127 cm), is spread fairly evenly throughout the year, though slightly less in the fall and winter. Mike's garden has both sunny and shady areas, and the soil is a sandy loam. Given the good ground, he does not need to use any special planting techniques, but he reminded me that this is attributable to his well-drained soil. As well as in the garden, Mike (who considers himself more of a plant collector than a gardener, per se) also grows many bulbs in pots that remain outdoors year-round. And because he uses a soilless potting mix for them, only the bulbs in containers receive any fertilizer. Mike prefers to use a time-release fertilizer. Squirrels are a nuisance, as they will dig, especially if the bulbs are in pots or newly planted, but gardeners everywhere experience this consistent, country-wide problem. Friends of mine in New York City may not have deer strolling down the avenue, but squirrels ("tree rats with furry tails," as they are sometimes called) are an aggravation.

Given the hot, humid weather around Greenville and the year-round precipitation, Mike finds, just as Bobby Ward points out, that bulbs from the Cape region of South Africa are unsuited. Further, the difference between Bobby's Zone 7 garden and Mike's location in Zone 8 means that Mike finds that many of the commonly grown bulbs of the Mid-Atlantic and Northeastern United States just don't do well farther south. Instead, his main interest is the subtropical amaryllids and irids of the Western Hemisphere, especially *Zephyranthes*, *Cooperia*, and *Habranthus*. He also grows other well-adapted, underused bulbs for the area, including *Rhodophiala bifida*, *Lycoris* spp., and many *Crinum*. When asked why he grew bulbs, Mike's concise reply says it all: "I enjoy the transient, fleeting nature of the individual blooms, which give me something to look forward to. Then there's their relative ease of culture, and their small size, which lets you forget about them when not in bloom, and makes a large collection easier to handle."

Arkansas

Bulbmeister.com is the name Kelly Irvin gave to his Web site, a name that reflects his passion for the bulbs he sells. His nursery is on the Ozark Plateau in Bentonville, in the northwestern corner of Arkansas. I think of Arkansas as part of the warm to hot and humid South, but Kelly offers a more accurate description: "This is temperate South/Central, often called 'the transition zone' among members of the horticultural community. Our temperatures never reach below −5°F, and rarely go above 95°F, but temperature extremes can be quite variable from year to year. And, the times, they are a changing." As Kelly points out, it is "very easy for us to experience a Zone 7 winter, sometimes a Zone 8. If you add the cultural practice of mulching and include microclimates, well, bulb growing can be very interesting in our area." The summer months of July and August have average high temperatures of 89°F (32°C), with a recorded high of 114°F (46°C). Average low temperatures in December, January, and February are, respectively, 26°, 22°, and 26°F (−3°, −6°, and −3°C), while the recorded low temperature for December and January is −14°F (−26°C). Technically, that places Bentonville in USDA Zone 6. But this USDA Zone 6 is different from the USDA Zone 6 I experience in New Jersey. For one thing, the further you get from an ocean or one of the Great Lakes, the greater the extremes when summer or winter temperatures stray from the "average," so Bentonville experiences more of a swing when this happens. For another, my winter weather stays cold for longer periods than does Kelly's.

I think I've finally found a good way to compare one region's winter conditions to another. The National Oceanographic and Atmospheric Administration, NOAA for short, provides all sorts of weather data. In the monthly summaries for its weather reporting stations, the data you might expect is included: average mean temperatures, average high temperatures, average low temperatures, and precipitation. In addition, information is provided for the number of days with temperatures of 32°F (0°C) or less in each winter month, and for degree days (heating in the winter months, cooling if it is summer). The average heating degree days for the month of December in Bentonville is 881. In December 1993, the figure for the weather site closest to where I live in New Jersey was 1011 heating degree days. Now that allows a somewhat more realistic means of making a comparison.

At the ripe old age of 13 years old, Kelly decided he was going to be a horticulturist, having fallen prey to the vegetable gardening "bug" and landscaping with trees. Twenty years later, he received his master's degree in horticulture. His previous interests (before bulbs) were forestry and then fruit culture. He did professional work in fruit and vegetable culture. But Kelly always enjoyed perennial plants and simply took an interest in bulbs through a combination of floral interest and the overall perennial behavior of flower bulbs. While a nursery is geared to production and sales, that differs from a garden, which is focused on aesthetics. In places where Kelly is trying to feature flower bulbs, he likes to intersperse low-growing shrubs and small trees, such as Japanese maples, to enhance interest throughout the year. He has no significant problem with deer or rabbits, just with moles. Although they do not seem inclined to eat his bulbs (Amaryllidaceae being among the least favored of geophytes), they can disrupt the soil environment. Kelly believes "even ground aesthetics to be important, and these are my greatest pests. I'm not good about doing this, but when I have sprayed the soil or lawn with concentrated castor oil in three-month intervals, mole tunneling has been significantly reduced. I simply add the oil to a hose end sprayer capable of low-ratio calibration and spray away." Though not a strict observer of rules on organic culture of plants, when it comes to fertilization of bulbs, Kelly likes to stick with steamed bone meal at planting time. Established plantings receive supplemental applications up to three times a year. Although others have reported problems with varmint attraction, he has not experienced any negative results. Kelly did mention, "I've been hearing reports here and there that 'experts' are defying the old rule to avoid nitrogen, but their explanations go against my horticultural training."

Often, Kelly notes, bulbs are busy growing and blooming in early spring and have, relative to the growing season, a short display time. Non-bulbous perennials offer visual interest during bulb dormancy, and Kelly avoids annuals purely as a matter of personal taste and the way he likes to garden. In the case of *Lycoris* and depending on which species, only foliage is present from fall or late winter through early spring. It then dies back, showing life again in late summer, when bloom spikes come rocketing out of the ground. Just one of those things, Kelly can't quite explain what triggered his directed enthusiasm toward *Lycoris*, which in turn sent him down the path of general interest in flower bulb culture.

Kelly says, "My most favorite flower bulb is the spider lily, *Lycoris radiata*. I've been collecting and selling various members of this genus, having a fairly wide range of hardiness adaptability. *Lycoris radiata* and many of the other lycoris that have fall foliage are best adapted to Zones 7 to 10. The species with spring foliage—surprise lily, *L. squamigera* being the most popular—are often recommended for Zones 5 to 9. I do grow *L. aurea* var. *surgens* in a winter house, which is kept above freezing. In my experience, *Lycoris* is a very tough genus, able to endure variable soil, moisture, and light conditions." That said, Kelly finds that flowering is best in locations with midday shade, adequate moisture in winter, and significant ample moisture in late summer. The soil conditions in Bentonville are generally acidic silt to clay loam, other than the

Narrow, iridescent red petals, dusted with a crystalline glitter, accessorized with elongated pollen-tipped stamen, give *Lycoris radiata* a fantastic beauty. Photo by Takeo Nihei.

Gardens are made of plants growing in combination, to better effect than individually. Here the fiery red beauty of *Lycoris radiata* is enhanced by the silver foliage of artemisia. Photo courtesy of Brent Heath/Brent and Becky's Bulbs.

extremely common rocky areas in the mountainous region. Kelly believes that lycoris will not perform well in shallow soils, but it seems tolerant of poor (infertile) soil.

"I have had excellent success with growing *Zephyranthes candida* and *Z. grandiflora* in the ground the last couple of years, but we have not had a classic winter in that period. I expect my other rain lilies to do well in the ground this winter (2003–2004). My main focus over the next five years is to test various *Zephyranthes* in the ground and have my nursery list focus on these, and *Lycoris* as bare-root sales throughout the year. And I do have some *Crinum* in the ground, planted only last spring. I am hopeful they will survive this particular winter, because it has been mild, but I don't intend to grow them commercially. None of them are recommended for my planting zone. Over the long haul, I will be testing *Crinum* through test plots of existing species and varieties and plant breeding to potentially incorporate into my nursery offers. None of them are recommended for my planting zone. In addition, *Hippeastrum* are presently a hobby. I only anticipate commercial sales based on business growth (additional greenhouse space for potted culture), or unusual discoveries in hardiness (which, already, I know exist)." In common with inland regions not adjacent to a large bodies of water with their moderating influence, weather conditions in Bentonville swing wildly, summer to winter. Particularly with unfamiliar, less common plants grown "out of zone" such as geophytes from South Africa or South America, this can be a challenge and offers a thoroughgoing test of their suitability for the area, something Kelly clearly recognizes. As he mentioned to me early one January, "Saturday reached past 70°F here, but this morning we woke up to almost 20°F temps. The harshest part of our winter is only just beginning, not to start letting up until sometime in February. We will have frosts as late as early May. I have some *Galanthus woronowii* (my favorite snowdrop so far) starting to bloom, and some of my spring foliage lycoris have sent up some leaves (not good) due to our warm spell in December/January."

CHAPTER 8

Geophytes for Damp to Wet Places

Two descriptive terms are used to characterize water-loving plants. One is *obligate*, and it refers to plants such as water lilies that are obliged to grow in wet places. The other term is *facultative*, and it pertains to plants that have the facility to grow in soggy soils but may also grow in average conditions. Some may be found in saturated soils most of the time, others only infrequently, but all are adaptable. On the whole, geophytes—be they bulb, corm, rhizome, or tuber—don't like wet feet, since their lumpy underground structure is prone to rot if the soil is wet. This is especially true if excess water arrives while they are dormant. Often they can tolerate astonishing amounts of water if it comes while they are in active growth. Mike Salmon of Monocot Nursery in England told me of seeing small species narcissus in Spain that were growing and flowering literally under water. When he went back later in the year to collect dormant bulbs, the same site was parched and dry. I had daffodils planted in rough grass on the far side of a pond for a client of mine in New Canaan, Connecticut. Spring rains would raise the water level until it appeared that some extraordinary yellow water lilies were floating their flowers on the surface. The water would recede a few days later, and all was well. Surplus water while the geophytes are in growth is a different situation from excess water when they are dormant. A few are happier about inundation than the majority, and these have the facility to grow where the soil is damp to drenched, even in standing water. Keep in mind that excess water while the geophytes are growing is preferable to waterlogged soils year-round. Another point: conditions where water is moving through the soil are preferable to stagnant water that just sits.

Winter-Hardy, Moisture-Tolerant Geophytes

If the real estate agent's mantra is "location, location, location," that of a bulb would be "drainage, drainage, drainage." In the garden, more failures with bulbs, corms, rhizomes, and tubers can be ascribed to wet soils (especially when they are dormant) than any other cause. Fortunately, for those of us who have areas with damp soils, some geophytes are less troubled by this than are the majority. After all, if there is a niche available, nature will find/adapt plants and animals to fill it.

Guinea hen flower

Guinea hen flower, *Fritillaria meleagris*, is a charming little bulb for mid-spring. From a naked little twin-scaled white bulb with a fringe of hairy dried roots at the base, it sends up a thin, sturdy stem from 8 to 12 inches (20 to 30 cm) tall. Four to six narrow, gray-green leaves alternate up the stem, which is crowned with one, occasionally two, flowers. Each alone appears too massive for such slender support—stout, bell-like flowers with square shoulders, tessellated in purple and grayish white. Some are more deeply flushed with purple, so dark that the dapple is barely noticeable, while a few are nearly white with faint green dappling. It is native to much of Europe, from northern Yugoslavia and southern Russia to Poland, and on into the central portion of France and southern England, where it is found in river floodplains.

Summer snowflake

Summer snowflake, *Leucojum aestivum*, flowers from mid- to late spring, depending on the mildness of the region where it is being grown. It differs from the spring snowflake, *L. vernum*, not only in flowering six to eight weeks later, but also in produc-

A wet meadow in Holland provides a suitable place to grow guinea hen flower, *Fritillaria meleagris*. Plants don't have a passport—it is the dampness and a temperate climate that is important, not the country. Photo by author.

ing from three to seven flowers on the stalk of an overall larger plant. Its ability to grow in such diverse places as Connecticut and Texas is explained by summer snowflake's native range, which encompasses Europe and southwestern Asia to northern Iran. Growing as it does in forests, wet fields, and riverside swamps, it proves tolerant of situations from average moisture levels in the soil to waterlogged conditions. I have noticed that the wetter the site, the longer the leaves remain green into summer. Interestingly, the swollen, air-filled seed pod floats on water as a means of dispersal.

The green-tipped, white bells of summer snowflake, *Leucojum aestivum*, make a welcome addition to the spring garden when sited near a pond bank, in a damp meadow, or in another suitably moist site. Photo courtesy of Brent Heath/Brent and Becky's Bulbs.

Three-cornered leek

Native from the western Mediterranean region of Italy to France and North Africa, three-cornered leek, *Allium triquetrum*, has naturalized in England. My friend Brian Whyer claims to dig and discard bushel baskets of this bulb on a regular basis. Found growing by streams in damp, shady places, a similar situation in the wilder, more casual parts of the garden would suit it well. In spring, the triangular stem with its few-flowered umbel of 3 to 15 bell-like, white flowers daintily marked with a central green stripe on each petal could make a graceful display without causing dismay.

Camass

Camass, camas, camosh, and quamash are all derived from a Native American name for *Camassia quamash*, one of the four species of this genus that are found in the Pacific Northwest, from southwestern British Columbia down to northern California, and eastward into Montana, Wyoming, and Utah. It was documented and gathered at the Weippe Prairie in what is today known as Clearwater County, Idaho, on 23 June 1806, near the end of the journey home of the great expedition of Meriwether Lewis and William Clark that began in St. Louis in the spring of 1804. Growing in wet meadows, where they thrive with heavy winter and spring moisture, this species often form large colonies. Camas was an important food source for native Americans, and there are accounts of battles over the gathering rights to meadows that were especially productive.

Growing to 2½ feet (76 cm) tall, their spike of starry blue flowers makes a handsome addition to the late spring garden. Flower color varies from white through deep blue and even purplish blue. Somewhat more compact than the other species, *Camassia* 'Orion' grows from 1 to 2 feet (30 to 60 cm) tall; it is a dwarf cultivar with deep blue flowers. 'Blue Melody' has mid-blue flowers set off by crisp white margins on the leaves. Camassia is one of the few bulbs I can laud for its tolerance of heavy New Jersey clay, coupled with deer- and vermin-resistant qualities. When we moved from Connecticut, I dug some, but not all, because the bulbs had lowered themselves beyond their original planting depth and I did not have time for lengthy excavations. The plastic grocery bag in which they huddled was tossed into a corner of the garage. When recovered three or four months later, sometime in September, the bulbs were still sound and had begun to root.

Fall is the planting time for camassia. Set the bulbs 4 to 5 inches (10 to 12.5 cm) deep, and since they can be left undisturbed for years give them ample room, spacing the bulbs about 12 to 18 inches (30 to 45 cm) apart. Camassia holds onto its foliage until early to midsummer, so some shade in the middle of the day is appreciated. They appreciate summer moisture, too, even when dormant in late summer. I prefer camassia when they are planted in groups, even to large colonies—the spikes of starry blue flowers have more appeal en masse. Though long-lived, I find that my bulbs are spartan about making offsets and do so in rather modest numbers.

Native to the Pacific Northwest, where it naturally occurs in wet meadows, *Camassia leichtlinii* adapts nicely to average situations in the garden, though I find its blue spires especially suitable in damp places where other plants fail to thrive. Photo by author.

Camassia cusickii is native to Oregon. The large bulbs produce clumps of narrow, blue-green leaves about 18 inches (45 cm) long and scarcely $1\frac{1}{2}$ inches (4 cm) wide. The pale blue, starry flowers are held on sturdy stems 30 to 36 inches (a little less than 1 m) tall. *Camassia leichtlinii* is somewhat taller, often reaching more than 3 feet (1 m). The leaves are 24 inches (60 cm) long and, at only 1 inch (2.5 cm) wide, have a ribbonlike appearance. Variable in color, selections have white, soft blue, or deep purplish blue flowers, and several forms have semi-double flowers. Wild hyacinth, *C. scilloides*, grows 2 feet (60 cm) tall with narrow leaves 1 inch (2.5 cm) wide. It has 8 to 10 flowers to a stem, and individual plants may vary in color from white through pale to medium and deep blue.

Turk's cap lily

Before the days of heavy development, highways, and office parks, the marshes of eastern New Jersey that are now along the turnpike were filled with *Lilium superbum*. It was said that you could stand in one spot and see at least 5000 plants blooming all together. Today the remaining remnants of marshland are filled with phragmites. In the mid-20th century, Mary Henry, a Pennsylvania resident, traveled widely in the eastern part of the United States in search of lilies. She is especially associated with this species, collecting outstanding forms with variant flower color from deep red to the clear yellow; unspotted 'Norman Henry' she named for her husband.

Superb, indeed, this Turk's cap lily can grow as much as 10 feet (3 m) tall, with up to 40 showy flowers (but usually less). Each flower nods at the end of a pedicel 6 inches (15 cm) tall that angles upward. The recurved orange petals curl backward, with their carmine-red tips actually touching at the back of the flower. Color varies from paler to deeper hues. Numerous dark brown spots are freckled toward the base of the petals, and a green star accents the throat. Blooming time is also variable, from the beginning of July through the middle of August in the United States, and individual plants remain consistent in their flowering period. It flourishes in wet meadows and marshes with acid soil, growing in full sun or filtered shade. Native from Massachusetts, Pennsylvania, and Virginia to southern Indiana, Alabama, northern Florida, and Arkansas, it would be well to match the northernmost and southernmost populations to gardens in those extremes—plants that originated from a Massachusetts population are unlikely to thrive in Florida, and vice

Growing in a wet meadow at the native plant garden of The New York Botanical Garden, the Turk's cap flowers of *Lilium superbum* easily rise above the surrounding perennials that help support the lily's stems. Photo by author.

versa. Plants can be raised from seed, remembering that this species exhibits *hypogeal*, or delayed, germination. The first growing season it sends down a root, and it will produce leaf growth in its second season. Stoloniferous, each year a new bulb is produced at the end of the fleshy rhizome. It is stem-rooting, and somewhat deeper planting will result in more seasonal roots on the buried portion to better nourish the bulb. In common with many other lilies, *Lilium superbum* likes its head in the sun and its feet in the shade. Planting it in combination with low shrubs or moisture-tolerant perennials helps not only with shading but also some buttressing support—just think of the numerous flowers and how they might cause the tall stem to bob and weave in a breeze.

Water-Tolerant Geophytes for Mild Winter Regions

Wet or dry are one set of parameters; seasonal temperature variations are another. A plant that requires mild winters is not necessarily growing at that time, so ample water can be lethal. Just as some cold-tolerant geophytes can thrive in wet meadows and similarly damp sites, some moisture-tolerant geophytes abhor cold winters.

Canna

Few gardeners are indifferent to cannas. Either they consider the plant to be low class, a trashy sort of plant, or they love it. If you can get beyond the idea that as a cutting-edge, in-the-know gardener you wouldn't be caught dead growing this Victorian favorite, you'll find yourself with a real workhorse for the summer garden. Cannas are quintessential plants in gardens where they're permanent residents and welcomed even in those where they are seasonal visitors. Nell Jean Campbell of Colquitt, Georgia, has cannas on the property that antedate her residency, red and yellow ones that grow around the smokehouse. Some people like the flowers, which are bold and colorful, to softer, more subtle shades as they range from creamy to sunny yellow, orange to red, pink, and bicolor. I prefer the flowers on the species such as *Canna iridiflora*, which are more refined and delicate in form. Hummingbirds agree with me, and I've had them visit the elegant red flowers of *C. warscewiczii* and the dainty peach-orange flowers of a purple-leaved canna (probably *C. indica* 'Purpurea') but not the large-flowered ones. And I'm especially fond of using cannas for their lush, bold, tropical foliage. There's green of course, and also a number of cultivars with lovely coppery bronze to reddish purple leaves such as 'Black Knight', 'Wyoming', and 'Red King Humbert', or 'Australia', with its shiny, purple-black leaves. I have a canna that Edith Eddleman gave me years ago, after digging a chunk from her Raleigh, North Carolina, garden. It is a flaccida type, with narrow leaves of a rich purple color and graceful peachy orange flowers. One guess is *C. indica* 'Purpurea', which in Ian Cooke's *The Gardener's Guide to*

Growing Cannas (2001) is described as a "fabulous foliage plant. It has a slender habit, rich purple leaves, and small, upright, orange flowers." He goes on to say "It can reach up to over 2.1 m (7 ft.) and seems to be one of the hardier types, tolerant of overwintering in the ground." The other choice would be 'Intrigue', which Ian mentions in his book as a recent introduction. However, I have had mine for well over a decade, and it is not listed in the Royal General Bulbgrowers' Association *International Checklist of Hyacinths and Miscellaneous Bulbs*, 1991 edition. Now, many years down the road from when I received it, I understand how Miss Edith could afford her generosity. The long, stout, white rhizomes happily branch. Each broken piece will regenerate and start growing again. Each winter I usually store enough rhizomes to fill four large boxes, packed in dry peat moss and stacked against an inside wall of my garage. In addition, those that are growing up against the house foundation appear to winter over easily with just a windrow of oak leaves piled over them, even through the severe cold and copious snow of the winter of 2002–2003. I have it in a narrow bed at the end of the deck, with gray-silver *Plectranthus argentatus*. Each summer I toss in some other geophyte to accent the combination; perhaps one year it is Abyssinian gladiolus, *Gladiolus callianthus* (syn. *Acidanthera bicolor*), with its swordlike leaves and maroon-blotched white flowers, or a green-flowered gladiolus another time.

Canna 'Pretoria', also known as 'Bengal Tiger', is nicely striped in yellow. I've partnered it with *Allium flavum* with soft yellow flowers and glaucous blue-green leaves and stem, and rue (*Ruta graveolens*) with lacy glaucous leaves. Another option sets it up with *Abutilon pictum* 'Thompsonii', a shrubby flowering maple with yellow-speckled leaves and bell-like apricot flowers. The two tender plants are backed up with *Berberis thunbergii* 'Aurea', a barberry with pleasant yellow leaves. Then there is *Canna* 'Durban', said to be a sport of purple-leaved 'Wyoming'. Its technicolor foliage is basically purple but veined in pinky red and developing peachy orange patches as the leaves mature. There is some confusion and legal issues involved with look-alike 'Phasion' (pronounced "passion"), registered with the United States Patent Office and offered for sale as

Clearly, cannas like wet feet, as exemplified by this *Canna* 'Pretoria' growing quite nicely in a pond. Photo by author.

At Beth Chatto's nursery in Essex, England, a happy combination of a dark-leaved canna and the soft mauve flowers of eupatorium offers both visual appeal and a planting scheme that requires little maintenance to keep it looking good. Photo by author.

'Tropicanna'. As long as you are not commercially propagating plants for sale, I don't think this is anything to lose sleep over. Plants of 'Durban' (or 'Phasion' or 'Tropicanna') grow vigorously, and the rhizomes branch freely. I have 'Tropicanna' growing in a soggy patch of soil at the bottom of my driveway. It is in combination with and as a backdrop to the magenta-flowered, wild type *Phlox paniculata*, the color that all the cultivars revert to if you don't deadhead and they manage to reseed. It also works with lavender-flowered horse mint (*Monarda fistulosa*) and tawny ditch lilies (*Hemerocallis fulva*), and a nearby towering *Silphium connatum* happily adds its 7 feet (2.1 m) tall stems of yellow daisies to the fray. I'm thinking of adding some nice, big Joe Pye weed, *Eupatorium purpureum*, to backstop the cannas.

A narrow-leaved cultivar named 'Stuttgart' has light-green leaves with broad patches of gray-green, further blotched with white. This is, however, a real fuss-budget of a canna. In the first phase of growth as plants are waking up in spring, the leaves often have peculiar constrictions, as if those parts that would be white if they were growing in summer are smaller than the greener portions of the leaf, causing this distortion in the leaf's shape. It wants strong light but not too much direct sun or the leaves, especially the white portions at the edge, turn brown. If it gets too dry, leaves turn brown—sometimes I think this is "just because," and not for any specific reason. Well-grown, it is a beautiful plant, but growing it well is the tricky part. I gave away two large pots full of rhizomes and focus my attention on just one, which summers by the front entry to our house, where it receives north light and seems relatively content. 'Stuttgart' does not flower; when it appears to do so, close observation will show that it is a green-leaved reversion that is actually in bloom.

Cannas take a surprising amount of moisture, and if you start the dormant tubers into growth in shallow water in early spring, just about any canna will adapt to a modest submersion by the time it is planted outdoors. Shallow water in a pond or pool that will quickly warm up in spring is better suited to the needs of heat-loving cannas than cool, moving water in a stream. 'Pretoria' is especially pretty, as its yellow-striped leaves reflect nicely on a pool surface. Those with narrow leaves readily thrive in shallow standing water. This may seem surprising, unless you are aware that *Canna flaccida*, a species 4 to 5 feet (1.2 to 1.5 m) tall with narrow, glaucous leaves and drooping yellow flowers is native to marshy areas in the southeastern United States, South Carolina to Florida. *Canna glauca* is similar in appearance, at 5 to 6 feet (1.5 to 1.8 m) tall is somewhat larger, and is native to wet areas and stream banks in Mexico, the West Indies, and South America. The latter was the species used, together with other hybrids, in the development of the Longwood water cannas in the 1970s. The four cultivars that were introduced all have narrow, glaucous leaves and iris-like flowers, but they vary in height and flower color. They thrive even with a foot

Reflected in the tropical lily pool at The New York Botanical Garden, *Canna* 'Red King Humbert' also pairs up nicely with the lotus behind it. Photo by author.

(30 cm) of water over their rhizomes. 'Endeavour' is 4 to 5 feet (1.2 to 1.5 m) tall, making a slender, graceful plant with clear, vivid-red flowers. At just 4 feet (1.2 m) tall, the shortest and most compact of the water cannas is 'Erebus', with sizeble clusters of pale, salmon-pink flowers. 'Ra' is tallest of the four and can reach 8 feet (2.4 m), with bright lemony yellow flowers. 'Taney' is also tall and open, rather loose growing, with soft apricot-orange flowers.

Rain lily

A diversity of *Zephyranthes candida* are discussed in Chapter 7, "Geophytes for the South and Southeastern United States." They all flower in response to rain, but rain as an interruption to otherwise dry conditions. However, one rain lily likes inundation. When I saw the elegant crocuslike white flowers of *Z. candida* in the water lily courtyard at Longwood Gardens in September 2003, masses of them were growing in shallow water, a lovely foreground display to papyrus and purple-stemmed taro, giant sagittaria, and lotus. I asked Tim Jennings, curator of the water gardens, about them. The first bulbs were planted about five years earlier. They're set out each year once the weather is mild and settled, and they flower all summer long and into fall. When cold weather approaches, they're lifted and potted up. Since foliage is evergreen, the plants are kept growing through the winter in a greenhouse. When the bulbs are lifted, Tim said, they've usually multiplied tenfold from the number that were planted out in spring.

And early the following month, as Boyce Tankersley and I were enjoying a stroll around the grounds of the Chicago Botanic Garden, what should I see but *Zephyranthes candida* growing quite nicely in the shallow waters of the lake-like lagoon. How delightful it was to see their clean white flowers glowing in the golden October sunshine. A light frost had kissed the tender dahlias and blackened their tops, but these zephyranthes were protected by the warmth held in the water. Of course, they'd be dug up and carried indoors before winter truly set in.

Zephyranthes candida is from south of the border, in Argentina and Uruguay. When it was discovered, way back in 1515, supposedly so many of the flowers were in bloom that the marshes along the river appeared white. Juan Diaz de Solis named the water course *Rio de la Plata*, Silver River, on that account. While it will tolerate average conditions, as might be expected this rain lily prefers a moist situation, even one that is seasonally flooded. Somewhat tender, to Zone 9, its starry white flowers (sometimes rose-tinted on the outside) close at night and in cloudy, shaded conditions. The narrow, rushlike, foot-long leaves are evergreen, and upright to arching. It has a tiny, 1 inch (2.5 cm) diameter bulb. Better to purchase it in growth, as dormant bulbs are often dry and unhappy and will take a year to reestablish themselves before consenting to flower.

Crinum

The riverboat *Delta Queen* was tied up at Oak Alley in Vacherie, Louisiana. Strolling down the alleé of live oaks from the levee toward the plantation house I could almost imagine my hoopskirts swaying. A double border of Saint Joseph's lily, *Hippeastrum ×johnsonii*, graced the garden on the left. At the opposite side of the building I found a mammoth bulb rearing halfway out of the soil. It was a veritable giant, with layer after layer of scales. This venerable crinum had clearly been there for quite some time, and just as obviously, here it would stay. No mere mortal would be able to change its location without the aid of machinery. Crinums are long-lived, persistent plants. They survive around abandoned houses, linger in old cemeteries, and find a roadside ditch a congenial habitat. Heavy clay is as accommodating to their needs as is the starvation situation in nutrient-poor sand. Native to tropical and subtropical regions, in the wild various crinum species are found in swamps, riverbanks, pond margins, and low-lying, seasonally flooded depressions. Other species grow in coastal dunes. Typical of other geophytes in the Amaryllidaceae, the flower stalk develops at the side of the leaves rather than in their center. (Perhaps you've noticed the same thing in amaryllis, *Hippeastrum* cultivars.) Bulbs the size of a football, even bigger, thrust up a veritable fountain of foliage in a whorled rosette. Give crinums a good start, since the roots on an ancient specimen can stretch as much as 6 feet (1.8 m) in every direction. Plant the bulb deeply to discourage production of offsets, since development of new bulbs decreases flower production. Feed them well, mulching over the entire root zone with old manure, which also provides a cooler root run. Water with manure tea, sloshed on as a foliar feed directly on the leaves as well as poured on the ground. Since crinums naturally grow in wet places, they are an excellent choice for use as semiaquatic plants in boggy places. Some crinums have drooping, lily-like flowers, while others have very narrow, widespread petals.

Southern swamp lily, *Crinum americanum*, is found growing in wet places, in anything up to a foot (30 cm) of water, along the Gulf Coast from Florida to Texas. It requires really wet conditions in a garden pond or bog. Narrow, straplike leaves are just 2 inches (5 cm) wide and 18 to 24 inches (45 to 60 cm) long. Threadlike violet stamens make a delicate accent to the very fragrant white flowers. Six elongated narrow petals look something like a spider lily's flowers but without the unifying central membraneous cup. Sweetly scented, the umbel of four to eight or twelve flowers makes an appearance in late summer or early autumn. The flowers appear almost ghostly, floating in the air in striking contrast to the black water in a Louisiana bayou.

Veld lily or Orange River lily, *Crinum bulbispermum* grows along riverbanks in the southern Transvaal, Natal, and the Free State of South Africa. It has anywhere from six to twelve funnel-shaped, sweetly fragrant white flowers streaked with pink or red—with a lot of variation: one plant may have all white flowers, another is pale pink; sometimes they have darker pink or wine colored markings down the center of each petal. Several cultivars have been selected. 'Album' has white flowers, 'Cape Dawn' has soft red to pink flowers on a stalk 6 feet (1.8 m) tall, and 'Roseum' has pink flowers. Bulbs grow to 6 inches (15 cm) in diameter, and sheathing leaves wrap around each other at the base, eventually form-

Florida swamp lily and southern swamp lily are both common names for *Crinum americanum*, a good indication that this elegant native bulb thrives in wet places. Photo by author.

ing a foot-long (30 cm) neck from which the tapering, bluish green leaves, 2 feet (60 cm) long, 3 to 4 inches (7.5 to 10.0 cm) wide at their base, erupt. Nell Jean Campbell of Colquitt, Georgia, has *C. zeylanicum* lilies that have been in her garden for 50 years or more. These are a familiar feature in gardens of the U.S. South, hybrid progeny from the crossing of *C. bulbispermum* and *C. scabrum*, which provided the wine-red striping on the blush colored, spicily fragrant flowers. Cynthia Mueller sees *C. bulbispermum* and its hybrids, especially *C. zeylanicum*, around College Station, Texas. Theresa Massey in Austin says crinums do well there, and some even naturalize.

Spider lily

Many plants that are commonly called *lily*—from the familiar daylily (*Hemerocallis*) or aquatic water lily (*Nymphaea*)—are not lilies at all. In this instance, spider lilies, *Hymenocallis*, happen to be Amaryllidaceae, the amaryllis family. The 30 or 40 species are mostly native to North, Central, or South America. All are tender to frost. The approximately six water-loving native American spider lilies are scarce and difficult to find, more for the collector than the everyday gardener, especially as not all of them are garden-worthy. A couple of species are worth seeking out, since their flowers are lovely and their bulbs are tolerant of, even favor, wet conditions.

Native in the southeastern United States, from Mobile Bay in Alabama westward to Texas, *Hymenocallis liriosome* flourishes in heavy clay soil, usually in shallow water perhaps 6 inches (15 cm) deep, or in boggy conditions. Dark green, glossy leaves, anywhere from 8 to 36 inches (20 to 90 cm) long, appear in mid- to late spring, together with the fragrant white flowers with a lilylike perfume. A small central cup acts as a base for six very narrow, long, gracefully arching petals. If the season is a wet one with good summer rains, the bulbs may rebloom irregularly in summer and into autumn.

Hymenocallis littoralis, an exotic (that is, nonnative) spider lily from Columbia, Surinam, and Mexico, is a popular garden plant in the U.S. South, where it thrives in shallow water; it has naturalized in Louisiana. Offsets form rather freely, helping its spread as a readily available pass-along plant. Numerous evergreen leaves, less than 2 inches (5 cm) wide and as much as 4 feet (1.2 m) long, make a good foliage presence in the garden. Attractive white flowers with the typically elegant, narrow spreading lobes add to their appeal. It sometimes becomes confused with a different species in garden centers. (Such places are rarely staffed by taxonomists!) Its surrogate, *H. caroliniana*, is native from Georgia to Indiana and Louisiana and has up to a dozen leaves, a half-inch (1.5 cm) wide by 18 inches (45 cm) long, and 5 to 10 flowers on a stalk 2 feet (60 cm) tall. In 'Variegata', *H. littoralis* has an unusual cultivar, with smaller, 20 inch (50 cm) long, dark green leaves nicely striped and edged in creamy white. Thriving in damp soil, *H. caribaea*, the species that Boyce Tankersley remembers growing en masse on Galveston Island, is a tropical evergreen species from the West Indies with numerous relatively broad leaves, 3 inches (7.5 cm) wide and 2 feet (60 cm) long. A flattened, sharp-edged scape 2 feet (60 cm) tall supports 8 to 10 or more elegant, sweetly fragrant white flowers. Even when not in bloom the mound of foliage provides a handsome foliage effect. A variegated form is offered for sale as *H. caribaea* 'Variegata', but that is probably not a valid name.

Caladium

When geophytes are discussed, it is commonly accepted that the majority will be found in three major plant families: the Liliaceae, Iridaceae, and Amaryllidaceae. Assorted other plant families provide some here and a few there. The aroid family, Araceae, includes an A-to-Z range of tuberous geophytes: from temperate *Arisaema*, *Arisarum*, and *Arum*, to such popular and practical tropical genera as *Alocasia*, *Colocasia*, *Xanthosoma*, and *Zantedeschia*. And *Caladium*. It is not that caladium have extravagantly attractive flowers that gives them their popularity. A greenish, sail-like spathe backs up a crudely erect spadix. In fact, removal of spathe and spadix is recommended as good cultural practice for caladium. Rather than a blooming beauty, it is the showy, colorful foliage—veined, marbled, and splashed in a seemingly endless set of variations in white, pink, and red—that provides the appeal. Moisture-loving and shade-tolerant, this tropical geophyte is popular with gardeners in tropical Gulf Coast regions (Zone 10) who can leave them in the ground year-round. In southern Florida, for example, caladium grow pretty much all year long, while in central Florida caladium are deciduous:

Caladium 'Red Flash' offers dull cardinal-red and forest-green leaves, touched with a sprinkling of white speckles. Photo by author.

leaves die back and the plants take a winter rest, but tubers remain viable. Caladium need to be dug and stored under protected conditions in northern Florida, as soil temperatures below 60°F (16°C) results in tuber death. In temperate climates, caladium are seasonal garden visitors, bedded out or grown in containers for summer color, after which the tubers may be dug and stored over the winter or allowed to freeze and replaced anew each season. One place where they won't work well is in the Pacific Northwest, for caladiums insist on hot, humid summer weather. And in the dry air of the desert Southwest, they shrivel to unhappy-looking, crinkled replicas of brown paper. What caladiums love are the dog days of midsummer, the heat and high humidity that sends gardeners fleeing for air-conditioned shelter. Some caladiums, 'Freida Hemple' for one, and basically any of the lance leaf cultivars, can tolerate more direct sunlight. Since numerous colorful plants are available for sunny sites, I prefer using caladium to add interest in shady places where the choice of flowering plants is much more restricted.

Broadly triangular, swordlike, or arrowhead-shaped leaves are more or less green. Their beauty lies in the greater or lesser amount of blotching, spotting, freckling, veining, or marbling in one or more colors: white, pink, or red. The generally accepted name *Caladium bicolor* is somewhat of a catchall, subsuming *C. picturatum* with narrower leaves and more acute basal lobes and *C. marmoratum* (meaning "marbled," "irregularly striped," or "veined") with gray, green, and white blotches. When considered as distinct, the three species are generally regarded to be the parents of what used to be named *C. ×hortulanum*. Taxonomists who prefer to divide things up (as opposed to lumping them together) separate those plants with mostly white-marbled leaves into *C. ×candidum*. Gardeners use a taxonomic divide of their own. Those with larger, broader leaves are usually grouped as fancy leaf, and those with narrower leaves in proportion to their length, generally derived from *C. picturatum*, are called lance leaf.

Caladium are graded by tuber size: mammoth are $3^1/_2$ inches (9 cm) or more in diameter, jumbo are $2^1/_2$ to $3^1/_2$ inches (6 to 9 cm), No. 1 are $1^1/_2$ to $2^1/_2$ inches (4 to 6 cm), and No. 2 are 1 to $1^1/_2$ inches (2.5 to 4 cm). The tubers are slow starters and need a long lead time before planting out in the garden, with high humidity and bottom warmth to start them off. My friend Delilah Smittle in Pennsylvania starts hers on top of the furnace, but a thermostatically controlled heat mat is a good alternative. In early spring, set the tubers knobby side up and buried halfway in a flat of damp peat moss. You have an option: tubers grown as they are received from a vendor will produce fewer but larger leaves. Remove the growing point by scooping with a grapefruit spoon or something similar, and the tuber will produce more leaves but they will be smaller. Keep the flat at 70° to 75°F (21° to 24°C), and mist regularly. When tubers are well-rooted, pot up in an open, coarse potting mix that will retain moisture but at the same time drain freely. The temperature may be lowered to 65°F (18°C). Water sparingly until the leaves start to grow, at which time it is important to maintain a moist, buoyant atmosphere and keep the plants in bright light but not direct sunlight. When the roots start to fill the individual pots, supplement with a liquid fertilizer. Caladium should always be given a fertilizer lower in nitrogen, as too much can turn leaves green. In any case, the mature leaf color is generally not apparent until plants have produced four or five leaves. Do not set out in the garden when the weather is merely settled; wait until there is dependable warmth night and day. The large leaves have a thin texture and substance and are easily damaged by windy or dry conditions. Cool autumn weather provides the signal for dormancy, and caladium's leaves slump to the ground.

Some beautiful white-leaved cultivars are excellent for moon gardens and brightening shady places. These include *Caladium* 'Aaron', with a creamy white center and narrow green border; green-edged 'June Bride'; heirloom 'Candidum' from 1868, whose lush white leaves are patterned with green veins and finished off with a green margin; and strap-leaved 'White Wing', with a deep green edge to the creamy white leaves. I still long for 'Caloosahatchie', a white lance leaf I once saw in a southern garden. 'Mrs Arno Nehrling', a more colorful variation, has large, white leaves, the smaller veins delicately traced in dark green and shaded crimson-red along the main veins. 'White Queen' is similar, with the addition of a green margin. 'Gingerland' is a particular favorite of mine, its white-ribbed, grayish white leaves splattered with maroon freckles and finished off with a tidy edging of dark green.

A relatively simple accent of red ribs against the central pink marbling decorates the green leaves of 'Pink Beauty'. 'Fannie Munson' has pale pink leaves, deeper pink main veins, a green tracery of veins, and a fine green edge, while transparent, rose-red 'Lord Derby' has darker ribs and a green border. 'Carolyn Whorton' has delicate, translucent rose-pink leaves, the larger veins marked in red, and shades toward the leaf margin with a deep, almost blackish green marbling. 'Freida Hemple' is a cutie, with somewhat smaller ruffled leaves, the bright red cen-

The rather uninteresting flowers of caladium resemble those of arisaema, to be expected since they are both in the aroid family. It is caladium's colorful leaves, as seen here with red-freckled green and white 'Gingerland', that make them welcome in our gardens. Photo by author.

ter and scarlet ribs contrasting with a wide, dark-green edge. 'Postman Joyner' is a softer version, with pale red leaves, darker veins, and a green edge. 'Red Frill' is a lance leaf with deep red leaves turning darker as they shade toward a deep green edge.

Native to Brazil and Venezuela, one species that sometimes shows up in the trade is *Caladium humboldtii*, a more diminutive plant with a tuber of 1 inch (2.5 cm) and dainty, long, dull green leaves of 4 inches (10 cm), nicely blotched and spotted with silvery white markings. Lovely in a larger grouping, it is used as an edging plant in the palm house of the Enid Haupt Conservatory of The New York Botanical Garden.

Partner caladiums with ferns, choosing something like evergreen holly fern (*Cyrtomium falcatum*) for the larger fancy-leaved types and southern maidenhair (*Adiantum venustum*) for lance leaf cultivars or the little *Caladium humboldtii*. Lily turf, *Liriope spicata*, with forest-green, straplike leaves, is another option. Just remember to select plants that also like to grow in high organic soils, constantly moist yet with good drainage, and dappled to moderate shade.

Elephant ear

Elephant ear looks like a great big all-green caladium, and indeed it was once sold just that way. Currently, with the popularity of water gardening and bold architectural plants for the tropical look, they're finding a popularity that's hard to beat. Unlike caladium that prefers merely a constantly moist soil, colocasia and alocasia can grow in standing water. Leaves of *Colocasia* point down from their attachment to the petiole, while *Alocasia* usually point upward, and *Xanthosoma* also has huge heart- or arrowhead-shaped leaves on a grandiose scale. The three can be difficult to tell apart, but since their requirements are much the same, why worry? These tropical plants grow from a large tuber, and cocoyam, also known as taro and dasheen, *C. esculenta* is an important food crop in the humid lowland tropics, where rainfall is often more than 100 inches (254 cm) a year. The large tubers are cultivated in the low-lying areas along streams and riverbanks. Grocery stores serving a Hispanic clientele often have tubers for sale in the produce department, labeled *yautia blanca*. If you are happy with a huge, green-leaved elephant ear, this is often the cheapest way to buy one, less expensive than an ornamental purchased from a garden center or by mail order.

It can be difficult to determine which end of the hairy brown tuber goes up. Look for the bull's eye rings and, if you're lucky, the small pinkish leaf buds. Both *Colocasia* and *Alocasia* are gross feeders that develop best with a soil enriched with compost and/or manure, and a once-a-week supplement with a high-nitrogen liquid fertilizer. Plant in full sun to partial shade in a moist to boggy site, or even, in Zones 10 to 11 where they are evergreen, standing water at the shallows of a pond. They will then produce enormous leaves, 4 to 6 feet (1.3 to 2.0 m) long, on a petiole 3 feet (1 m) long. The apple-green leaves are attractive in their own right, but gardeners looking for more panache might prefer the cultivars with leaves in other colors. Imperial taro or black caladium, *C. esculenta* 'Illustris', has somewhat smaller light green leaves blotched and stained blue-black between the main veins and along the edges. Leaves grow almost 3 feet (1 m) long and half as wide, with overall height of the plant around 3 to 4 feet (1.0 to 1.3 m). *Colocasia esculenta* 'Jet Black Wonder', sometimes offered for sale as *C. esculenta* 'Black Magic', has dark eggplant-purple leaves and petioles. When a breeze ruffles their sail-like surface, the somewhat lighter, dusty-looking purple on the underside of the bold leaves is revealed. Avoid a very windy site, however, as leaves can be tattered by strong gusts. They are ground hardy in Zones 8 and 9 but will be deciduous, and in colder areas the tubers should be dug and stored indoors after the foliage has been kissed by a frost.

Alocasia are just as flashy as their *Colocasia* elephant ear cousins. Growing conditions are basically the same: partial shade for most, ample water at all times, and a soil high in organic matter. The larger cultivars and species should be fertilized every week with a high-nitrogen liquid fertilizer, while the smaller ones are content with an every other week supplement to their diet. Remember that smaller is a relative term, and these may grow as tall as 18 inches (45 cm) to 3 feet (1 m). *Alocasia* 'Hilo Beauty' is a smaller cultivar with apple-green leaves spotted with lighter green, cream, and white. Giant elephant ear, *A. macrorrhiza*, can reach 8 to 10 feet (2.6 to 3.3 m) tall, with immense leaves 3 to 4 feet (1.0 to 1.3 m) long on petioles 4 feet (1.3 m) long, pointing skyward as they unfold but later drooping downward as they mature. As you no doubt

Foliage can provide elegant options in the garden, as seen here at Windrush Gardens in Tennessee, where the bold, cool, glaucous blue leaves of elephant ear ramble about with the more vivid green, needlelike leaves of saw palmetto. Photo by author.

anticipate from the scale of this Brobdingnagian plant, it needs more of everything: ample water, rich soil, and abundant fertilizer. *Xanthosoma sagittifolium* 'Chartreuse Giant' has heart-shaped leaves 2 feet (60 cm) long, glowing and golden yellow, on petioles 1 to 2 feet (30 to 60 cm) tall. Partial shade produces more vibrant color, and the leaf stalks grow even longer. With 2 to 3 feet (60 to 90 cm) long, dark purple leaf stalks and triangular, 2 feet (60 cm) long dark green leaves enhanced with dark reddish purple veins and leaf margins, blue taro, *X. violaceum*, is not as swarthy as 'Jet Black Wonder' yet is still a stunning plant.

Give these big beauties playmates on a similar scale: towering ornamental grasses such as giant reed grass (*Arundo donax*) and the biggest astilbe you can find, perhaps 4 feet (1.3 m) tall *Astilbe thunbergii* 'Professor van der Wielen', with its nodding white panicles of flowers, or 3½ feet (1 m) tall, salmon-pink 'Straussenfeder'.

Calla lily

A ditch lily found in wetlands and as a common roadside wildflower in South Africa, where it is native, *Zantedeschia aethiopica* is given short shrift, like goldenrod in the

Another aroid family member, the great green leaves of *Zantedeschia aethiopica* 'Childsiana' are best considered as a backdrop to the pristine white flowers of this rhizomatous South African perennial, which has been in cultivation for more than a century. Photo courtesy of Brent Heath/Brent and Becky's Bulbs.

For a variation on a theme, consider this relatively hardy cultivar, *Zantedeschia aethiopica* 'Green Goddess', with liberal amounts of chlorophyll modifying the flowers' spathe back into leaves. Photo courtesy of Brent Heath/Brent and Becky's Bulbs.

United States. Brought in from abroad, American gardeners regard the elegantly curled white flowers of this aroid as an exquisite florists' flower, and we pay from $5 to $10 per stem, depending on the time of year. Triangular, spearhead, or arrow-shaped leaves, as much as 18 inches (45 cm) long on long petioles, grow from the tips of the branching, tuberlike rhizomes. Evergreen in milder climates, calla lily will be deciduous in cooler Zone 8 climates. The dark green leaves with an undulating margin may sometimes be spotted with white. Grown as a plant for the margins of a pond in as much as 2 feet (60 cm) of water, calla lily will also perform in a marshy situation or even in a site with constantly moist soil. If it is planted in standing water, provide a gradual transition rather than submerging it all at once and perhaps inundating the leaves. Add water as the plant grows and petioles lengthen, or lower the pot in which the tubers are planted. The tubers are generally hardy to brief periods of below-freezing temperatures, and of course the temperature in the muddy bottom of a pond, below a layer of ice but with free water between ice and mud, remains above 32°F (0°C). *Zantedeschia aethiopica* 'Crowborough' is a cultivar with large white spathes that was selected in England for its cold-hardiness, but cold-hardy in the British Isles, warmed and moderated by the Gulf Stream, and cold-hardy in the northeastern United States are very different matters.

CHAPTER 9

Geophytes for the Rock Garden

Many years ago I worked at Libner Grain Company on Commerce Street in Norwalk, Connecticut. The retail store sold all sorts of things: various kinds of seed for feeding wild birds, scooped out and weighed in bulk from waist-high bins along the back wall; bulk grass seed; hand tools; fertilizers and flower pots; and peat moss and potting soil. In the autumn we sold flower bulbs. One day a man came in and asked for 100 *Scilla siberica*. As I was counting the small bulbs with their red-purple tunics into a bag, I made polite conversation by mentioning that I thought these smaller bulbs were often more charming than the larger ones. "Oh," he said, "then you will like the American Rock Garden Society." Little did I know that I was talking to Larry Hochheimer, membership chairman for the national organization. In due time a membership form came to my house. I joined, and later I attended a few of the local chapter's meetings. These people were serious! They raised all sorts of plants I had never heard of, and some from seed. They talked about plants using their Latin names. And they were also some of the kindest, most generous, and caring/sharing gardeners I had ever met. I was hooked.

One thing I observed when visiting various rock gardens to which I'd been invited (and rarely did I depart without some plants) was that these gardens were very different from those with which I was familiar. Plants in perennial gardens were carefully arranged by height and color on flat ground. These rock gardens were built on slopes. If a slope did not exist at the site, it was built, and the plants were set out to look like a natural scene on a mountainside. Should the garden be shaded, these gardeners grew more than pachysandra. Their woodland rock gardens focused on shade-tolerant native plants and their counterparts from Europe and Asia. The year following my joining the society, people in the Connecticut chapter decided to place a group order for bulbs. Libner Grain Company was all well and good for big yellow daffodils and opulent red tulips, and the blue Siberian squills, but these folks wanted little treasures that would be in keeping with the scale of things in their rock gardens. So an order was placed with John D. Lyons Company, on Alewife Brook Parkway, in Leominster, Massachusetts (now long out of business), and Mary Mattison Van Schaik in Vermont. I volunteered to help repackage the bags of bulbs into the individual orders. It was a long time ago, but I remember sorting out little bulbs of species tulips and daffodils, crocus I was told would flower in winter, and other bulbs, corms, and tubers I had never heard about. As well, I was told these bulbs were not especially difficult to grow. They were small and dainty, and thus needed placement with other plants of suitable scale. Most of them would grow best with full sun, good drainage, and a gravel mulch—conditions that would be found in a rock garden. I was hooked all over again.

This was all happening while we lived on an eighth of an acre in Norwalk, Connecticut. I planted lady tulip, *Tulipa clusiana*, with its dainty red and white flowers on graceful stems 8 inches (20 cm) high; dwarf water lily tulip, *T. kaufmanniana*, with soft yellow and creamy white flowers; and *T. greigii*, with chocolate-striped leaves and large red flowers on short stems. Several cultivars of little, early-blooming snow crocus, *Crocus chrysanthus*, were nestled in against some rocks in a microhabitat next to a basement window on the south side of the house: 'Cream Beauty', 'Pearl Beauty', 'Snow Bunting', and 'Violet Queen'. I took a class with Linc and Timmy Foster at the Brooklyn Botanic Garden in October 1970. After the class was over, we were sent home with some plants and bulbs: one each *Erythronium* 'White Beauty' and *Narcissus assoanus* (at the time named *N. juncifolius*), two each *Puschkinia scilloides* var. *libanotica* and *Iris danfordiae*, and three winter crocus corms. From de Jager Bulb Company I ordered, among other geophytes, 12 *Crocus laevigatus* 'Fontenayi'. My garden notes from that time mention that they were planted on 13 October, with some peat moss, sand, bone meal, superphosphate, and wood ashes dug into the soil, and the little corms were bedded in a layer of sand. Of course, today I would not bother with bone meal. While skunks and wandering dogs did not eat the geophytes, they scattered them around the landscape as they dug for the bone meal, from where I had to collect and replant them. The sand layer, however, was a good idea then and it is still useful now. It is not so much for improved drainage as an *aide-mémoir*—dig into a layer of yellow sand and it reminds you that some choice geophytes are lurking in this stratum. And my little winter crocus flowered in December!

I expanded my efforts to the north side of the house. It was shaded but quite bright since the area was open to the sky, and both our house and that of our neighbor across the driveway were white, bouncing around what light there was. After some rearrangement of rocks (they always seem to need to move uphill), a small *Rhododendron* 'Purple Gem', and more little corms and bulbs, on 18 September 1970 I planted a dozen each *Crocus* 'Cream Beauty' with buttery yellow flowers, lemon-yellow 'E. A. Bowles' with purplish feathered edges, and somewhat smaller lemon-yellow 'E. P. Bowles'. I also planted 12 each of 'Snow Bunting', white when it opened in sunshine but with an inconspicuous grayish exterior, and *C. chrysanthus* 'Warley', white with a brownish yellow blotch inside and grayish white outside, with a broad purple streak down the center. A month later, on 16 October, I planted 13 *Narcissus obvallaris*. Clearly, these lumpy packages with their plain brown wrappers had taken a firm hold of my fancy.

I am not alone in my fondness for little geophytes to grow among the rocks. Mark McDonough lives in Massachusetts, and he has a particular fondness for alliums, the ornamental onions, and raises a great diversity of uncommon species from seed. It's not a matter of blind craving for anything not yet in cultivation. Mark has a discerning eye and carefully selects and chooses the best of what he brings to flowering size. This ability to differentiate between the excitement of "it's in bloom!" and "garden-worthy" is a lesson all gardeners would do well to remember. The right plant in an appropriate place is worth admiring. The same plant in a different site is often just not right. Rock gardens are a place for the miniature and exquisite. Since not all of us live high in the mountains, where true alpine plants that grow above the tree line can prosper, we make do with saxicole plants, those that thrive when growing among rocks and have the appropriately dwarfed and refined character. When it comes to geophytes for the rock garden, Mark points out that in their jewel box settings, rock gardeners prefer to grow species crocus rather than the inflated Dutch crocus. Dwarf narcissus are preferred, but with *Narcissus*, he finds even full-sized daffodils are admissible. Various other minor bulbs are good, from dwarf reticulata iris to galanthus; scilla; muscari; any fritillaria that will grow, no matter the size; and, Mark added with a grin, "the enlightened also grow *Allium*."

Crocus

A postcard sent from my friend Bobby Ward in Raleigh, North Carolina, one February happily reported snow crocus, *Crocus* 'Gipsy Girl', *C.* 'Ladykiller', *C. imperati*, *C. sieberi*, and cloth-of-gold crocus (*C. angustifolius*, syn. *C. susianus*) in flower. That is earlier than in my Connecticut garden, but only by a month. His postcard was dated 16 February, and I could report much the same by mid-March.

Crocuses prefer full sun and good drainage. Damp soils, especially while they are dormant, is an anathema. Planting a low ground cover serves several purposes: it prevents accidental disturbance while the crocuses are dormant, lends interest to the garden when the crocus are dormant, and, lastly, the actively growing ground cover uses at least some of the moisture from summer rains. Prostrate, flat-growing thymes such as *Thymus serpyllum* are very useful as is low-growing, spring-flowering moss pink, *Phlox subulata*, with its prickly looking foliage and numerous small flowers in shades of blue, pink, or white. Small violas are attractive partners for those crocuses that flower as their partners. Pansies are too big to be in scale. Keep in mind that crocuses are popular with all sorts of vermin: deer and rabbits will eat their top growth, while mice and chipmunks devour the corms. Planting in the gravel-rich substrate of a rock garden is some help with the latter, but a concerted effort through the use of repellent sprays, fencing of the garden, or some other means is necessary to keep at bay the larger critters who come to dine. On sunny days crocuses open their flowers wide, closing at night and in cloudy weather.

Commonly called snow crocus, *Crocus chrysanthus* is a variable species with lilac, sulfur-yellow, orange, or white flowers. Outside, flowers may be self-colored (the same as the inside) or they can be suffused, freckled, feathered, or striped with brown, gray, or purple. They all have a golden yellow throat, orange stamens, and a rounded flower. As you might expect from such a variable species, numerous clones have been selected and named. Good yellows are available in a range from pale to deeper shades. They include the following: 'Advance' is peachy yellow inside and bluish violet and white outside; 'Brassband' is straw-yellow inside, with a warm, tawny glow, and apricot-yellow outside, with a bronze, green-veined blotch; 'Cream Beauty' is the color of clotted cream, a light, creamy yellow and a darker interior; 'E. A. Bowles' is golden yellow with a dark bronze throat; 'E. P. Bowles' is lemon-yellow, with a bronze-yellow base and purplish brown blotch; 'Gipsy Girl' is yellow inside with striking, deep bronze-purple feathering on the outside; 'Saturnus' is dark yellow inside and out, with dark purple stripes on the outside; 'Snow Bunting' is pure white, accented with a bronze-yellow throat and dark lilac-purple feathering on the outside; and 'Zwanenburg Bronze' is

The early flowers of *Crocus chrysanthus* 'Blue Pearl' offer a welcome source of pollen and nectar to hungry honeybees. That's only on sunny days, for the crocus close their flowers at night and on overcast or rainy days, when the bees would not be flying anyhow. Photo by author.

saffron-yellow inside and nearly all burgundy to bronze outside, with an attractive yellow margin. Some blue-hued clones include 'Blue Bird', which is creamy, old ivory–colored inside and grayish violet-blue outside; 'Blue Pearl' is soft blue inside and out with a bronze-yellow base; and 'Ladykiller' is white inside and purple-violet with a white edge on the outside. The corm of snow crocus is wrapped in a tough, papery, pale tan, annulate tunic, ring-marked as it splits from the base, rather than fibrous and netted.

Crocus biflorus is so named because it produces its flowers in pairs from each growing point. Understand that each corm is capable of producing several growing points, so it can display a veritable bunch of flowers. Scotch crocus is a sterile, free-flowering, old-garden form, with white flowers neatly feathered with five or so bluish purple stripes on the outside, accented with a yellow throat. Since it makes numerous cormlets, propagation is quick and easy. *Crocus biflorus* subsp. *alexandri* has a white interior and a white or golden yellow throat, while the exterior is suffused with deep violet-purple. *Crocus biflorus* subsp. *weldenii* has paler flowers, flushed with pale blue and a white or pale blue throat. 'Fairy' is a cultivar with a white interior accented with a purple blotch, and finely speckled with violet-purple on the outside. All of these are included in the winter-flowering crocuses, since they bloom so early in the year. These also have annulate tunics.

Crocus sieberi is another popular species, no doubt attributable to its showy flowers, which are white within, lilac on the outside, and have a golden heart. *Crocus sieberi* subsp. *atticus* has purple-tinted white petals with distinct purple veins and flowers in late winter or early spring. *Crocus sieberi* 'Bowles' White' is small and has pure white

I rather imagine that *Verbascum thapsus* with its large, velvet-soft leaves grew here accidentally. Surely I didn't plant it on top of the little corms of *Crocus biflorus*. No matter, because I like the results. Serendipity works for me. Photo by author.

flowers. 'Firefly' is nearly white, at least on the outside, suffused with lavender on the inside of the petals and a yellow throat. 'Hubert Edelstein' has deep purple flowers with a white blotch at the tips of the petals. And *C. sieberi* subsp. *sublimis* f. *tricolor*, which you may see listed in catalogs as *C. sieberi* subsp. *sublimis* 'Tricolor' (whatever happened to Linnaeus's intention to name all plants with binomial nomenclature?) is sublime indeed, with its flowers distinctly marked with three bands of color—lilac, pure white, and golden yellow. Corms have a reticulated tunic.

A handful of other species to watch for in the mail-order catalogs of specialty bulb nurseries can extend the diversity of crocuses in your garden. *Crocus ancyrensis* 'Golden Bunch' is among the earliest to flower in spring, warming the chilly day with a bunch of tangerine-yellow flowers. An heirloom variety, 'Golden Bunch' has been in cultivation since 1879. Corms have a reticulate to fibrous tunic. *Crocus angustifolius* 'Cloth of Gold' has been around in gardens significantly longer, since 1587. Its golden yellow flowers striped or flushed with maroon nestle down in the leaves. The tunic is reticulate to fibrous. *Crocus imperati* is usually offered as 'De Jager', a cultivar with flowers that are lilac inside with alternating buff and purple stripes outside. The corm has a parallel fibrous tunic. *Crocus minimus* is a sweetie, in late winter or early spring displaying lovely mid- to deep purple petals around a tiny yellow heart, and plum-colored stripes, veins, or shading on a bronze exterior. Tunics are parallel fibrous in appearance. To go with cloth of gold, of course we need cloth of silver, *C. versicolor* 'Picturatus', which has white flowers feathered with purple on the outside, and a papery tunic that splits until it becomes parallel fibrous.

If you have ever planted a bag of mixed Dutch hybrid crocus, no doubt you have noticed that those with yellow flowers bloom earlier than the white, striped, lilac-to-lavender crocuses. While *Crocus vernus* is primarily responsible for the latter type, the golden yellow traces its ancestry to *C. flavus*. If you prefer planting different colors as you choose rather than random chance, buy these larger crocuses by name. Look for large white *C. vernus* 'Jeanne d'Arc', and then select 'King of the Striped' or 'Pickwick' for large grayish white flowers with lilac-blue stripes, and 'Remembrance' or 'Vanguard' if a violet or light mauve to purple flower flushed with silver suits your taste. 'Golden Yellow' is actually classed as *C. flavus*, but this is the one to purchase if you want a larger yellow crocus. The tunic is papery, but it splits lengthwise into fibers.

Fall to winter-flowering crocus will be discussed in Chapter 10, "Geophytes for the Autumn Garden."

Bulbocodium vernum

Every year I forget about this sweet charmer of early spring, until sometime in March, up pop their dainty fuchsia-pink flowers from beneath the disguise of a mat of creeping thyme. The timing varies with what winter chose to throw at us—submerged in snow and cold or relatively mild. I planted six corms several years ago, in a sunny spot toward the base of the slope behind my house. Since my soil is heavy clay, I amended it to improve the drainage by using some red shale gravel that color-coordinates with the rocks that are naturally embedded in the clay. And by now several flowers are emerging at each point of planting, suggesting that the corms are slowly multiplying away underground. At the time I planted, I was struck by the corms' appearance—a smaller version of colchicum. They have the same smooth, papery, rich-brown tunic, tapered toward the top and with a little footlike protrusion to one side of the basal plate. Actually, at one time they were named *Colchicum bulbocodium*; then they were shifted out to a genus of their own as *Bulbocodium vernum*. According to Brian Mathew, the rational for the shift is that *Bulbocodium* has one style, separating into three at the tip, while in *Colchicum* all have three separate styles. Others, such as E. A. Bowles, state that the tepals of *Bulbocodium* are free from each other rather than joined in a tube as are those of *Colchicum*. This means that when picked, *Bulbocodium* flowers fall apart in my hand.

A chain of commentary exists in classic rock garden literature. In *The English Rock Garden* (1919), author Reginald Farrer, a plant hunter who is a passionately opinionated rock gardener, refers to *Bulbocodium vernum* as "a pleasant cousin to autumn crocus that is not a *Crocus*, nor even a *Colchicum*, and does not bloom in autumn." He goes on to describe its appearance in earliest spring high on the flanks of the Alps. In Louise Beebe Wilder's *Pleasures and Problems of a Rock Garden* (1928), she mentions *Bulbocodium* as "having been cultivated for at least three hundred years." This dovetails with *The International Checklist of Hyacinths and Miscellaneous Bulbs*, which gives 1629 as the date of its first mention. Today we can add another seven-and-a-half decades to that span. Wilder gives *Bulbocodium* a paragraph, saying, "It is not now often seen, however, which is a pity, since its promptness in making its bow to the spring world, despite storms and cold, should alone recommend it." And H. Lincoln Foster, doyen of American rock gardeners, calls *Bulbocodium* "a bright and luminous spot in the very earliest days of spring."

Bulbocodium vernum welcomes spring with its vivid, rose-pink flowers before the calendar quite agrees that winter is over. Photo by author.

Native to the Pyrenees, southwestern and south-central Alps, to southern Russia, the small violet flowers appear close to the ground, spreading perhaps 1½ inches (4 cm) wide when fully open. Three small leaves appear with or just after the flower fades; then they fade away themselves in late spring. I rarely see *Bulbocodium* grown or mentioned, which is unfortunate since, as the name suggests, it is a welcome harbinger of spring.

Daffodils

Daffodils are an integral part of the spring scene, immortalized in William Words-worth's poem "Daffodils," which commemorates "a crowd, a host, of golden daffodils." If you are familiar only with the big yellow varieties, these dainty rock garden species will seem like something out of a fairy tale. Daffodils are pest-resistant, poisonous to rodents who might chew on the bulbs below ground or any grazing creatures that eat the leaves and flowers on other geophytes. Though some are better cosseted in an alpine house (a greenhouse heated just above the freezing point), several daffodils' dainty size belies a rugged constitution.

Narcissus asturiensis (syn. *N. minimus*) comes from northern Portugal and north-western and north-central Spain. Since it is found in the mountains, this gives it more resistance to cold than one might expect, and it is hardy to Zone 4. Picture a yellow trumpet daffodil. Now minimize it until the flower is barely the size of a dime, and there you have it. Soft yellow, usually slightly nodding, and the slightly twisted petals

Narcissus asturiensis has little trumpet flowers barely as large as a dime. Dainty size belies their sturdy nature; neither snow nor cold delay or diminish their performance. Charming in the rock garden and perfectly in scale for a dollhouse garden. Photo by author.

all combine to give the tiny flower an insouciant charm. This is one daffodil whose small size conceals a rugged nature. Snow and freezing temperatures do nothing to deter it once it has begun to bloom. On one occasion I entered a specimen in a local daffodil show sponsored by the American Cancer Society in conjunction with its Daffodil Days sale of flowers. I think it got an award because they didn't know what to make of it, such a wee little thing amidst all the trumpets, large cups, doubles, and other more common, standard-sized garden daffodils.

Hoop petticoat daffodil, *Narcissus bulbocodium*, is similarly small but looks quite different. The dark yellow to citron-yellow flower resembles nothing so much as a megaphone for fairies, with tiny, twisted petals that stick out like little spikes. From 4 to 6 inches (10 to 15 cm) tall, it needs careful siting so you won't step on it by accident. The straight species does just fine in the garden. 'Golden Bells' is a vigorous, free-flowering cultivar, with from four to eight flowers from each bulb. There's a handful of varieties—*N. bulbocodium* var. *bulbocodium*, *N. bulbocodium* var. *conspicuus*, *N. bulbocodium* subsp. *obesus*—most of which you'll need to raise from seed (and good luck finding any) if you really must have them. The ethereal white-flowered ones have been separated out and are now called *N. cantabricus*. Most rock garden enthusiasts who possess the forms, subspecies, and varieties keep them in an alpine house in a pot, rather than risk them out in the open garden.

It's hard to believe that dainty little *Narcissus bulbocodium* (seen here) is related to big, yellow trumpet daffodils—sort of like a Chihuahua and a Great Dane. Photo by author.

The dwarf cultivars that grow around 6 inches (15 cm) tall are listed as miniatures by the American Daffodil Society. Though of suitable scale for rock gardens, they prefer conditions less lean and not so well-drained as the gravelly soil provides.

Tulips

Tulips are a puzzlement. Gardeners in Colorado find them perennial, whereas most of my shenanigans in attempting to perennialize the larger mid-spring–blooming kinds are of no avail. Plant them deeper so they won't split, one authority pontificates. Indeed, I emulate a squirrel heading for China, only to dig and delve for their removal when yet again I end up with lots of bulbs sending up a single outsize rabbit-ear leaf. Christopher Lloyd wrote that 'White Triumphator' (a graceful lily-flowered tulip with petals drawn to a narrow point, then reflexed backward in a casual manner) was perennial. Perhaps they are in England, but not so in my garden. So I consider Darwin and Triumph, lily-flowered and parrots, and all such to be annual tulips—planted in fall, blooming in spring, and then discarded.

Mark McDonough posted a thoughtful discussion of tulips on the Pacific Bulb Society's forum, noting, "I've never been a fan of tulips, finding them too tall and fancy, the foliage corpulent and unrefined. The flowers are sumptuous to be sure, but that's beside the point. I plant 'Red Emperor' and 'Yellow Emperor' for my mom; she adores them. And when, 3 to 4 years hence, I must dig them out, the waning bulbs sputtering feeble distorted foliage and few diminished blooms, to be replaced with freshly planted Holland-grown bulbs in a continuing cycle.

"Rock gardeners tend to shun tulips; the allure of growing them spoiled by centuries of selection and over hybridization. We think of tulips as bedding plants suitable for seasonal floral display in parks, corporate landscapes, and botanical gardens; definitely not for the rock garden in the true sense. Even the lovely *Tulipa greigii* × *T. kaufmanniana* hybrids, though dwarf enough for rock garden consideration, are still too portly and ostentatious for inclusion.

The Duc van Tol tulips are close to the wild species *Tulipa schrenkii*, and caused great excitement when they were introduced in 1595. In size and habit they would be an interesting addition to today's rock garden. Photo by author.

Tulipa species are poorly represented in rock gardens, perhaps not because they are deliberately shunned, but because we fail to consider them. It wasn't until recent years that I discovered the charm of dwarf tulip species. Reluctantly I tried a couple with the conviction that the bulbs would fizzle out in a few years, as their fancy brethren do. Instead they continued to grow, increase, and flower reliably for many years without signs of decline. Dwarf species of tulips are now among my favorite bulbs, and my journey in search of dwarf tulips is just beginning. I still hold the line at species with coarse fat foliage, preferring instead those that are less 'tulip-like,' with smaller concise herbage, fascinatingly undulate basal leaves, or fine linear strands of gray or green vegetation."

I, too, enjoy the greigii, kaufmanniana, and fosteriana species tulips and their cultivars, which are earlier blooming and dwarf in stature and return year after year to flower in the garden. Keep in mind that tulips are edible: chipmunks and mice will eat the bulbs, while deer and rabbits eat the flowers. Indeed, during the German occupation and the Hunger Winter of World War II, the Dutch people ate tulip bulbs, too.

Tulipa greigii and its cultivars grow 10, 12, or perhaps 14 inches (25, 30, or 35 cm) tall. Their leaves are deliciously marked in chocolate-brown stripes and streaks. Often wavy along the edge, the leaves stay close to the ground. Flowers, when open wide on a sunny day, can be as large as 6 inches (15 cm) across. Hardy to Zone 5, these make a great addition to the rock garden. 'Cape Cod' is yellow with a buff to apricot overtone and a sharply contrasting red stripe. 'Donna Bella' is cream-colored, marked with

Tulipa 'Plaisir', a greigii hybrid, pairs up beautifully with *Anemone blanda* 'White Splendour'. Photo by author.

flamelike carmine red on the outside and an interior black blotch at the base of the petals. 'Oratorio' is soft rosy red, tinted apricot on the inside with a black blotch at the bottom of the petals. 'Oriental Splendour' has large, deep yellow flowers marked with red flames. 'Plaisir' is creamy, with broad, vermilion-red flames and yellow flushes. 'Red Riding Hood' is solid scarlet red, with a small black marking at the base of each petal. Multiflowered 'Toronto' has deep salmon-pink flowers, tangerine-red inside, with a yellow basal blotch edged with bronzy green. Since they flower later than *T. kaufmanniana*, the greigii cultivars extend the tulip season.

Waterlily tulip, *Tulipa kaufmanniana*, is early flowering and overlaps with early and mid-season daffodils. Though rather short, the largest only 8 inches (20 cm) tall, they produce large flowers in proportion to their stature. Some have mottled leaves. 'Ancilla' has rose-red flowers edged with soft pink, white inside with a yellow blotch at the base of each petal, circled by a red ring. 'Heart's Delight' is carmine-red edged with milky pink outside, pink inside with a yellow throat, and mottled leaves. 'Stresa' displays currant-red flames on the outside, yellow on the inside with a red mark at the throat, and mottled leaves. 'Vivaldi' has carmine-rose flowers edged with yellow, sulfur-yellow inside and golden at the base, also with mottled leaves.

Tulipa fosteriana and its cultivars have very broad, grayish green leaves, and a large oval to oblong flower. Color ranges from white 'Purissima' (syn. 'White Emperor') to creamy white and pale yellow 'Sweetheart', and vivid orange 'Orange Emperor' with a yellow blotch at each petal's base. 'Madame Lefeber' (syn. 'Red Emperor') has fiery flowers of "give-me-a-ticket" red (like an overpowered convertible that attracts a cop's attention, even while it is parked), with each petal's black basal blotch edged with yellow. They grow 12 to 14 inches (30 to 35 cm) tall and bloom at the end of the early tulip season, the beginning of the midseason.

As well, a handful of other species tulips are excellent when grown in the rock garden. *Tulipa bakeri* has lilac to purple flowers and a yellow basal blotch inside, blooming in mid-spring and growing 6 to 8 inches (15 to 20 cm) tall. 'Lilac Wonder' is a cultivar with lilac-pink petals. It is a difficult color to match with other pinks and lilacs, so instead choose the easy way out and avoid such consorting colors. Evergreen candytuft, *Iberis sempervirens*, with nice little mounds of white flowers is a good choice, as is *Veronica incana* 'Nana', with silver foliage. *Tulipa batalinii* reminds me of an egg yolk, one from supermarket eggs, soft golden yellow. When it first appears, it balances close to the ground, and then as the stem continues to grow it reaches its full height of about 5 inches (12.5 cm). 'Apricot Jewel' is a buff apricot with a hint of rose; 'Bright Gem' is sulfur-yellow with an orange blush; and 'Bronze Charm' is also sulfur-yellow with apricot-bronze feathering. Dwarf bearded iris bloom at the same time and come in a rainbow of colors. Or go for a single-color theme and pair this tulip with *Aurinia saxatilis* (syn. *Alyssum saxatile*) with golden flowers and grayish leaves on a prostrate, mat-forming

This tight cluster of flowers signals the underground multiplication of *Tulipa aucheriana*—several now growing where I had planted only one. Good drainage and a sunny, sloping site provided the right conditions, even though Connecticut is far from its native haunts in Iran. Photo by author.

plant. Only 6 to 8 inches (15 to 20 cm) tall, *T. hageri* 'Splendens' has unusual, dark dull-red flowers with a coppery bronze red interior and an olive to black basal blotch. Multiflowered, they are much handsomer than this description, especially when they open wide in sunshine. Highly variable, *T. humilis* offers a series of little tulips 4 to 6 inches (10 to 15 cm) high for early spring bloom in the rock garden. Cup-shaped flowers open wide, like a little pale pink star with a yellow center. 'Eastern Star' is magenta-rose with some bronze-green markings on the outside. 'Magenta Queen' is what I'd call lilac-purple, with ferny green marking on the outside. 'Odalisque' is light purple outside and reddish purple with a yellow blotch inside. 'Persian Pearl' is light magenta outside, cyclamen-purple inside, contrasting with a yellow blotch at the base of the petals.

Tulipa aucheriana is similar to *T. humilis*, but with star-shaped flowers and undulate edges to the leaves, which lie on the ground. I had bought three from John D. Lyons and planted them in my Wilton, Connecticut, rock garden. It was a west-facing slope, with sand and gravel at least 2 feet (60 cm) down (the furthest I ever bothered to dig). The three little tulips loved it there, slowly multiplying by offsets until they made a nice group each spring when they came into bloom (until, that is, the deer came ambling down the slope to dine). *Tulipa tarda* is a popular, bunch-flowering little tulip with white and yellow flowers. *Tulipa turkestanica* is also multiflowering, with a nodding spray of white flowers that have an orange center.

Bulbous iris

Gardeners have long had a love affair with iris, from the rainbow array of German or bearded iris to the easy-care Siberian iris, yellow flag iris that grows in anything from average conditions to standing water, and more. Many gardeners, however, are unaware of bulbous iris, how hardy they are, and that the three species most generally available flower so early in the spring. Plant them in groups of a half-dozen or so. The flowers look elegant simply displayed against a gravel mulch, but the elongating leaves will need some disguise as they lengthen afterward.

Iris reticulata is named for the reticulated, netlike tunic that covers the bulb. Two or three narrow leaves, topped with a whitish hook that helps them pierce the still cold ground, appear together with the flower. They are nicely in proportion then but will continue to lengthen after the flower disappears, before the leaves themselves fade away in late spring or early summer. The bulbs make numerous offsets, which need to grow on to reach flowering size and reduce the vigor of the parent bulb. Planting some fresh bulbs each fall will ensure the most reliable display the following spring, when they will make a nice contrast to various soft-hued crocus. The true species has narrow, royal-purple standards and falls marked with a smooth yellow bee guide. It is rarely grown, preference being given to selections and its hybrids with *I. histrioides*. *Iris reticulata* 'Cantab' has flax-blue flowers, lighter at the tips, with a yellow blotch. 'Edward' has darker blue flowers, marked with an orange blotch. 'Gordon' has light to medium-blue falls, with an orange blotch on whitish ground, which is in turn lightly penciled with blue stripes. 'J. S. Dijt' is one of the latest to bloom, with dark reddish purple falls and purple standards. 'Natascha' is a still somewhat expensive newcomer, with ivory flowers, both standards and falls chilled with a flush of blue, the falls veined in green with a golden yellow blotch.

The rich purple flowers of *Iris reticulata* add early color to the rock garden. Photo by author.

Iris histrioides has somewhat broader petals than *I. reticulata* and a violet-tinged blue color. The two species have been crossed to give us a wide range of cultivars. Photo by author.

Iris histrioides is the most reliable repeat bloomer. The flowers are up to $3^{1}/_{2}$ inches (9 cm) across and appear shortly before the leaves. Flowers of the straight species are blue, with paler falls spotted with blue and a smooth yellow bee guide. 'George' is a delightful dark plum-purple with somewhat darker falls. 'Katherine Hodgkin' is coming down in price. She's still an indulgence, but what a lovely one. Light greenish blue standards with smoky blue stripes rise above paler falls penciled with charcoal stripes and the yellow blotch freckled with charcoal spots. Two other older cultivars, mid-blue 'Lady Beatrix Stanley' and purple-blue 'Major', have white-spotted falls, but they are both becoming hard to find.

Iris danfordiae is a gem—plump yellow flowers with greenish brown spots, all of 2 to 3 inches (5 to 7.5 cm) tall when in bloom, which it manages to do even earlier than the other two species. The falls are what carry the display, since the standards are reduced until they are barely there. It has the unfortunate habit of splitting into rice-grain offsets, all of nonflowering size. Some say to plant bulbs extra deeply, which in this case would be about 6 inches (15 cm) down. A dose of high potash liquid fertilizer (potassium, the third number on the package) might help things move along back to flowering size. It is worth planting anew each autumn, since this Turkish plant from the snow-melt zone up in the mountains will flower before winter is truly gone.

Iris histrioides 'Katherine Hodgkin', a fey fairy of a flower, with hints of bluish green, greenish blue, and streaks and spots of yellow. It's easy to see why enthusiastic gardeners pay the higher prices charged for this choice beauty. Photo by author.

Buttery yellow petals on plump *Iris danfordiae* add sunny color and a sweet fragrance to the early rock garden. The grasslike leaves will extend as the flowers fade and grow to an awkward height before withering. Photo by author.

CHAPTER 10

Geophytes for the Autumn Garden

Autumn is the time of year when bulbs dart out in front of me, hurling themselves in my path. Garden centers display bright yellow banners to announce the arrival of the new crop of bulbs, while discount stores and home centers have bags of mixed tulips (deer fodder), perhaps an assortment of four different purple-flowering bulbs (tulips, alliums, crocus, and hyacinths), and other snares for eager gardeners. I admit to being an impulse buyer. (Are there gardeners who are not?) Perforce I must wait for results, since the vast majority of fall-planted geophytes will not blossom until spring. However, some instant gratification is not amiss, and I especially enjoy those geophytes that bloom within a few weeks of planting and then continue to return year after year. They take more effort to procure, as these are not what the chain stores tend to stock. The drawback, as far as nurseries are concerned, is that these autumn-blooming geophytes do not hold as well as a daffodil or tulip, and they are not willing to languish in a bag, box, or bin until some kindly soul takes them home and plants them. Colchicum is noted for flowering on a windowsill. Fall-flowering crocus will shrivel to their demise if not promptly planted. And others—the various surprise lilies, naked ladies, and magic lilies—resent disturbance and may sulk away underground for a year or more before even surfacing with foliage, let alone flowers. Some winter-hardy geophytes do just fine in Zones 5 and 6, while others prefer a milder winter. While it may be rushing the season, I intend to cast my net wide enough to include geophytes that begin their growth and/or flower from late summer (mid- to late August here), and others that perform in the traditional fall and winter seasons. This allows me to make a fine catch that includes geophytes such as colchicum that flower in fall but delay leaf growth until spring, and others such as hardy begonia, *Begonia grandis*, which begins growth in late spring and then flowers in autumn.

A few terms are useful to know. If the focus is on leaf growth, you would say *synanthus* to refer to leaves that appear at the same time as flowers, while *hysterogenic*, meaning "late-produced," refers to those whose leaves develop after flowering. *Anthesis* refers to the period during which the flower is open. You would correctly say that leaves are present at anthesis if you were talking about all of the spring-blooming crocus, but it applies only to a few of the fall-flowering species. *Precocious* is used for flowers that appear before the leaves develop. *Cyclamen hederifolium* is precocious, since flowers appear in late summer and leaves develop in early fall. Different species of autumn-blooming crocus may be precocious, flowering before the leaves are fully developed, and some flower before the leaves can even be seen above ground.

The degree of development of the leaf at anthesis is one trait by which different species may be characterized and are identified. Brian Mathew, author of *The Crocus* (1982), considers leaves to be synanthus if even just the tips are visible at flowering. *Crocus medius*, which flowers in late autumn, is hysterogenic, and early to mid-fall blooming *C. kotschyanus* (syn. *C. zonatus*) flowers without the leaves. The overall pattern is that fall-blooming crocus species tend to flower before the leaves develop, though some, such as saffron crocus (*C. sativus*) and mid- to late-fall flowering *C. cartwrightianus* and *C. ochroleucus*, have visible leaves at flowering.

Geophytes may behave one way in the wild and another way in cultivation, where temperature, day length, quantity of moisture, and regularity of its arrival might be different. All sorts of options are possible: leaves that grow and are dying back when the geophyte is in flower, as so many of the larger ornamental onions insist on doing. While the cycle of dormancy, leaf growth, and then flower production—such as that for tulips, daffodils, and hyacinths—is what we are familiar with, other geophytes have a dormant period, then flower, and then produce leaves part way into their blooming period, such as *Cyclamen hederifolium*.

When we move beyond spring- and summer-blooming geophytes to explore those that flower in autumn, it becomes clear that many flower first and may wait until spring to produce foliage. This odd way of doing things has fascinated gardeners. Think of all the so-called naked ladies, surprise lilies, and magic lilies that pull this trick. One old common name for colchicum was "son before the father." People observed spring foliage and seeds, followed by flowers in autumn, and made an incorrect but more familiar sequence of connection—spring, summer, fall—when it should have been fall bloom through winter dormancy to springtime foliage and seed production.

Winter-Hardy, Autumn-Flowering Geophytes

Summer days contract in length, taking on a golden haze toward dusk. Bags and boxes of geophytes accumulate in the toolshed, awaiting autumnal burial for springtime resurrection. Yet a certain few geophytes turn the seasons around, blooming as the first leaves come tumbling to the ground.

Colchicum

Perhaps my favorite autumn-flowering geophyte is colchicum, also known as naked ladies, son before the father (for its habit of producing seed in spring yet flowering in fall), fall crocus (a confusing epithet), and more. Looking like crocus on steroids, the large, cuplike flowers arise naked, sans any foliage, in mid-autumn (September and October in the United States). Surprisingly, they make long-lasting cut flowers. The corms of colchicum, wrapped as they are in a brown tunic, look rather like tulip bulbs, except they are uniformly rounded and have a footlike portion protruding below the basal plate. Colchicums have much to recommend them. As well as flowering in autumn when relatively few geophytes choose to bloom, they are resistant to deer, rabbits, pine voles, mice, and other such vermin. The primary difficulty is acquiring the corms as early as late summer, which is when they're best planted. Though occasionally offered for sale at quality nurseries, the usual course of action is to mail order them from a catalog and hope that their idea of shipment at the appropriate time for your area is correct.

The two more readily available species are the somewhat smaller *Colchicum autumnale* and larger *C. speciosum*. Both have white-throated lavender flowers. Both species have white forms, though *C. autumnale* 'Album' seems easier to find. 'Lavender Lady' and 'Violet Queen' are two readily available cultivars. *Colchicum* 'Waterlily', a double-flowered form, collects water when it rains and quickly collapses. Taking a tip from

The double flowers of *Colchicum* 'Waterlily' appear in autumn without their leaves. A mass of low-growing asters offers subtle pairing of color and very practical support for the colchicum's heavy flowers. Photo by author.

Nina Lambert, I planted 'Waterlily' among some pachysandra. Not only do the flowers look fantastic with the dark green, polished foliage, but it acts as a support and holds the flowers nicely upright. *Colchicum autumnale* 'Pleniforum' is the dainty double form of this species, and the rare *C. autumnale* 'Alboplenum' is the choice, quite scarce, double-white form.

I tend to favor colchicums to the fall-flowering crocus since the deer and pine voles that saunter and burrow through my garden enjoy the crocus as appetizers to more serious nibbling but leave the colchicums alone. I prefer to plant colchicums in groups of three to five or more, selecting a site at the edge of woodland or in full sun. Unfussy, they tolerate my heavy, clay-based soil, though I do amend with compost and also dig in gypsum or land lime to help flocculate (clump up) the clay. It appears to help in my garden, though opinions are mixed as to its efficacy. The coarse foliage of colchicum appears in spring and collapses in early summer, necessitating sturdy neighbors that will not be smothered by this foliar decline and descent.

Nina Lambert also grows colchicum in her meticulously maintained Ithaca, New York, garden. She mentions, "I have a few of the larger colchicums planted in clumps in bright deciduous shade in vinca. The foliage looks no worse than unfolding hosta in the spring and the flowers are held up nicely in the fall. A friend plants his colchicum in a geranium bed that he cuts back—actually mows (yes, with a lawn mower set high)—in the late summer. The geraniums start making new growth but their foliage (ground cover) is sufficiently restrained (and the flower color doused) to allow the colchicum flowers to have the stage."

Colchicum agrippinum is a particular favorite of mine, with neatly tessellated flowers checkered in rosy purple and pinkish white. Mine usually begin flowering at the end of August, with each established corm sending up five or more flowers. That's another pleas-

I'm pleased with the way *Colchicum autumnale* 'Album' matches up nicely with variegated brunnera at Belle-Wood Garden. Flower and foliage look good in autumn, and the brunnera is vigorous enough to survive the collapse of the coarse mass of aging colchicum leaves in June. Photo by author.

ant thing about colchicums. Nina also grows this species and has it sited at the base of a wall and in a raised bed where it shows well in late August to early September. She finds that the foliage lasts no longer, and is no coarser, than that of *Scilla litardieri* (syn. *S. pratensis*) that is nearby. She utilizes the space in summer thusly: "I let *Silene armeria* and the annual larkspur self-sow next to or over it. They fill in (and mark the spot) during the summer and if need be, can be cut off when the colchicum come into bloom."

In August 2002 I had the pleasure of traveling to The Netherlands for the International Stauden Union conference, staying at De Nachtegaal in Lisse, in the heart of the bulb district at the height of the bulb harvesting season. Call it horticultural lust if you want, but with a gardener's usual impetuous acquisitiveness I was determined to obtain geophytes generally unavailable in the United States. I e-mailed Rene Zijerveld of Dix and Zijerveld (a wholesale-only nursery) in advance of my travels, and after some dialogue back and forth I ordered several choice cultivars and species of *Colchicum*, to be handed over once I had arrived in Lisse. And once I was there, my good friend Leo van Tol took me to visit Rita van der Zalm, proprietress of a specialty bulb nursery in Noordwijk. I expected the usual complications of bringing any plant material back into the United States so I had my import permit and made arrangements for a phytosanitary inspection the morning of the day I would fly home. Nonetheless, I was envisioning the agriculture inspection station at Kennedy Airport in New York City closed for the weekend by the time I arrived on a Friday evening. This might result in a delayed inspection, and the need to drive more than two hours each way to pick up the geophytes the following week. So when a friend who works for a large wholesale bulb exporter offered to ship them over for me, I leaped at the opportunity. It was interesting to see what the colchicums had been up to in their travels. When the carton was delivered to my doorstep a couple of weeks later, some had broken dormancy and were sending forth nascent flower shoots, while others were still at rest.

Colchicum cilicicum 'Purpureum' were fat handfuls, each corm more than 2 inches (5 cm) tall by 3 inches (7.5 cm) wide at the base, with a polished, smooth, chestnut-hued tunic that was cracked and peeling away from the corm. Small signs of growth were visible at the base but no flower shoots were showing. The deep violet-purple flowers soon came into bloom and performed even better the following year, elegant in combination with the spike of pale purple bell-like flowers of late-blooming *Hosta lancifolia* and *Tricyrtis formosana* 'Amethystina', with white-throated amethyst flowers. The corms of *Colchicum* 'Rosy Dawn' were somewhat larger, at 2½ inches (6.5 cm) tall and wide, with a striated, chestnut-brown tunic and flower bud-shoots of 2 inches (5 cm) already showing. When it quickly came into bloom I was delighted with the lightly checkered, bright rosy flowers, set off with a white throat. *Colchicum* 'Zephyr' had corms with a small footlike extension beyond the basal plate, clearly vertical orientation, 2 inches tall by 2 inches (5 cm) thick at the base, and two impatient shoots obviously ready to flower.

They settled down to display rich, purple flowers with a starlike, greenish white base inside. The corms of *C.* 'Autumn Herald' were a squatty 2 by 2 inches (5 by 5 cm), with a dark chestnut-brown tunic and flower shoots an inch (2.5 cm) or so long. Amethyst-violet on the outside, the inner petals were a deeper violet-purple, with a broad, ivory-white base. *Colchicum* 'Daendels' had corms with a more vertical shape, 4 inches (10 cm) high and nearly 2 inches (5 cm) wide at the base, covered with a tight-fitting, chestnut-brown tunic with a somewhat blistered texture. Pale flower shoots were well extended upon arrival and developed into rounded, rather globular pale lilac flowers. In my garden journal entry for 15 September 2003, I noted that *C.* 'Daendels' had been in bloom for about 10 days, followed by 'Violet Queen', and then 'Autumn Herald' and 'Harlekijn'. And the *C. speciosum* were beginning to peek through the ground.

'Harlekijn' also had corms with a more vertical, elongated shape, but they were smaller than the preceding cultivar, only about 2^1/$_2$ inches (6.5 cm) tall and 1^1/$_4$ inches (3 cm) thick at the base, with a similarly blistery chestnut-brown tunic but not yet in growth. The flowers are amethyst-white at the very base and white for most of their length. In both years that they've bloomed in my garden, the flower petals displayed a curious in-rolled effect at their edges, similar to but not as extreme as a cactus dahlia. *Colchicum macrophyllum* has an unusually slim boomerang shape, with one "leg" (that portion beyond the basal plate) as much as 4 inches (10 cm) long but less than an inch (2.5 cm) thick, with a firmly dormant, tight, smooth, dark brown jacket. Rosy purple, moderately tessellated flowers are paler, almost white, with just a tinge of violet in the throat. *Colchicum variegatum* was also somewhat gently curved, each leg an inch (2.5 cm) or somewhat greater and approximately a half-inch (1.5 cm) thick, and covered by a golden tunic, firmly attached, with vertical striations. The strongly tessellated, deep reddish purple flowers are elegant.

Colchicum hungaricum had the daintiest corms of them all, a petite inch (2.5 cm) high by an 1^1/$_2$ inches (4 cm) or less wide at the base, with a smooth, medium-brown tunic and no signs of growth. This late winter to early spring–flowering species made one gasp of effort, attempting to show me what it could do before succumbing and becoming compost.

Autumn-flowering crocus

Fall crocus (the real thing, and not colchicums) need full sun, gritty soil, and protection from the varmints. The addition of crushed stone to the soil not only improves drainage, it deters voles and chipmunks. Growing fall crocus in pots kept in an alpine house (greenhouse heated to just a couple of degrees above freezing) may be the solution for gardens with hungry populations of voles, mice, chipmunks, and deer. Some species of *Crocus* bloom in the dead of winter (December, January, and even February in the United States), encouraging signs that winter has not put an end to gardening.

While colchicums will flower with their corms sitting exposed on a windowsill or tabletop, autumn-blooming crocus require prompt planting if they are to perform well. Late fall-blooming *Crocus speciosus* and its cultivars 'Aitchisonii', 'Artabir', and others bloom in late-autumn, pairing up nicely with *Sedum sieboldii*, whose creeping stems and rosy flowers make a pleasing partner for the lavender crocus flowers. 'Conqueror' has large, sky-blue flowers in early to mid-autumn and grows 5 to 6 inches (12.5 to 15.0 cm) tall. 'Oxonian' blooms in mid-fall and has rich, violet-blue flowers, accentuated with darker veins. Another combination, seen in Gertrude Wister's garden near Philadelphia, has masses of crocus at the feet of *Aster lateriflorus*. The aster's numerous small flowers have a yellow center that ages to rose-red after pollination, attractive with the lavender crocus and further accented by the red fruits of *Cotoneaster horizontalis* nearby. Since these crocus are dainty, I'd suggest planting 10, 25, or more to have an effective display the first year. Though their leaves also wait until spring, it will be the typical grassy crocus foliage that inconspicuously withers away.

In her Zone 5 Ithica garden, Nina Lambert finds that various *Crocus speciosus* have been the most enduring of the fall-blooming crocus, and the two cultivars she has are 'Cassiope' and 'Oxonian'. They are both strong seeders and get recycled via the mulch pile or the resifting of the gravel, thus moving about the garden even without the additional help that is always provided by chipmunks and squirrels. *Crocus ochroleucus* has

Autumn is welcomed at BelleWood Garden with the lavender flowers of *Crocus speciosus* 'Aitchisonii' peeking through the chartreuse-yellow leaves of golden feverfew (made more vivid by a summer trimming to encourage new growth). Photo by author.

remained, but not increased. She thinks that she lost all the *C. kotschyanus* (syn. *C. zonatus*) quite a while back, and late autumn–flowering lilac to deep purple *C. medius* has not been reliably hardy. While Bill Hamilton, who also gardened in Ithaca, successfully grew *C. sativus*, Nina has had to replace it several times.

Other autumn-flowering crocus to look for include *Crocus goulimyi*, with three darker lavender-blue outer petals and paler, softer, lilac-blue inner petals, that produces leaves together with the autumn flowers. As it has a very long and slender perianth tube, its flowers tend to loll about and it is best planted with a supporting ground cover. *Crocus kotschyanus* is usually an easily grown species that flowers in mid-autumn (September or October in the United States), with pale lilac flowers laced with darker violet-purple veins and accented with a yellow throat. All that is true if you get the right one. The clone that is most generally available never seems to flower. It just splits, and splits, and splits again. The 10 misshapened and sort of flattened corms (like a large chocolate chip) that I planted produced an endless array of nonflowering, teensy-tiny cormlets. In disgust, I finally dug the entire sod of crocus and pitched them into the trash. If I can find a reliable source I'll try again, though I'm beginning to think that I'd be better off with seed. After all, the parent corm had to flower in order to produce them.

Late-blooming, anywhere from October to February in the States, and among my favorites (I know, I say that about everything, but in this case it's true) is *Crocus laevigatus* 'Fontenayi', with lilac-purple flowers feathered and striped in darker purple, with a deep yellow throat. It blooms quite late and could readily be classed with the winter-blooming crocus. The dainty flowers are fragrant but are so small and far from an upright gardener's nose that in seasonably cold weather this is difficult to detect. Kneel, cup your hands around the flower, and gently exhale. The warmth of your hands and your breath will release the violetlike scent. The typical narrow, grasslike crocus leaves, with a silvery white stripe down the center, accompany the flowers. *Crocus longiflorus* is even more fragrant, but you must still kneel in homage to the globular lilac flowers whose yellow throat glows through to the outer petals. The strain I had flowered in late autumn—October to November—together with its leaves as is generally the case for this species. Other clones are said to bloom somewhat earlier, in mid-autumn.

I had read about *Crocus niveus*, said to be the finest of the white-flowering autumn crocus. But every time I tried to order it, the suppliers printed "out of stock" on the invoice. One autumn I was in England and staying with my friends Simon and Pippa Wills, who at that time lived in Clevedon, Avon. I was well entertained by visits to nurseries, including Mike Salmon's Monocot Nursery in Somerset—beds of colchicum in bloom whetted my appetite, and the good conversation was a pleasure. I was explaining my frustration about obtaining the snow crocus to him, really more as a gardener's generalized gripe over frustrated plant lust than anything else. With a grin around the pipe he was smoking, Mike reached under a bench and picked up a paper bag. He

The luminous flowers of *Crocus goulimyi* appear to glow in the slanting light of an autumn afternoon. The airy mulch of pine needles makes a good background and also serves to keep the flowers (which appear without the leaves) clean. Photo courtesy of Brent Heath/Brent and Becky's Bulbs.

A window box of *Crocus goulimyi* on the author's toolshed shows the sort of instant gratification these fall-blooming geophytes can offer a gardener. Planted just a couple of weeks previously, they add a welcome promise to autumn's turn into winter. Photo by author.

counted out 10 large corms, each covered in a finely netted tunic. Remarking that they should "make up to a nice potful for you," he completed my quest. Knowing something exists is just the starting point, because then you know to look for it. Good-sized white flowers set off with orange-red styles appear in late autumn, together with the foliage.

Crocus ochroleucus is easier to obtain, with yellow-throated, creamy white flowers in late autumn/early winter, blooming before the leaves appear or while they are still quite short. Though somewhat small flowered, it has been very reliable for me. I have hopes for *C. cartwrightianus* 'Albus', tempered with the understanding that it may not like New Jersey. The species itself is most likely the wild parent of sterile *C. sativus*, the saffron crocus. *Crocus cartwrightianus* grows around Athens and on most of the Cyclades Islands in Greece. It enjoys a Mediterranean climate, which I fail to provide, for one thing being too wet in summer. 'Albus' is the white form of the usually lilac to lavender or purple crocus, white-flowered forms being something that this species ap-

parently does fairly regularly, in contrast to other species that only rarely have white-flowered forms. And unlike other crocus, which close at night or on cloudy days, once *C. cartwrightianus* opens, its flowers remain open. They bloom here from October to December, so we will see if the shoots peering forth from the earth at October's end will open before the snow flies.

Deciding when winter ends and spring begins is a variable and perplexing question that varies from year to year, depending on the depths to which winter descends. Gardeners who play around with microclimates, finding a sunny stone wall or, even better, a house foundation with a trickle of warmth seeping through the stones, concrete, or concrete blocks can jump one hardiness zone and at least a couple of weeks ahead of the rest of the garden. In the United States, crocus that flower in December and January are clearly winter-blooming. March can be assigned to spring. That leaves February in a does/

We consider pairing perennials with other perennials, annuals, or bulbs. If shrubs are added to the gardener's palette, we get such stunning combinations as *Crocus medius* with the clusters of intense violet berries of *Callicarpa*. Photo courtesy of Brent Heath/ Brent and Becky's Bulbs.

does not situation. Some crocus mentioned in Chapter 9, "Geophytes for the Rock Garden," such as *Crocus biflorus* subsp. *weldenii*, bloom in February or March. That's either extra early or very late, depending on your point of view. Whatever the viewpoint, summer is the only season when no crocus are in flower.

Sternbergia

In late August 2003 I happened to visit Young's Nursery in Wilton, Connecticut. Four cardboard boxes were stacked on the counter, holding three different kinds of fall-blooming crocus—*Crocus ochroleucus*, *C. zonatus*, and *C. sativus*—and *Sternbergia lutea*. I really adore it when I find geophytes in boxes, where they can be fondled and selected one by one, rather than sequestered away from touch in mesh bags. Priced at 10 for $7.00, I was helpless. Seduced, I succumbed, and 10 plump bulbs came home with me.

Called autumn daffodil, *Sternbergia lutea* looks more like a rich, golden yellow crocus. Interestingly enough, since it is in the family Amaryllidaceae, it is a closer relative (botanically speaking) to the daffodil than the crocus. Native to Turkey and growing westward into Spain and eastward into Kashmir, the genus includes several species that have gotten well and truly muddled in the trade. For years, the bulbs were collected from the wild. That meant what was purchased as *S. lutea* could easily be something else. And the only clue was when the leaves appeared in relation to when the

Another autumn option for matching geophyte and shrub connects the rich yellow flowers of *Sternbergia lutea* with the blue flowers of *Caryopteris*. Photo by author.

bulbs flowered: do leaves appear before, together with, or long after the flowers withered away? If the leaves appeared long after the flowers faded away, then you had *S. clusiana*. If the leaves appeared before, together with, or just after the flowers, you had either *S. lutea* or *S. sicula*, and a closer inspection of the leaves was the best way to distinguish these two species. *Sternbergia lutea* has bright, shiny green leaves while those of *S. sicula* are darker green with a gray central stripe. Together with *Galanthus* and *Cyclamen*, *Sternbergia* is now protected under CITES Appendix II and may not be sold without governmental paperwork for both export and import. Currently, vendors are more likely to provide nursery-propagated material.

In the wild, *Sternbergia* are generally found on very freely draining limestone soils, in full sun. In the United States, *Sternbergia lutea* flowers from September to November, depending on the season, while *S. clusiana* and *S. sicula* bloom in October and November. Even though *S. clusiana* has been known in Europe since the 16th century, it has never been what could be called widespread in gardens. Indeed, the same might be said of the other species. While said to be hardy down to 28°F (−2°C), garden literature suggests that one err on the side of caution—that anything less than perfect drainage and dry winter conditions has a tendency to rot the bulbs. Further, they need a hot, dry summer rest, and unless conditions are ideal, as in a Mediterranean climate, cultivation in containers protected in a bulb frame or alpine house is recommended. Planting advice varies a good deal, from do not disturb for several years, to Raymond Foster's suggestion in *The Garden in Autumn and Winter* (1983) that sternbergia "can often be grown and flowered successfully as temporary pot-plants before planting out," but keep in mind that his advice is intended for gardeners in Great Britain. A good summer baking is the general suggestion, yet Elizabeth Lawrence mentions "the most brilliant patch I ever saw was under a great live oak in Tarboro, North Carolina." That would surely be dry, but hardly sun-baked. And advice on how deep to plant varies from 5 or 6 inches (12.5 to 15.0 cm) to a quite shallow planting with the neck of the bulbs exposed.

However, reports from gardeners who are growing sternbergia today seem to indicate it is more tolerant of cold and less fussy about conditions than the literature suggests. Angelo Porcelli lives in Italy, where *Sternbergia lutea* grows in a variety of soils, from a rather neutral red clay to an alkaline loam, so he doubts that pH is an issue. The soil is stony, and the bulbs are deeply embedded. Unlike the *Cyclamen hederifolium* that shares the same habitat, he finds that sternbergia grows only in open areas, never or only rarely under shrubs, and in that case they are weak and flower poorly. Jim Shields in central Indiana (USDA Zone 5) has poor luck growing *S. lutea* in containers. While they survive, the bulbs do not bloom. Rather, he plants them out in his garden, finding that they survive, grow, and flower. His soil is over limestone bedrock, deep under the surface, and the water is very hard, also full of calcium. (When I lived in Angola, Indiana, many, many years ago I used to catch rainwater to wash my hair. What came out of the tap was so hard that soap didn't lather.) Bill Lee also lives in the Midwest. He was given several sternbergia a few years ago, bare bulbs with their foliage still green. He planted them in two different places in the garden, in unamended southwestern Ohio clay. One group is on flat ground at the edge of a patch of pachysandra, and the other is at the top of a slope. Bill put it rather simply: "They have flourished. I would say from my experience that sternbergia are not fussy."

James Waddick in Kansas City, Missouri, where the soils are alkaline and the summers hot and dry, finds that *Sternbergia lutea* is hardy and, for the most part, trouble-free. They are slow to multiply but do so eventually. James made an interesting observation: "One year I bought some [sternbergia] mail order, and one of them turned out to be the uncommon species *S. colchiciflora* with distinct foliage and flower. It has neither offset or set seed, but remains a single bulb." *Sternbergia colchiciflora* is a small-flowered species that blooms in mid-autumn. Inch-wide (2.5 cm), funnel-shaped, pale yellow flowers practically rest on the ground, since the scape is hidden in the soil below. Four to six narrow, twisted leaves appear after the flowers. Native to southeastern Spain and Italy, and into Iran, in the wild it grows in open, stony, dry sites. James and I agree that the appearance of this émigré intermixed with the *S. lutea* he had ordered is a clear indication that the sternbergia bulbs he received had to have been collected in the wild.

Jane McGary has experience with a wider range of sternbergia than do most folks. If, as is the current taxonomic inclination, you count *Sternbergia sicula* as a separate species from *S. lutea*, she grows six different species. All of hers are in a mildly acid soil mix; thus Jane believes that, from her observations, none need lime to flower. She does add that *S. candida* (a winter/early spring-blooming species from southwestern Turkey with white flowers) has not flowered for her in northwestern Oregon, even though she has three different clones and has had one of them for almost 10 years. Her recommendation: "I believe the main prerequisite for flowering in this genus is a warm position. They don't flower well in the open garden for me. I suppose the spring is wet for too long. However, I have seen them in Oregon gardens at slightly lower elevation, flowering well for years, up against a south-facing wall. For that reason I grow them all in a bulb frame and occasionally commit some *S. lutea* or *S. sicula* to the garden, where they make leaves but no flowers. In the frame, with very limited water from May through September, they bloom prodigiously."

Moving eastward across the country to northern Massachusetts, Mark McDonough finds that both *Sternbergia lutea* and *S. fischeriana* perform well, flowering beautifully for him out in the open garden. Both are grown on small embankments on the south—that is, the warm—side of the house, in full sun. The first species is growing in a clay-loam soil amended with some sand for improved drainage. Mark's approach is a clever one: "I plant bulbs around the base of deciduous shrubs, with the theory that the shrub roots take up much of the summer moisture and allow the bulbs to dry out properly. So far, this technique has worked very well." He mentions that the handsome, shiny, straplike green foliage of *S. lutea*, planted on the southerly-facing base of a rose-of-Sharon shrub, "remains amazingly evergreen in spite of ice and snow through the winter. The late autumn flowers are glorious." *Sternbergia fischeriana* is also given high praise; he calls it "a beautiful species. Buds might show in very late autumn/early winter in a mild autumn season, but they don't open until early spring here. The flowers are very large, and the glaucous foliage attractive and narcissus-like. This species is grown in very sandy soil amended with some leaf humus, and seems easy enough to grow."

I suppose I could have planted three of my bulbs here, three there, and scattered the remaining four elsewhere. Perhaps because it was raining at the time I chose the cautious route and potted them up. Next summer I'll plant them out in the garden. Perhaps.

Snowdrops

Should this topsy-turvy flurry of bulbs flowering in fall take hold of your fancy, set your sights on *Galanthus reginae-olgae* (syn. *G. nivalis regina-olgae*). Why it is named for Queen Olga of Greece I have no idea. Though royally named, this uncommon, funny snowdrop that flowers in the autumn, emerging amid the falling leaves, is most typically shared among friends as a pass-along plant. The flower looks just like other snowdrops that bloom in spring, other than the fact that in common with several other autumn-flowering bulbs, it waits to produce foliage. There is something unsettling about walking along, scuffing the fresh-fallen leaves and seeing snowdrops. One year I set a couple of miniature pumpkins around the flowers and took a picture, as otherwise, I discovered, the image gives no sense of the season. Charles Cresson gave me three bulbs in trade for some plants I had given him. I found a suitable place adjacent to a path down into the woods that I traverse regularly. They settled in and in their second year began flowering in mid-October. Apparently they were quite happy with the site I had chosen for them. My garden journal entry for 19 October 1999 notes that there were 19 buds. On 24 October 2000, 26 buds and flowers appeared. And two years later, there were none. In hindsight, perhaps I should have lifted and separated the bulbs, replanting them in a couple of new locations as a precautionary safety measure. But these things happen. Carol Lim, in Bucks County, Pennsylvania, suffered the same loss, and her *G. nivalis regina-olgae* also grew and flowered for a while, then emerged but did not bloom, and then died. Perhaps even though she was referring to the double snowdrops, Nina Lambert's comment that those which bulk up to form clumps need to be lifted and divided and/or drenched with a fungicide, could well have been advice applied to my lost queen.

Another of my autumn-blooming snowdrops was acquired as *Galanthus caucasicus* var. *hiemalis*. In late November or early December, up come good-sized white snowdrops together with their leaves. They remain through the winter, now frozen and listing at an acute angle, then buried in snow, resurfacing and straightening up in a thaw. There doesn't appear to be much in the way of multiplication, as the few that I moved from Connecticut in 1995 remain as individuals rather than bulking up into nice groups. I still have the plant, but the name it came with has disappeared. In his 1999 monograph, *The Genus Galanthus*, Aaron P. Davis suggests that the early-flowering forms of *G. caucasicus*, though popular in gardens where it has long been cultivated, are merely the early-flowering variety of *G. elwesii* var. *hyemalis*. Further complicating the issue, Mark Smyth, a galanthophile from Northern Ireland, advised me that I should now call them *G. elwesii* var. *monostictus* (Hiemalis Group). Only thing is, I always thought that the distinguishing characteristic of *G. elwesii* were two green markings on the central tube, one at the sinus and the other at the base, sometimes fusing together. And the snowdrop in question in my garden has only one green marking, at the sinus. But that's okay. Maybe I'll just call it "that early-blooming snowdrop down in the woods."

Hardy begonia

Hardy begonia, *Begonia grandis* subsp. *evansiana* (syn. *Begonia evansiana*), resembles a cane-stem begonia that wandered into the garden for the summer. Rather than needing protected winter conditions indoors, it snuggles down under a blanket of autumn leaves and makes a repeat appearance in my garden year after year. It shows itself late in spring, developing stems 15 to 18 inches (35 to 45 cm) tall, sometimes taller, with the typical angel-wing leaves. Pink flowers appear in early autumn. Also at about this time, small tubercles form at the leaf/petiole and petiole/stem juncture. Where the growing season is lengthy—say, around Atlanta, Georgia—the tubercles mature, fall to the ground, and develop into new plants. Hardy begonia also does quite well on the bay side of Long Island. On the Atlantic Ocean side it survives but does not multiply as freely. In Connecticut and New Jersey I find it more prudent to collect the tubercles prior to frost. If they're ripe enough, the pointy little red-flushed spheres easily come off with a little gentle urging. Either loosen the soil, scatter them, and cover with some compost and mulch, or sow in a flat, keeping them cool over the winter. Two things to keep in mind: hardy begonia collapses with the first hard frost of autumn, and even though deer do not eat fibrous-rooted begonias, they do chow down on the hardy begonia.

Allium thunbergii

The ornamental onions most commonly seen in gardens are those that flower in late spring to early summer. These are moderate to tall species and cultivars with the unfortunate trait of losing their leaves around the time they bloom, and then going dormant. *Allium thunbergii* is different in size, temperament, and bloom time. Native to lower mountain slopes on Honshu, Shikoku, and Kyushu in Japan, and extending into South Korea, *A. thunbergii* is one of my autumn favorites for its ease of maintenance and attractive late-season flowers. Emerging from its winter rest in spring, established plants make a neat tussock of fresh, green, rushlike leaves, 6 to 8 inches (15 to 20 cm) tall, that remain through summer and fall. In my garden, in October they produce elegant, small umbels of rose-purple flowers, which have an elongated style and stamens, creating a larger, if somewhat blurred effect. Well behaved, it does not seed about. The narrow bulbs have fibrous roots, and larger clumps respond quite nicely to division in spring after the foliage is well developed. Given its dainty size, it needs placement at the very forefront of the border, perhaps partnered with *Crocus speciosus* and *Sedum sieboldii* for an autumn-enhancing display. The same trio would work quite nicely in the rock garden.

The grassy mound of *Allium thunbergii* leaves makes an underpinning for the rich pink flowers that appear in autumn. Modest in size, this charmer is a front-of-the-border plant that needs similarly sized companions if it is not to be overrun. Photo by author.

Cyclamen hederifolium

There is something enticing about cyclamen. Their dainty flowers hover over the ground like a flight of badminton shuttlecocks, and the foliage has a remarkable beauty of its own. What a pity that many gardeners are familiar only with the bloated versions of *Cyclamen persicum* that are offered as holiday gift plants from Thanksgiving onward. Actually, there's even hope in that department, as "miniatures" (still larger than the true species but not as gross as the oversize version) are fast becoming a popular alternative. The species itself is quite attractive and astonishingly long-lived. In 1973 my sister and her family emigrated to Israel, eventually settling in Jerusalem. Our parents went to visit them that winter and came home that December, bringing me a tuber of *C. persicum* that had been found at a roadside work site. Thirty years later, the tuber, somewhat irregular in form, is 6 inches (15 cm) long by 5 inches (12.5 cm) wide. Planted in a large, shallow bulb pan kept in my lean-to greenhouse, it is ignored in the summer while dormant. Sometime in October I'll notice the first signs of new growth, little pimples of foliage forming on the floral trunks. A good soaking, and then not another drink until growth is well under way. A goodly number of flowers appear in January, dancing over the silver-laced, dark green leaves. Thirty years is a respectable age and a tribute to a well-traveled plant that has "done its thing" when kept under basement grow lights, in a chilly spare bedroom, and now in the palatial accommodations of a cool greenhouse.

Even more than cyclamen in pots, I enjoy cyclamen in gardens. The three most reliable for me are early spring-flowering *Cyclamen coum*, summer-blooming *C. purpureum*, and autumn-blooming *C. hederifolium*. The well-named ivy-leaved cyclamen has ivylike leaves, from somewhat rounded to lanceolate, dark green with apple-green blotches or lacelike, silver-gray markings. The leaf can be mostly dark green, mostly ghost gray, or anything in between. Hysterogenous, its leaves appear a month or so after flowering begins in late summer. Flower color varies from light to deep pink, often with a darker blotch at the base, or white, though rarely without some pale pink markings at the opening. Cyclamen grow from tubers and do not make offsets. Though I suppose it is possible to chop one apart, being careful to retain growing points on each segment, that would be the only way to obtain identical plants. Since cyclamen are seed-raised, variation occurs, but it is astonishing how uniform some seed strains can be. The Silver-leaved Group, for example, has principally silvery gray leaves. *Cyclamen hederifolium* 'Silver Cloud' has very silver leaves and pink flowers. I find that an occasional silver-leaved cyclamen in a planting of silver-marked green leaved ones is visually more appealing to me than a large group of only silver-gray leaved plants. 'Album' has pure white flowers and was introduced back in 1601. 'Bowles' Apollo' has pink flowers and dark green leaves with paler blotches, heavily marked with two silver blotches separated by a green ring, often with a red flush over the entire leaf (or at least while they are young). 'Ruby Glow' has dark magenta flowers, and 'Rosenteppich' is a variable strain with pink to deep pink to red flowers. Plant cyclamen on the shallow side, with only an

The luminous white flowers of *Cyclamen hederifolium* 'Album' brighten the shady ground. Look carefully, and you'll see the first leaves and a few coiled "watch springs" as pollinated flowers emerge during the process of seed maturation. Photo by author.

inch or two (2.5 to 5 cm) of soil over the top, though they may pull themselves deeper with time. Choose a site in a woodland, with good drainage. End of summer, as weather is cooling off and plants are coming out of their summer rest, is a good time for planting. One handsome combination uses *Ajuga reptans* 'Burgundy Glow' as a ground cover for pink, ivy-leaved cyclamen. The silvery green ajuga leaves, splashed with deep red, are especially attractive in the first stages of growth when the cyclamen has flowers but no foliage. Japanese painted fern, *Athyrium niponicum* 'Pictum', is a handsome companion but should not be planted over the top of the cyclamen.

Arum italicum

Since it is of autumn interest, I'm placing this arum here by default, even though it does not flower at this time of year. Instead, it takes the fall flowers/spring foliage cycle and reverses it. The leaves of *Arum italicum* and its cultivars 'Pictum' and 'Chameleon' make their appearance in autumn and are generally able to remain right through winter for me. If 'Pictum' does get frozen down in a harsh winter with little snow cover, a new crop of leaves will be produced in spring. Flowers appear in spring, and then everything disappears for a summer rest. Come the following autumn, up come coblike clusters of red seeds, and then the leaves. Very confusing.

Arum grows from warty, sticklike tubers. *Arum italicum* 'Pictum' has leaves 6 to 10 inches (15 to 25 cm) long, strongly arrow-shaped, dark green with creamy-white markings along the veins. Often I find that purchased tubers produce only all-green leaves

Winter comes, and the leaves of *Arum italicum* 'Pictum' barely make it above a blanketing snowfall that protects them from the worst of the cold weather. Photo by author.

In spring, the flowers of *Arum italicum* offer a family resemblance to its aroid cousins such as arisaema and caladium. Photo by author.

their first season after fall planting, settling down and displaying their handsome, gray netlike markings in the second year. I like to combine 'Pictum' with evergreen Christmas fern, *Polystichum acrostichoides*. 'Chameleon' has much larger leaves, marbled in apple green and grayish green with a distinct border. It has never shown any winter damage; even when its leaves get so frozen they slump to the ground, they'll hoist themselves back up with better weather.

Lycoris: A Variably Hardy Genus

Magic lily, surprise lily, naked lady, and mystery lily are names attached to various geophytes that flower in fall unaccompanied by foliage. With naked lady, for example, referring to *Colchicum*, *Amaryllis belladonna*, and various *Lycoris* species, such common names can easily lead to confusion. These bulbs and corms are an interesting addition to the garden, providing fresh flowers at a time when other plants in the garden are winding down and looking somewhat weary. They also make good cut flowers.

Remember the childhood ditty "April showers bring May flowers"? Even in summer rainfall areas, end-of-summer storms bring autumn flowers, an effect all the more striking after a dry spell. James Waddick of Kansas City, Missouri, is a lycoris fancier who grows not only the somewhat familiar species of *Lycoris* but also many recently imported species as yet unavailable to the general gardening public. Though he was commenting on rare species, his observations and remarks are fascinating. The summer of 2003 had been quite dry in his area, with six weeks of near total drought. A patch of 25 *L. chinensis* (a winter-dormant species related to *L. aurea*, with leaves in spring and pure yellow flowers) managed to produce a single, short flower stalk. Late in summer the region had a tropical deluge, 7 inches (17.5 cm) of rain over a weekend, and it soaked in very nicely. Within 24 hours and almost visibly, this same patch of bulbs produced 40 flowering stalks. Some were even blooming as they emerged from the ground (very odd), and some reached nearly full size. James cannot recall another occasion when stalks emerged with such synchrony and speed. And just a few days afterward, *L. caldwellii* (another Chinese species, also with leaves appearing in spring and pure yellow flowers that fade to cream as they mature) that are traditionally later to bloom also made their appearance, normal in regard to numbers and height. Clearly, lycoris respond to rainfall just as much as do rain lilies, *Zephyranthes* and *Habranthus*.

When I was in Japan late one September, *Lycoris radiata* in the ditches bordering rice fields were in full bloom, solid bands of scarlet red. Narrow petals reflexed backward, and their threadlike stamens stuck out like the antenna of some shrimplike creature, providing yet another common name, spider lily. The red spider lily also grows throughout the U.S. South, in North Carolina, Tennessee, Georgia, and elsewhere.

They first arrived on American shores when Captain William Roberts brought three rather dried-out bulbs to his garden in New Bern, North Carolina. The captain had been with Commodore Perry when the black ships made their 1852–1854 expedition to Japan that ended the country's self-imposed isolation. Red spider lily sends up its exotic flowers in autumn, and four to seven narrow, dark green leaves marked with a central whitish stripe follow soon afterward. In cold winter climates, this can be a problem since foliage damage usually weakens the plants. Choose a sheltered location, however, and the plants can be remarkable hardy. In September 2003 I saw three in bloom at the T. H. Everett Rock Garden of The New York Botanical Garden, which had been planted three years previously. Two had sent up only a single flower stem, but one bulb, clearly happy and establishing itself well, was producing three bloom stalks. The clone usually found growing here is *L. radiata radiata*, a sterile triploid. One of Edith Eddleman's inspired plant combinations is a wonderful pairing of red spider lily with Japanese blood grass, *Imperata cylindrica* 'Rubra', in the perennial border at the J. C. Raulston Arboretum in Raleigh, North Carolina.

The long-necked bulbs resent disturbance and should be replanted in short order after they have been dug up. Permanent fleshy roots are part of their life style, and if these are cut off or become dried out it really sets back their reestablishment. The withered bulbs that Captain Roberts brought home in the mid-1850s were anecdotally reported not to grow, showing neither flowers nor foliage, for 10 years. Red spider lily often makes no growth at all, not even producing leaves, in the first cycle after disturbance. They should send up foliage the following season and flower thereafter. In general, lycoris move more easily if unearthed and replanted just after flowering. They will be making root growth in the fall, and this helps their reestablishment more successfully than if dug and reset as foliage fades away in early summer, which is before their resting period. More recent introductions from Japan are the fertile diploid form, with a slightly earlier, perhaps by two weeks, flowering period. Red spider lily seems to prefer light to moderate summer shade while dormant.

Lycoris squamigera is the species more commonly grown in the U.S. Northeast, since it sensibly waits until spring to send up its flat, straplike, somewhat grayish green leaves. At least that's the pattern they follow where winters are colder. I'm told that in mild climates they often send up leaves in autumn and refresh themselves with a second flush of foliage in spring. Leaves wither away in early summer. Then in mid- to late summer, the bulb sends up a naked stalk 20 to 28 inches (50 to 70 cm) high crowned with four to six rose-pink, trumpetlike flowers. For a while this was classified as *Amaryllis hallii*, and anyone familiar with *A. belladonna* can see a resemblance. It was introduced from Japan in 1862 by Dr. George H. Hall of Bristol, Rhode Island. A young American doctor turned trader, he also introduced Japanese wisteria, several magnolias, some conifers, and a crabapple to his country. I occasionally see these magic lilies as I travel around Hunterdon County, New Jersey, perhaps growing next to an old barn, even coming up as a clump in the middle of a lawn where once there might have been a flowerbed. They also appear in the occasional Pennsylvania garden, and I've seen them as far afield as the Shaw Arboretum in Gray Summit, Missouri, left from the days when the property was a farm. Mine are paired up with hostas and ferns, to provide some foliage when the naked flowers pop up in midsummer and to shield the ground from inadvertent disturbance when bare of the lycoris foliage earlier in summer.

There we were, checking in to the hotel in Davis, California, on a day late in August. And sitting on the counter was a vase with several stems of some warm, golden yellow, trumpetlike flowers. Leaving my husband to deal with the luggage, I questioned the desk clerk on duty about these hurricane lilies, and found out it was the evening clerk who brought them in. When we finally met up, it turned out she lived within walking distance of the motel, and she even drew me a map to see the plants in her garden. As I had thought, they were *Lycoris aurea*, a beautiful Chinese species with four to seven sunny flowers, the petal edges undulate and adding to their appeal. Flower stems are from 1 to 2 feet (30 to 60 cm) tall, with four to seven flowers. Native from China and Japan to Burma and Vietnam, it is often seen growing at the edges of cultivated fields. This tender species is popular with Florida gardeners, especially around Saint Augustine. The common name hurricane lily pairs its time of bloom with the season of great storms. The plants I saw had autumn foliage together with their flowers. Technically those with stamens barely longer than the petals should be named *L. aurea* var. *aurea* and may be distinguished from var. *angustipetala*, which has long stamens as much as twice as long as the narrower petals.

Other spider lilies are making their way into wider distribution. They are valued for their beautiful flowers in late summer and early autumn. Generally hysteranthous, their leaves appear after the flowers (very much after in the case of *Lycoris squamigera*, which flowers in late summer and produces leaves the following spring). *Lycoris incarnata* has six to eight fragrant, flesh-pink or rose-colored flowers on stalks 18 inches (45 cm) tall in late summer or early autumn, and it waits until spring to produce foliage. *Lycoris sprengeri* is a Japanese species very similar to *L. squamigera*, differing in a shorter flower stalk, a foot (30 cm) tall, and rose-pink flowers with electric-blue tips to their petals. *Lycoris sanguinea* is native to China and Japan (but remember that the Japanese have been cultivating Chinese plants for centuries, long enough for some to naturalize). The dark green leaves appear in spring, and four to six orange-red flowers on a stalk 18 inches (35 cm) tall appear in summer. *Lycoris albiflora* looks like a white *L. radiata*, often with a hint of yellow or pink, with narrow reflexed petals and long stamens that extend far beyond them. It is considered likely that these are actually hybrids between *L. radiata* and *L. traubii*, a saffron-yellow–flowered species found on southern Japan and Taiwan, with leaves appearing in late autumn.

Gardeners who wish to push the envelope might try the species with spring foliage as probably hardier than those with autumn or winter leaves. A sheltered site and free-draining soil would also aid in getting them through the winter. If you decide to play it safe and grow them in pots sheltered indoors for the winter, remember that all lycoris dislike disturbance. Top-dressing, removing the top few inches of soil and replacing it with fresh potting mix, is less upsetting to the bulbs than the more disruptive act of repotting. While they like a summer rest, they need not be kept as dry as South African geophytes. Try standing the pots in a tray of sand, which is kept moist.

Amaryllis belladonna: An Autumn-Flowering Geophyte for the Mediterranean Garden

The quintessential late summer /early autumn–flowering geophyte in California and regions with similar climate is *Amaryllis belladonna*. I was amazed the first time I saw them, tall naked stalks crowned with pink, trumpetlike flowers emerging from bare ground. "Stop the car!" I'd entreat, and jump out for another picture. I was able to calm down after the day I saw a long driveway, both sides of its entire length, solidly lined with naked ladies. I tried to buy a bulb at a garden center, only to be told they were rarely offered for sale—a classic example of the pass-along plant. It is hysteranthous,

A garden must have been here once upon a time, for this abandoned field is in Mendocino, California, not the South African Cape region. It is home to a sizable display of the beautiful pink flowers of *Amaryllis belladonna* that are thriving on their own, returning each September to surprise onlookers with their beautiful pink flowers. Photo by author.

with 5 to 11 straplike leaves appearing soon after the flowering stalk withers away. This winter leaf growth is a problem in colder climates, though I successfully had it flower for several years in Wilton, Connecticut. It was planted in the ground under the roof overhang, to restrict moisture while dormant in the summer months, and near the house foundation for additional protection. In winter I would cover the leaves with a pile of some dry, lightweight mulch, such as pine needles. This was more an act of pushing at the envelope than routine gardening.

Several cultivars are variations on the theme of pink trumpet flowers. *Amaryllis belladonna* 'Barberton' has dark rose-pink flowers, those of 'Capetown' are deep rose colored, while 'Jagersfontein' flowers are deep pink, and free-flowering 'Johannesburg' has pale pink flowers, lighter in the center. 'Pallida' is said to be a robust clone with large, abundant, rose-pink flowers, and the flowers of 'Hathor' are white.

It depends on the weather, just when the naked ladies make an appearance—not solely temperature, I think, but also early moisture. Sue Haffner had them flowering in late July 2003: "Darned if those naked ladies aren't blooming already in my front yard here in Clovis, California. It's been very hot and unusually humid here, though the clouds are finally going away. We are about to set a new record for consecutive 100°F days." Mary Sue Ittner noticed the first three in flower on 12 August 2003. The species had already been out and about where she lives in coastal Mendocino County, California, but those in her garden had not bloomed for three years, even though they used to. She was sure their bulbs were large enough. (The bulb can be as much as 4 inches [10 cm] in diameter, taller than it is wide.) Perhaps, Mary Sue speculated, it was too shady where they were planted. And maybe they need to be divided when they get that large. Was it possible they were too overcrowded to bloom properly? Apparently she was right on track, because Ann Marie Rametta, whose garden is in southern California's San Gabriel Valley, suggested that naked ladies do better in full sun. She advised Mary Sue that "they also do better if divided every three years, as they multiply so much that they tend to push the older bulbs up out of the ground. Only the newer ones that are in the ground will bloom. If you separate the older ones, and/or replant the ones out of the ground, they too will bloom. But the roots like to be at least touching the ground. I have several I've divided and due to lack of pots just lay them in a planter and they are all blooming now, too. I have over a hundred in bloom right now (mid-August) throughout the garden."

Jim Lycos, in Springwood, Australia, had somewhat different advice. In his experience, division of the bulbs just helps in producing larger sized bulbs. The larger the bulb, the more flowers will appear in an umbel, but once a bulb is large enough to flower, increased size does not mean it is more likely to do so. Jim commented that "In the southern dry inland parts of my state I have seen 120-year-old grave plots with around four layers of *Amaryllis belladonna* filling the grave area, and given the right rainfall conditions they have hundreds of flower stalks. Last year (2002) we experienced the driest year on record—a drought throughout the eastern states of Australia. In my area, outside Sydney, the drought broke in the last month of summer (February) with a 6-inch downpour. Rather than a field day I had a field month photographing the marvelous flowerings of large clumps of amaryllis. In areas and suburbs where in previous years one would at best see half a dozen flowering stalks from a clump, this year there were 30 to 50 stalks in bloom in some garden clumps of amaryllis. A friend who grows ×*Amarygia multiflora* (formerly *Amaryllis multiflora*) varieties in clay loam in full sun with half the bulbs exposed, never divided, and watered only by rainfall, commented to me that it was the best flowering he has ever experienced! I actually achieved the same result in my garden by heavily watering the amaryllis clumps from midsummer on. By heavy watering I mean drip watering each clump for a whole day each fortnight during mid- to late summer (one month altogether). A dry, hot summer followed by inundation is a reliable way of inducing heavy flowering in amaryllis." Note that *A.* 'Multiflora' is the name of a two-generation hybridization program. First stage is ×*Amarygia bidwillii*, a bigeneric cross between *Amaryllis belladonna* and ×*Amarygia multiflora*, with large, deep rose-pink flowers on stems 18 to 24 inches (45 to 60 cm) tall. When this is crossed back onto its amaryllis parent, the offspring are known in the trade as *Amaryllis* 'Multiflora'.

In the wild, *Amaryllis belladonna* is found growing in loamy soils in seasonally moist sites, on coastal hills and stream banks on the southwestern coast of the Cape Province of South Africa.

Bulbs Going Wild

Territorially Ambitious Geophytes

Some geophytes grow quite nicely in our gardens, while others are more difficult. And then there are those that do all too well, geophytes with territorial ambitions that see no need to hang around home but would rather spread far and wide. They may do so through seed, or they may manage things asexually; perhaps they do both. And it can prove difficult to evict them.

Few gardeners would knowingly disturb a natural site. Yet we feel free to add what we will to our gardens. It is when plants move out of the garden that they present us with difficulties. From ignorance or disregard, too many plants have been introduced that have over time become a problem: Kudzu, Japanese honeysuckle, multiflora rose. It is a worldwide problem that is not confined to perennials or shrubs or annuals or any other category of plants, and it does include several geophytes. Consider your climate, investigate the habits of the plants you are considering adding to your garden, and then make an informed decision if that must-have plant with "vigorous," "freely spreading," or other warning phrases in its description is really something you should be planting.

Allium

There's that pernicious weed, onion grass, crow garlic, or false garlic—*Allium vineale*. Native to Europe, North Africa, and western Asia, I cannot imagine that anyone ever planted it on purpose. However it arrived on our shores, it's definitely here to stay and has naturalized in the American mid-Atlantic States, upper South, and Pacific Northwest. It sprouts in early spring, with grasslike clumps of waxy coated, hollow green leaves a foot (30 cm) or more tall. Onion grass grows equally well in sunny lawns and shaded woodland, and it is summer dormant. The white mother bulb underground produces lots of hard-shelled brown offsets. When the original bulb is pulled, these offsets remain behind to grow. All things considered, onion grass is hard to kill. Dig it up, and the cloves remaining underground will sprout next year. The only effective way to use a weed-killer such as glyphosate requires that you cut the leaves in half and then spray the herbicide down the hollow shaft.

Seeds are not the problem, since onion grass seems to flower quite rarely. Instead, it bears a cluster of little bulblets in place of flowers. These often sprout while still attached to the long stalk, giving a Beatle-esque mop-headed appearance. This, says Dilys Davies in her book *Alliums: The Ornamental Onions* (1992), is something to beware of. "Any *Allium* with bulbils in the head should be viewed with suspicion." She goes on to suggest that once identified, "incarcerate them in heavy duty plastic or tins, dump into the incinerator or bin, grind them underfoot in the centre of a large concrete carpark, then wait for the inevitable germination next year."

Some alliums have a habit of seeding about, as anyone who has grown chives, *Allium schoenoprasum*, knows only too well. Plant a few in the herb garden, allow the attractive, soft purple flower heads to set seed, and stand back next spring when the numerous offspring jump into growth. This problem can be avoided if you remove the flowers before they go to seed, starting right from the first year. As always, keep in mind the old folk saying that "one year's seeding means seven years of weeding." One summer my British friend, Brian Whyer, was complaining about an invasively seeding onion. "I have been at Banbury digging up the *Allium triquetrum* as part of my general tidy up of the garden. Want a bucket full? It is a real pain, even if you don't pull off the flower heads each year, which of course I have forgotten to do some years. This is from a single pot of a few bulbs about 10 years ago."

Ornithogalum umbellatum

While I doubt that anyone will deliberately plant onion grass, other geophytes with attractive good looks are sometimes, nay make that often, planted, to the hapless gardener's ultimate regret. Star of Bethlehem, *Ornithogalum umbellatum*, is one such cheerful immigrant thriving in New York City and elsewhere. Found throughout the Middle East, it happily settles in—in lawns, in cracks in pavement, and anywhere else it gains a foothold. John C. Wister warns against it in *Bulbs for American Gardens*: "It should not be planted in the garden because it becomes a weed, but it is pretty and it is nice in a wild or fairly wild position"—from which I am confident he would have found it migrating into the garden. The leaves look like those of a crocus—straplike, narrow, medium-green, with a paler whitish stripe down the center. Eight to ten starlike, white flowers cluster on a stem 6 to 8 inches (15 to 20 cm) high, with a tidy green stripe on the outside of each petal. Blooming in spring, the flowers open late in the morning and close in the afternoon. Once it gains a foothold, star of Bethlehem is difficult to evict since even the tiniest offset seems capable of rapid regeneration. Nell Jean Campbell in

Colquitt, Georgia, has it naturalized in the front lawn and in the grass at an old house site elsewhere. She thinks it could become a pest, except that the "lawn" is not a focal point, and centipede grass is a tough competitor in poor soil.

Ranunculus ficaria

Another pernicious pest is the lesser celandine, *Ranunculus ficaria*. Oh, there are cultivars with double flowers, white flowers, copper-hued leaves, and more. I'm thinking of the straight species, with dark green leaves that are sometimes blotched with brown or silver. They lie flat to the ground and in spring are spangled with golden flowers before they disappear for the summer. The prolific root tubers quickly turn a few plants into a widespread carpet. I once saw a furtive visitor to The New York Botanical Garden taking a small portion. Thinking I should say something, perhaps along the lines that plant thieves would most likely be composted, I reconsidered. It would be punishment enough once the lesser celandine took hold in her garden.

Hyacinthoides hispanica

Many visually pleasing memories have stayed with me from my first visit to the Netherlands. One is of a park across the street from the Hotel Bel Air in The Hague. It was in April, and the ground beneath ancient beech trees was carpeted by masses of English bluebells, *Hyacinthoides non-scripta*, creating a soft blue haze. (Don't confuse this geophyte with the Scottish bluebell, *Campanula rotundifolia*.) In England, in spring, the woods are similarly filled with wild English bluebells. This species has the bell-like flowers arranged on one side of the flower stem, which nods gently at its tip. The species most generally offered for sale is the Spanish bluebell, *H. hispanica*, with flowers arranged loosely around the stem and the uppermost flowers remaining erect. The Royal Horticultural Society *Manual of Bulbs* (1996) mentions the fact that "Plants cultivated as *H. hispanica* are often hybrids between this species and *H. non-scripta*." Apparently where the two species are grown in relative proximity in the bulb fields of Holland, bees are cross-pollinating the two. That is bad enough, but it gets worse. Pollen from Spanish bluebells growing in English gardens is being carried by bees to English bluebells growing wild in nearby forests. The resulting hybrid offspring are more vigorous and are crowding out the native species.

Romulea, Watsonia, and Sparaxis

What's well behaved (or perhaps what merely conducts itself more politely) in one region can prove problematic in another. South African geophytes act one way at home, are controlled by the weather in winter-rainfall and cold-winter regions, and some are going berserk in Mediterranean climates elsewhere in the world. Australia has serious problems with major rogues, including watsonia and romulea.

In general, the 90 or so different species of *Romulea* are native to the Mediterranean region and South Africa. They grow from small corms, rather flattened at the base and covered in a stiff, fibrous tunic. The flowers resemble those of a crocus but appear in the leaf axils, in clusters of two to several. Several of the species are, where hardy, rather on the weedy side. At this point a distinction should be drawn between geophytes that make expanding clumps but remain essentially where they have been planted and those that enlarge their territory and spread beyond the garden's boundaries. In Australia, they appear as garden escapes—around towns, old farms, on nearby roadsides, dispersed by dumping garden debris, cutting roadsides while plants are in seed, or movement of contaminated soil. Onion grass, *R. rosea*, grows about 6 inches (12 cm) tall. Native to the Cape Province of South Africa, it has grasslike leaves and small mauve or white starlike flowers with the outer segments lightly striped in purple and shaded with green at the base. *Romulea minutiflora* is said to be really weedy in western Australia, naturalizing in a wide-spreading, invasive manner. Although, given that the flower is well named, with tepals ¼ inch (½ cm) to barely ½ inch (1 cm) long, I'm unclear why anyone planted it in the first place.

Another South African genus, *Watsonia*, includes about 70 species, and so far 6 have escaped from gardens and are naturalized in western Australia. Probably the worst is *W. meriana* var. *bulbillifera*, which is difficult if not impossible to control. This salmon form of *W. meriana* has a three-fold technique for multiplying, including the usual production of seeds from the flowers and underground cormlets as well. However, *bulbillifera* also produces many small cormlets at each node on the stalk, which get scattered well away from the parent plant. This expands their territory in a dramatic manner. The production of cormlets along the stalk is a genetic variation that apparently shows up only on plants with salmon-colored flowers. It is so bad that farmers are advised not to make hay from fields where this *bulbillifera* is growing, to prevent accidental contamination of new areas through transport of cormlets baled with the hay.

Not everyone agrees that *Watsonia meriana* var. *bulbillifera* should be eradicated, and I came across a diametrically opposite point of view on a Web site that asked, "Are all exotic species to be removed and only indigenous species to remain?" The line of contention went something like this: Few native grasses remain on the hillsides in California. The majority of grasses are imports from Europe. *Cortaderia jubata* is a nonnative grass that is a fire hazard, and it is sensible and prudent that it should be eliminated. But why, if *W. meriana* var. *bulbillifera* is such a problem in Australia and elsewhere, has it not become a problem in its native habitat in South Africa?

The problem with *Watsonia meriana* var. *bulbillifera* is not confined to Australia. Along Highway 1 on the northern California coast, near Mendocino and at Salt Point State Park, it is crowding out the native plants. Parts of eastern Uruguay and some milder regions of Argentina are being affected. Even though the growth of other South

African bulbous plants is influenced by year-round rains in those areas of South America, it seems to have little effect on this watsonia. Gardeners might be safe if they plant the other color forms of *W. meriana*, with red to orange, pink, or mauve flowers, which apparently are better behaved, not invasive, and flower for a longer season. However, *bulbillifera* is already widespread in the southwestern portion of Western Australia. Other watsonias that have also naturalized include the following species: *W. marginata* is recorded from the Darling Range near Perth to Albany; rosy watsonia, *W. borbonica*, is also a problem, as is *W. versfeldii*, which grows up to 6 feet (2 m) tall, forming a showy plant with white, pink to cerise, or red flowers and has become a serious weed of roadsides and rocky granite outcrops between Perth and Albany.

Weather patterns in many parts of the United States will control the growth of watsonias, since they are winter-growing. They need rainfall at that time, yet while in growth they cannot deal well with cold temperatures. Conversely, warm, wet summers can rot the dormant corms. Regions with Mediterranean climates, winter rains, and moderate temperatures, followed by dry summers—places such as France, Italy, Spain, and Portugal—could be risky.

Other iridaceous South African genera have also naturalized in western Australia, including three of the six species of *Sparaxis*. The most commonly seen is *S. bulbifera*, with large, cream-colored flowers in spring. It is a serious invader of clay wetlands on the Swan coastal plain and in the Avon Valley. A second species, *S. grandiflora*, has purple or white flowers. The two species are known to crossbreed, with offspring displaying the usual resulting hybrid vigor. Harlequin flower, *S. pillansii*, is found around old settlements from Perth to Albany. Its common name refers to the striking tricolor petals, which are red, pink, or purple at the end of each petal, yellow toward the base, and with a black center. *Tritonia crocata* and *T. lineata*, and *Homeria flaccida* and *H. collina* spread both from seed and offsets. *Chasmanthe floribunda*, which is easily mistaken for watsonia, has also naturalized. Montbretia, *Crocosmia ×crocosmiiflora*, spreads by underground runners. Additionally, some species of *Gladiolus* will occasionally naturalize, spreading around from old farmsteads and town gardens where they had originally been planted.

Oxalis

Oxalis can be a pest in just about every garden. It spreads by seed, shoots, and root fragments. Some have tubers. Of the 800 species in the genus, 50 are tuberous. Of the 14 species of *Oxalis* that occur in western Australia, only 1 is native. Three that are pests in the bushland are soursob or Bermuda buttercup, *O. pes-caprae*; four o'clock, *O. purpurea*; and finger leaf, *O. glabra*. Soursob was introduced to Australia in 1839 as an ornamental plant for the garden. It is now a weed on a wide range of habitats from disturbed areas to its most prolific occurrences on heavy but well-drained, fertile soils.

Though it originated in South Africa as a Mediterranean climate plant, soursob copes just fine with subtropical and semi-arid conditions. In milder climates anywhere, it naturalizes widely, becoming a serious weed. While it sets seed very rarely in European gardens, the plant manages just fine through the production of numerous bulbils. The parent bulb develops into two bulbs during the growing season, and an additional bulb forms on the fleshy tuber at the end of the underground stem. Twenty or more bulbils develop on the rhizomatous stem above the original bulb. At minimum, that's a 23:1 rate of increase. In *Garden Bulbs for the South* (1994), Scott Ogden mentions that although soursob is a vigorous spreader, hard frost quickly damages the tender foliage.

Four o'clock, *Oxalis purpurea*, is also thought to be an escapee from gardens. Flower color is very variable, from rose-purple to deep rose, violet to pale violet, yellow, cream, or white, all with a yellow throat. It prefers moist, heavier soils and is tender to frost. Finger leaf, *O. glabra*, has short, narrow leaves in clusters along the upright stems 6 inches (15 cm) tall, and pinkish purple flowers with a yellow throat. In Australia, all three—soursob, four o'clock, and finger leaf—are winter-growing plants, sending their leaves up as temperatures drop in autumn, and then going dormant as temperatures rise in late spring.

In Chapter 7, "Geophytes for the South and Southeastern United States," Nell Jean Campbell mentions two oxalis that grow on her property, *Oxalis crassipes* and *O. rubra*. Interestingly, the former is not mentioned in the RHS *Manual of Bulbs*. Elizabeth Lawrence grew a pink-flowered oxalis with "a pale green cloverlike leaf and tuberous roots. It has a habit of coming up at odd and unexpected places, and is certainly too great a spreader for a choice spot." She mentions that it is one of the commonest garden flowers around Raleigh, North Carolina, and that her mother grew it also. When she received an identical plant from a Mr. Houdyshel, he identified it as *O. crassipes* and said that in southern California it is evergreen and almost ever-blooming. Scott Ogden says that it is a sturdy native to the Argentinean pampas and is especially drought-tolerant. In southern U.S. states it will start blooming in February and continue into summer, especially if it gets some shade from intense, late-day sun. After a brief hiatus, a repeat period of bloom often occurs in late fall that may, given a sheltered site, continue into the winter.

Sources

Every autumn, gardeners gravitate toward garden centers and nurseries, drawn like iron toward a lodestone. What draws us are those lovely bags, boxes, and bins of bulbs, corms, and tubers. The "usual suspects" are readily found: a range of tulips and daffodils, hyacinths, and a host of smaller geophytes such as crocus, snowdrops, scillas, and more. Occasionally you can serendipitously come across something out of the ordinary. (I remember my delight one September at finding *Oxalis adenophylla* and *Ornithogalum nutans* as I strolled down the aisle of bulbs at a nursery where I'd stopped on impulse.) In general, however, a wider range will be found through mail-order sources, and this is the better way to obtain less-common geophytes. The best way is to raise them from seed, but this is suitable only for the patient gardener.

The following list does not claim to include every possible source, nor do I pretend to have ordered from each one (pleasant though that might be). Keep in mind that printing and mailing a paper catalog costs the nursery money. Unless the catalog is just a simple list, the nursery will usually charge a few dollars, especially if it is an overseas nursery.

Mail-Order Sources for Geophytes

Brent and Becky's Bulbs
Brent and Becky Heath
7463 Heath Trail
Gloucester, VA 23061
Telephone: 877-661-2852 (toll-free, orders only)
Telephone: 804-693-3966 (for questions, catalog requests, other business)
Fax: 804-693-9436
Web site: www.brentandbeckysbulbs.com
E-mail: bbheath@aol.com
Offers a superb range of familiar bulbs from tulips, daffodils, and hyacinths right through the minor bulbs, and with an excellent selection of others less commonly available. Separate catalog of spring-planted summer bulbs. Illustrated color catalog, good Web site, with comments and suggestions for companion plants.

Chicago Horticultural Society

Contact person: Martin King
1000 Lake Cook Road
Glencoe, IL 60022
Telephone: 847-835-8357
Fax: 847-835-1635
Web site: www.chicagobotanic.org
E-mail: mking@chicagobotanic.org

Offer a once-a-year bulb sale in early October, primarily at the Chicago Botanic Garden but with mail order available as of 2003. Not all bulbs that are available may be purchased by mail order, and mail order appears to have minimums of 25. That's not a problem with daffodils, but it sure is a lot of *Fritillaria imperialis*!

Colorblends/Schipper & Co.

Box 7584
Greenwich, CT 06836-7584
Telephone: 888-847-8637 (for orders only)
Telephone: 203-625-0638 (for questions, information, other business)
Fax: 203-862-8909
Web site: www.colorblends.com
E-mail: info@colorblends.com

Primarily tulips, but also daffodils and a few other bulbs. Some of their offerings are available only in preblended mixes of two different tulips or as suggested combinations of two different hyacinths, hyacinths and daffodils, hyacinths and Grecian windflower to be ordered separately, and so on.

The Daffodil Mart

30 Irene Street
Torrington, CT 06790-6668
Telephone: 800-255-2852
Fax: 800-420-2852

The Daffodil Mart is the bulb department of White Flower Farm.

Dutch Gardens

128 Intervale Road
Burlington, VT 05401
Telephone: 802-660-3500
Fax: 802-660-3501
Web site: www.dutchgardens.com

Dutch Gardens is now the bulb department of Gardener's Supply Company.

Grant Mitsch Daffodils

Richard and Elise Havens
P.O. Box 218
Hubbard, OR 97032
Telephone: 503-651-2742
Fax: 503-651-2792
Web site: www.web-ster.com/havensr/mitsch
E-mail: havensr@web-ster.com

Daffodil specialists with commensurate prices. Get your 'King Alfred' somewhere else. (They don't sell these kinds of daffodils.) Come here for choice treasures, many of their own breeding. No Internet orders; no Internet catalog. Paper catalog is $3 in the U.S., $4 overseas. Orders are taken March through fall, shipping in September and October.

McClure & Zimmerman

108 W. Winnebago
P.O. Box 368
Friesland, WI 53935-0368
Telephone: 800-883-6998
Fax: 800-374-6120
Web site: www.mzbulb.com
E-mail: info@mzbulb.com

A nice selection of familiar bulbs—tulips, daffodils, crocus, and so on—as well as a good selection of less frequently available offerings such as *Lachenalia*, *Veltheimia*, and more. Their paper catalog has a few botanical-style drawings, but no color pictures.

Old House Gardens—Heirloom Bulbs

Scott Kunst
536 Third St.
Ann Arbor, MI 48103-4957
Telephone: 734-995-1486
Fax: 734-995-1687
Web site: www.oldhousegardens.com
E-mail: OHGBulbs@aol.com

Heirloom bulbs, the very ones our grand-
parents used to grow. Old cultivars of tulips,
tazetta daffodils, hyacinths, cannas, and
more. Some of their offerings date back to the
13th century, and the cut-off date is around
1950. Paper catalog with color illustrations.

John Scheepers, Inc.

23 Tulip Drive
Bantam, CT 06750
Telephone: 860-567-0838
Fax: 860-567-5323
Web site: www.johnscheepers.com
E-mail: catalog@johnscheepers.com

Good selection of typical spring-flowering
bulbs, and a pleasing selection of tender
summer-blooming varieties such as *Eucomis
bicolor*, *Galtonia candicans*, and more.

TulipWorld B.V.

Grasweg 71
1031 HX Amsterdam
The Netherlands
Telephone: 31-20-6944171
(Remember that their local time is +6 hours
U.S. East Coast, and +9 hours U.S. West
Coast)
Fax: 31-20-6944307
Web site: www.tulipworld.com
E-mail: office@tulipworld.com

An Internet company offering Dutch-grown
bulbs direct to the consumer. Web site offers
all sorts of information on selecting, growing,
combining, and using flower bulbs. They can
also be reached in the United States:

TulipWorld USA

P.O. Box 758
Chadds Ford, PA 19317

Van Engelen, Inc.

23 Tulip Drive
Bantam, CT 06750
Telephone: 860-567-8734
Fax: 860-567-5323
Web site: www.vanengelen.com
E-mail: customerservice@vanengelen.com

This is the wholesale side of John Scheepers,
Inc., with modestly large minimums (a $50
minimum order) for their offerings of daffodils, tulips, hyacinths, and other bulbs at
lower per-bulb prices.

Nancy R. Wilson

6525 Briceland-Thorn Road
Garberville, CA 95542
Web site: www.asis.com/~nwilson
E-mail: nwilson@asis.com
Species and miniature narcissus

U.S. Sources for Geophytes

Appalachian Wildflower Nursery

Don Hackenberry
723 Honey Creek Road
Reedsville, PA 17084
Telephone: 717-667-6998

Arrowhead Alpines

P.O. Box 857
Fowlerville, MI 48836
Telephone: 517-223-3581
Fax: 517-223-8750
Web site: www.arrowhead-alpines.com

Some uncommon geophytes are included
among the wide range of alpines that they
offer.

Asiatica Rare Plant Resource
Barry Yinger and Andrew Wong
P.O. Box 270
Lewisberry, PA 17339
Telephone: 717-938-8677
Web site: www.asiaticanursery.com
E-mail: asiatica@nni.com
Specializing in shade-tolerant plants from
Japan and China, including arisaema and
trillium.

Bulbmeister
Kelly M. Irvin
4407 Town Vu Road
Bentonville, AR 72712
Web site: www.bulbmeister.com
E-mail: bulbmeister@bulbmeister.com
Specializing in *Lycoris* "in the green," also sell-
ing spring and fall bulbs. Price list available
on the Web.

Bulbmania
M & C Willetts
P.O. Box 446
Moss Landing, CA 95039-0446
Telephone: 831-728-BULB
Web site: www.bulbmania.com
E-mail: sales@bulbmania.com

Caladium Bulb Company
1231 E. Magnolia St.
Lakeland, FL 33801
Telephone: 800-974-2558
Fax: 863-683-8479
International calls: 863-680-8080
Web site: www.caladiumbulbs.com
E-mail: caladium@caladiumbulbs.com
Offers 21 different caladiums, elephant ears,
and also tuberose.

Caladiums Online
81 Bates Road
Lake Placid, FL 33852
Telephone: 863-465-3274
Fax: 863-465-9568
Web site: www.caladiumsonline.com
Offers nice selection of premium jumbo and
large number 1 size fancy leaf, strap leaf, and
dwarf caladiums. Family-owned firm in busi-
ness for more than 50 years.

Caladium World
P.O. Box 629
Sebring, FL 33871
Telephone: 863-385-7661
Fax: 863-385-5836
Web site: www.caladium.com
Specializing in caladiums only. Order online
or request a free print catalog.

Collector's Nursery
16804 NE 102nd Ave.
Battle Ground, WA 98604
Telephone: 360-574-3832
Fax: 360-571-8540
Web site: www.collectorsnursery.com
E-mail: dianar@collectorsnursery.com
Excellent mail-order source for unusual bulbs
from arisaema and arum to zantedeschia.
Also lots of uncommon perennials to grow
as companion plants with your bulbs.

Jim Duggan Flower Nursery
1452 Santa Fe Drive
Encinitas, CA 92024
Telephone: 619-943-1658
Web site: www.thebulbman.com
E-mail: jimsflowers@thebulbman.com
An extensive selection of South African geo-
phytes for Mediterranean-climate gardens.

Far West Bulb Farm

Ames and Nancy Gilbert
14499 Lower Colfax Rd.
Grass Valley, CA 95945
Telephone: 530-272-4775
Fax: 530-272-4775 (call first to let them
know you are sending a fax)
Web site: www.californianativebulbs.com
E-mail: nancyames@accessbee.com

California native bulb species (shipped only
while dormant, 1 September to 1 November
each year): *Allium, Brodiaea, Calochortus,
Chlorogalum, Dichelostemma, Erythronium,
Lilium, Triteleia.*

Hansen Nursery

Robin Hansen
P.O. Box 1228
North Bend, OR 97459
Telephone: 541-756-1156
E-mail: hansen.nursery@verizon.net

Cyclamen galore, and also other Northwest
native bulbs, corms, and tubers such as alliums, brodiaeas, camassia, triteleias, and
more.

Horn Canna Farm

Route 1, Box 94
Carnegie, OK 73015
Telephone: 580-637-2327
Fax 580-637-2295
Web site: www.cannas.net

Cannas only, around 25 varieties.

Munchkin Nursery & Garden

Gene Bush
323 Woodside Drive NW
Depauw, IN 47115-9039
Telephone: 812-633-4858
Web site: www.munchkinnursery.com
E-mail: genebush@munchkinnursery.com

Specializing in woodland plants, Munchkin
Nursery includes trillium, arisaema, and a few
other geophytes, both North American
natives and their Asian counterparts.

NorthWest Native Seeds

Ron Ratko
17595 Vierra Canyon Rd. #172
Prunedale, CA 93907
E-mail: tvrozil@juno.com
Seeds.

Odyssey Bulbs

Russell Stafford
8984 Meadow Lane
Berrien Springs, MI 49103
Telephone: 877-220-1651 (toll-free, for
orders only)
Fax: 616-471-4642
Web site: www.odysseybulbs.com
E-mail: odysseybulbs@earthlink.net

A fantastic list of choice and uncommon
bulbs: alliums, arums, colchicum, corydalis,
crocus, ornithogalum, oxalis, scilla, tulips,
and more. This is not the place to go for the
usual selection of daffodils and tulips.

Plant Delights Nursery Inc.

Tony Avent
9241 Sauls Road
Raleigh, NC 27603
Telephone: 919-772-4794
Fax: 919-662-0370
Web site: www.plantdel.com
E-mail: office@plantdel.com

An eclectic mix of incredible plants with a
goodly number of geophytes mixed in. Alocasia, arisaema, arum, arisarum, colocasia,
corydalis, crinum, crocosmia, cyclamen,
hymenocallis, lycoris, trillium, and more.

Roslyn Nursery

211 Burrs Lane
Dix Hills, NY 11746
Telephone: 631-643-9347
Fax: 631-427-0894
Web site: www.roslynnursery.com
E-mail: roslyn@roslynnursery.com

Primarily a source for rhododendrons, azaleas, and other shrubs, they do offer a few

companion plants that include the occasional geophyte.

Seneca Hill Perennials

Ellen Hornig
3712 County Route 57
Oswego, NY 13126
Telephone: 315-342-5915
Fax: 315-342-5573
Web site: www.senecahill.com

This lady knows how to grow plants and satisfy her customers. Seed-raised cyclamen selected for unusual leaf patterns and silver color, hardy aroids, and other uncommon, small, hardy bulbs such as corydalis, arum, and high-altitude hardy South African species like dierama and moraea. She's experimenting with eucomis as hardy plants and getting positive results.

Shields Gardens Ltd.

Jim Shields
P.O. Box 92
Westfield, IN 46074
Telephone: 317-867-3344
Fax: 317-896-5126
Web site: www.shieldsgardens.com
E-mail: jim@shieldsgardens.com

Especially fond of clivias, they do some breeding of clivias and other tender geophytes. A good range of tender-to-cold geophytes are available, such as crinum, cyrtanthus, galtonia, gladiolus, hippeastrum, hymenocallis, lachenalia, nerine, and more. Seeds of some bulbs and clivias also available.

Tejas Native Bulbs

Web site: www.tejasnativebulbs.com

Offers only geophytes native to Texas, often of limited availability elsewhere. One drawback—geophytes are listed by common, rather than Latin names. However, each has a color image to go with it, so know what you are looking for.

Telos Rare Bulbs

Diana Chapman
P.O. Box 4147
Arcata, CA 95518
Web site: www.telosrarebulbs.com
E-mail: rarebulbs@earthlink.net

An excellent source for a wide selection of hard-to-find native bulbs of California and the western United States, also South African, and Central and South American tender bulbs for Mediterranean-climate gardens.

The Temple Nursery

Hitch Lyman
Box 591
Trumansburg, NY 14886

Specialize in galanthus shipped "in the green" (as growing plants rather than dormant bulbs).

Yucca Do Nursery Inc.

Rt. 3 Box 104
Hempstead, TX 77445
Telephone: 409-826-4580
Fax: 409-826-0522
Web site: www.yuccado.com
E-mail: info@yuccado.com

The place for rain lilies (zephyranthes and habranthus) as well as a wide range of other geophytes, tender-to-cold geophytes, including species raised from seed of their collecting trips to Mexico.

Foreign Sources for Geophytes

Note: To import plants and/or seeds from abroad, you will need both an import permit and a phytosanitary (plant health) certificate. The vendor provides the phytosanitary certificate and will include an additional charge for this. Applications for an import permit are made through the United States

Department of Agriculture, reachable at the following address:

APHIS
PEQ/Permit Unit
136 4700 River Road
Riverdale, MD 20737
Telephone: 301-734-8645

Keep in mind that you must first fill out a form, and then it must be processed before the document is sent to you, so don't expect an overnight turnaround. As well as your name and address, they'll want to know what you intend to import, the country of origin, and where it will enter the United States. You'll have an easier time (quicker service) if shipments come in through a port with an agricultural inspection station on site: JFK Airport in New York rather than Newark Liberty Airport in New Jersey, for example.

United Kingdom

Avon Bulbs
Burnt House Farm
Mid-Lambrook
South Petherton, Somerset TA13 5HE
U.K.
Telephone: +44-(0)1460-242-177
Fax: +44-(0)1460-242-177

Jim & Jenny Archibald
Bryn Collen
Ffostrasol
Llandysul
Dyfed, Wales SA44 5SB
U.K.
Seeds of rare and unusual and alpine plants.

Chiltern Seeds, U.K.
Bortree Style
Ulverston, Cumbria LA12 7PB
U.K.
Web site: www.chilternseeds.co.uk
E-mail: chilternseeds@compuserve.com
Seeds.

Paul Christian
Rare Plants
P.O. Box 468
Wrexham LL13 9XR
U.K.
Telephone: +44-(0)1978-366-399
Fax: +44-(0)1978-266-466
Web site: www.rareplants.co.uk
E-mail: paul@rareplants.co.uk
Bulbs: lovely Web site, with an enticing display of their wide range of uncommon geophytes.

Monocot Nursery
Mike Salmon
St. Michaels
Littleton
Somerton, Somerset TA11 6NT
U.K.
Specializing in seed-raised geophytes from wild-collected seed, since he believes that much of what's being offered is no longer true to name. Lovely colchicums, narcissus from Spain, all sorts of delicious things.

Potterton & Martin
Robert Potterton
The Cottage Nursery
Moortown Road
Nettleton
Caistor, Lincolnshire LN7 6HX
U.K.
Telephone: +44-(0)1472-851-714
Web site: www.pottertons.com.uk
E-Mail: rob@pottertons.co.uk
Offers a wide range of species; rare and choice geophytes from narcissus and tulips

to colchicum, cyclamen, fritillaria, galanthus, and many other small bulbs; and also a seed list in autumn.

South Africa

Rust-en-Vrede Nursery
Alan Horstmann
P.O. Box 753
Brackenfell 7561
Republic of South Africa
Telephone: 27-21-981-4515
Fax: 27-21-981-0050
E-mail: rustenvrede@hotmail.com
Seeds and a few bulb species from the Cape Floral Kingdom, mainly winter rainfall species and especially Amaryllidaceae. Primarily a hobbyist operation selling limited quantities.

Silverhill Seeds
Rachel and Rod Saunders
P.O. Box 53108
Kenilworth, Cape Town 7745
Republic of South Africa
Telephone: 27-21-705-2095
Fax: 27-21-706-7987
Web site: www.silverhillseeds.co.za
E-mail: rachel@silverhillseeds.co.za
Seeds of all type of South African plants, including many, many bulbous species.

Summerfield's Indigenous Bulbs & Seed
P.O. Box 5150
Helderberg
Somerset West 7135
Republic of South Africa
Telephone: 27-21-855-2442
Fax: 27-21-855-2442
Cultivators of select South African indigenous bulbs and corms, mainly of winter-rainfall species. Seeds also available.

African Bulbs (formerly The Croft Wild Bulbs Nursery)
Rhoda and Cameron McMaster
P.O. Box 26
Napier 7270
Republic of South Africa
Telephone and fax: 27-28-423-3651
Mobile: 27-82-774-2075
Web site: www.africanbulbs.com
E-mail: africanbulbs@haznet.co.za
Seeds and bulbs of Eastern Cape species and some winter-rainfall species. Some good ones that they can supply include crinum, eucomis, scadoxus, veltheimia, and watsonia.

Cape Seed & Bulbs
Jim Holmes
P.O. Box 6363
Uniedal 7612
Republic of South Africa
Telephone 21-21-887-9418
Fax: 27-21-887-0823
Web site: www.clivia.co.za
E-mail: capeseed@iafrica.com
Seeds and bulbs of winter and some summer rainfall species, especially Amaryllidaceae, Iridaceae, and some Hyacinthaceae.

Penrock Seeds and Plants
P.O. Box 70587
Bryanston 2021
Gauteng
Republic of South Africa
Fax: 27-11-462-1998
Web site: www.penroc.co.za
E-mail: seeds@penroc.co.za
Specializing in the export of bulbous, caduciform, and succulent plants.

Cape Flora Nursery
P.O. Box 10556
Linton Grange 6015
Republic of South Africa
Telephone: 27-41-379-2096
Fax: 27-41-379-3188
Web site: users.iafrica.com/c/ca/capeflor
E-mail: capeflor@iafrica.com
Seeds and bulbs of primarily Eastern Cape species.

Other Countries

Bulb'Argence
Lauw de Jager
Mas D'Argence
30300 Fourques
France
Telephone: 33-466-016-519
Fax: 33-466-011-245
Web site: www.bulbargence.com
E-mail: dejager@bulbargence.com
The nursery is situated in Zone 9 on the southern coast of France and specializes in bulbs for the Mediterranean climate. They offer mainly summer-dormant, winter-growing geophytes from the Mediterranean area, South Africa, Chile, California, and Asia. The separate winter catalog also, to a lesser extent, includes summer growers.

Pacific Rim Native Plant Nursery
Paige Woodward
44305 Old Orchard Road
Chilliwack, BC V2R 1A9
Canada
Telephone: 604-792-9279
Fax: 604-792-1891
Web site: www.hillkeep.ca
E-mail: paige@hillkeep.ca
The focus is on species. While they occasionally sell plants that are genuine rescues from construction sites, the majority of what they offer is propagated from wild-collected seeds. Their list includes nursery-propagated lilies

and other hardy geophytes such as arisaema, erythronium, fritillaria, and trillium, as well as alpine and woodland plants of eastern Asia and western North America.

Bulb Nursery
Janis Ruksans
LV-4150 Rozula, Cesu raj.
Latvia
Telephone: 371-941-84-40, 371-41-00-326
Fax: 371-41-33-223
E-mail: janis.bulb@hawk.lv
This nursery offers rare and unusual geophytes from Central Asia, such as allium, anemone, arisaema, arum, colchicum, corydalis, crocus, erythronium, fritillaria, muscari, scilla, sternbergia, tulips, and more.

Tools

Stillbrook Horticultural Supplies
P.O. Box 600
Bantam, CT 06750
Telephone: 800-414-4468
Fax: 860-567-5323
Web site: www.stillbrook.com
E-mail: bill@stillbrook.com and dee@stillbrook.com
Several of the vendors on the general list of mail-order companies also offer a few hand tools. This place specializes in tools and has a good selection of sturdy, quality items.

Organizations, Web Sites, and Plant Societies

Pacific Bulb Society E-mail List
Mary Sue Ittner, List Administrator
Web site: http://lists.ibiblio.org/mailman/listinfo/pbs
E-mail: pbs-request@lists.ibiblio.org
Active forum open to all, with a topic of the week as well as general questions and answers provided by experienced individuals. Extensive photo library on the Web. As well, mem-

bers receive a periodic bulletin and, for a nominal charge to cover shipping and handling, have access to seeds and bulbs donated by other members.

International Bulb Society

Web site: www.bulbsociety.org

Portions of the Web site are open to the general public; others are restricted to members only. Members have access to a seed exchange.

Botanical Society of South Africa

Private Bag X10
Claremont 7735
Republic of South Africa
Telephone: 27-(0)21-797-2090
Fax: 27-(0)21-797-2376
Web site:
http://www.botanicalsociety.org.za
E-mail: info@botanicalsociety.org.za

Focus on indigenous plants of South Africa, including geophytes.

Indigenous Bulb Association of South Africa

P.O. Box 12265
N1 City 7463
Republic of South Africa
E-mail: sa.da.@mweb.co.za and
rachel@silverhillseeds.co.za

Membership benefits include a seed exchange, bulletin, and bulb chat forum. Note that the e-mail addresses are subject to change with change of officers.

North American Rock Garden Society

Membership: Executive Secretary
NARGS
P.O. Box 67
Millwood, NY 10546
Web site: www.nargs.org

Members have access to an extensive seed exchange of alpines and other uncommon plants including geophytes, as well as a quarterly bulletin and other benefits.

The Scottish Rock Garden Club

Membership Secretary, SRGC
P.O. Box 14063
Edinburgh, EH10 4YE
Web site: www.srgc.org.uk

Benefits of membership include an annual seed list with thousands of items, as well as a twice yearly journal, and more.

American Daffodil Society

Naomi Liggett
4126 Winfield Rd.
Columbus, OH 43220
Telephone: 614-451-4747
Fax: 614-451-2177
Web site: www.daffodilusa.org
E-mail: NLiggett@compuserve.com

Has a listing of vendors specializing in daffodils, and also general bulb suppliers.

Netherlands Flower Bulb Information Center

Web site: www.bulb.com

Supported by the Associated Dutch Bulb Growers, this is a useful site for general information about bulbs, with details on selection and care, bulbs for containers, forcing bulbs, and more, including some lore and legend.

Garden Web Forums—Bulbs

Web site:
www.gardenweb.com/forums/bulbs

This is just one of a plethora of Garden Web forums. You can just lurk and read messages, or register (simple to do) to post questions of your own and supply answers to others. Most questions/answers on the Bulb Forum are rather basic (which way is up, how long can I wait before planting, and so on).

Quick Picks

Geophytes for Spring Bedding

Mass planting of spring-blooming geophytes, such as tulips, daffodils, and hyacinths, provides a colorful display. Keep in mind that foliage must be allowed to grow and mature after the flowers fade. Allowing approximately 15 percent of the space in a herbaceous border for these spring-flowering bulbs provides a good display without leaving an awkward gap afterward. The space can be concealed by the expanding foliage of adjacent perennials such as peonies, daylilies, Siberian iris, or hostas. Or annuals may be planted directly over the now-dormant bulbs. Consider pairing the "big three" of hyacinths, tulips, and daffodils with other geophytes that bloom at the same time: hyacinths or early tulips with *Anemone blanda* or daffodils with *Muscari armeniacum*.

Geophytes for Planting Under Ground Covers

The critical point to keep in mind is that the geophyte must be vigorous enough to reach daylight from beneath the ground cover. In shady sites where pachysandra or running myrtle are familiar choices, select larger geophytes. Daffodils are better suited to use with pachysandra, which is too vigorous for small geophytes such as *Eranthis hyemalis* or even *Galanthus nivalis*. Daffodils and hyacinths may also be grown under *Vinca minor*, and Dutch hybrid crocus will grow in lightly shaded area. In sunny areas try species crocus with thyme.

Geophytes for the Woodland Garden

A wide range of geophytes will grow quite well in woodland areas, springing into growth, flowering, and then going dormant as the trees leaf out. In light to moderate shade, at the edge of woodland or under a small tree such as a flowering dogwood,

276

Cornus florida, grown as a specimen in a lawn, consider planting Grecian windflower, *Anemone blanda*; glory of the snow, *Chionodoxa* species; cyclamen, *Cyclamen coum* and *C. hederifolium*; winter aconite, *Eranthis hyemalis*; dog's tooth violet, *Erythronium* species; guinea hen flower, *Fritillaria meleagris*; snowdrop, *Galanthus* species; wood hyacinth and English bluebell, *Hyacinthoides hispanica* and *H. non-scriptus*; spring snowflake, *Leucojum vernum*; grape hyacinth, *Muscari* species, in light shade; daffodils, *Narcissus* species and cultivars; and both *Scilla siberica* and *S. mischtschenkoana*. Asian species of *Arisaema* are excellent choices, and *Caladium* adds wonderfully colorful foliage to the summer garden.

Do not overlook all the wonderful native woodland wildflowers that have lumpy underground storage structures: *Dicentra cucullaria* and *D. canadensis*, *Claytonia virginica*, *Erythronium* species and cultivars, *Arisaema triphyllum*, *Sanguinaria canadensis*, and trilliums.

Geophytes for the Rock Garden

A rock garden is, for preference, located in full sun; has a well-drained, gritty soil; and generally has a mineralized, infertile soil. Choose small, dwarf geophytes that will appear in proportion to the other plants such as *Phlox subulata*, *Iberis sempervirens*, and thymes. Both spring- and fall-flowering crocus are good choices, as are little tulips such as *Tulipa kaufmanniana* and *T. greigii* and their cultivars, as well as species such as *T. bakeri*, *T. hageri* 'Splendens', *T. clusiana*, and others. Dwarf species of *Allium* will do well. Spring-flowering *Bulbocodium vernum* is another good choice, along with *Iris danfordiae*, *I. histrioides*, and *I. reticulata*.

Geophytes for Wet Sites

For a damp meadow, a sunny, grassy place that might be temporarily inundated but then subside merely to moist, consider growing guinea hen flower, *Fritillaria meleagris*; three-cornered leek, *Allium triquetrum*; camassia, *Camassia quamash*; or *Lilium superbum*. *Caladium* will take the same moisture regimen but prefers shade. Cannas will grow in a sunny damp place, but they also thrive in standing water, provided it is not too deep. Dainty white flower of the west wind, *Zephyranthes candida*, grows in shallow water in sunny sites. For gardens in the U.S. South, consider southern swamp lily, *Crinum americanum* and other crinums; spider lilies such as *Hymenocallis liriosome*; and any of the elephant ears, *Alocasia*, *Colocasia*, and *Xanthosoma*. Don't forget calla lily, *Zantedeschia aethiopica*, which also likes it wet.

Cut Flowers

While just about any geophyte can be used as a cut flower, some are preferable to others. One important consideration is how long will they last—and, possibly, how they smell. I cannot recommend using crown imperial, *Fritillaria imperialis*, as a cut flower. Forget all the Dutch flower paintings—the skunklike aroma will be unbearable indoors. Daffodils and tulips are commonplace cut flowers. Do not mix and match these two, since freshly cut daffodils ooze a substance that causes tulips sharing their water to collapse. Hyacinths are another good choice but sometimes sag and droop. One florists' trick—run a fine wire through the stem on the inside with a small bend at the top to hook through the stem wall just below the topmost flower. Snowdrops, *Galanthus nivalis*, are charming, as are grape hyacinths, *Muscari* species. I like to set a vase of these little flowers on a mirror to reflect the flowers and double my pleasure. Lilies are popular, but remember that their pollen will indelibly stain fabric. Some flower arrangers remove the stamens for that reason. Surprisingly, colchicums make a very good cut flower, lasting quite well. Hippeastrum is elegant as a cut flower, but use a piece of green florists' tape around the base of the stem or it will split and curl. Nerines and lycoris are also popular, as is zantedeschia. Caladium leaves add a special, colorful touch to arrangements.

Fragrant Geophytes

Hyacinths are wonderfully fragrant. The occasional tulip is fragrant. Look for heirloom 'Prince of Austria', a single, early, orange-scarlet tulip introduced in 1860, and its orange-flowered sport, 'Generaal de Wet' that dates from 1904. 'Prinses Irene' is another sweetly fragrant tulip, with orange flowers lightly brushed with a hint of purple. Other fragrant tulips include 'Ballerina', a lily-flowered tulip with blood-red markings on the lemon-yellow petals and marigold-orange on the inside; and 'Ellen Willmott', another fragrant lily-flowered tulip, this time with primrose-yellow flowers. 'Angélique' is a popular double-flowered, late-blooming, blush pink, fragrant tulip; and 'Peach Blossom' is also double-flowered, like a little peony, but it flowers earlier. Tazetta daffodils are fragrant, with a strong, rather musky scent that can be overwhelming indoors. 'Soleil d'Or' and Chinese sacred lily have lighter, more floral scent. *Narcissus poeticus* 'Plenus' is sweetly scented. If you want fragrant lilies, look to the oriental hybrids, developed from *Lilium speciosum* and *L. auratum*. The species themselves are fragrant and pass that trait to their offspring. Trumpet lilies are also quite fragrant. Two tender geophytes worth growing for their fragrance are lemon-scented freesias and the powerfully fragrant tuberose.

Heirloom Geophytes

You can hold history in your hand and plant it in your garden. Heirloom bulbs, corms, rhizomes, and tubers are among that cast of characters that have been growing in gardens for a century or more and are likely to be reliable stalwarts. Of course, species have been around in gardens since they first entered into cultivation. It's the cultivars that are the real historical players. A number of heirloom daffodil cultivars are mentioned in Chapters 5, 6, and 7. Tulips have been cultivated for so long that the origin of many of the oldest cultivars is unclear. The "broken" virus-infected tulips of the "tulipomania" are no longer commercially available, though a few continue to be grown by English enthusiasts. Many of the old tulip cultivars are held in historical collections and are not readily available. Among these are 'Duc van Tol' and its cultivars, dating back to the16th and 17th centuries. In season they may be seen in bloom at the Hortus Bulborum in Limmen, The Netherlands. 'Generaal de Wet', a tulip in the single early group, was introduced in 1904 and is one of the heirloom cultivars that may still be found for sale. 'Murillo' was introduced in 1860 and is the parent from which so many early-flowering double-tulip sports were selected. Venerable hyacinths are available, such as 'King of the Blues' from 1863; 'L'Innocence', which is still one of the best whites for early forcing that was also introduced in 1863; and rose-pink 'Lady Derby' from 1883. *Crocus versicolor* 'Picturatus' has been in cultivation since around 1574. *Galanthus nivalis* 'Flore Pleno', a double snowdrop that continues to grow well in gardens, has been in cultivation since 1731. *Anemone nemorosa* 'Robinsoniana' was introduced by William Robinson around 1870. 'Red King Humbert' is a canna that was introduced just over a century ago in 1902, and it continues in popularity today. Old House Gardens, mentioned in "Sources," specializes in heirloom varieties, and Brent and Becky's Bulbs, also listed, often provides the date of introduction for their older cultivars.

Deer-Resistant Geophytes

If they are driven by hunger, deer will eat anything. They digest their food not with enzymes as we do, but with bacteria living in their gut. Different family groups apparently have dissimilar intestinal flora and have different diets. For this reason, deer can adapt to a changing diet. With that caveat and explanation out of the way, following is a basic list of geophytes that, in general, deer will avoid eating—at least, most of the time they won't eat them.

Anything in the Amaryllidaceae: *Amaryllis, Crinum, Galanthus, Habranthus, Hippeastrum, Hymenocallis, Leucojum, Lycoris, Narcissus, Nerine, Rhodophiala, Sternbergia,* and *Zephyranthes*. While tulips and lilies are dined upon with delight, some of the Liliaceae are low in appeal, such as *Camassia, Chionodoxa, Colchicum, Fritillaria, Hyacinthoides, Hyacinthus, Muscari,* and *Scilla*. Ornamental onions, also in the Liliaceae (or if you want to follow Dahlgren's Balkanization of 1985, in the Alliaceae) are also left alone, at least by deer if not by taxonomists. Deer do not dine on aroids such as caladium, callas, arisaema, pinellia, and arisarum; on winter aconite, *Eranthis hyemalis*, in the Ranunculaceae; or on cannas, in Cannaceae. For more on deer-resistant bulbs, see the section in Chapter 2, "Geophyte Care and Cultivation."

Geophytes for the Pacific Northwest

The Pacific Northwest—Oregon, Washington, the northern part of California, and Canada's British Columbia—has the soft climate gardeners tend to associate with England. Understand that this is an overview and regional differences exist. The rain shadow to the east of the mountains gives that area more of a Mediterranean climate. West of the mountains the winters never get very cold (except at high elevations in the Sierra, Olympic, and Cascade ranges), and summers are temperate rather than torrid. Despite the Northwest's reputation for a wet climate, it's not that the area is plagued by floods and deluges, at least not most of the time, but rather that showers are frequent. It is a great place to grow geophytes, and Washington's Skagit Valley is home to nurseries that produce daffodils, tulips, lilies, and dahlias as garden plants and also for cut flowers. While tulips are a good crop, they do not necessarily perennialize in the Pacific Northwest any better than they do elsewhere in the country. Daffodils grow wonderfully well in Pacific Northwest gardens as do a host of smaller geophytes. These include various anemones such as *Anemone blanda* as well as the somewhat more tender *A. hortensis* and *A. pavonina*. Glory of the snow, *Chionodoxa* species; *Cyclamen coum* and *C. hederifolium*; dog's tooth violet, *Erythronium* species and cultivars; snowdrops, *Galanthus* species and cultivars; and several scillas such as the familiar *Scilla siberica* and less common *S. scilloides, S. peruviana, S. litardieri,* and *S. autumnalis* are popular. Woodlanders, from *Arisaema, Arum,* and *Cardiocrinum* to trilliums, all prosper.

A wide range of lilies, both cultivars and species, thrive, as one would expect in a region where native lilies abound. After all, the northern Willamette valley, south of Portland, Oregon, is where Jan de Graff had his Oregon Bulb Farm for several decades. Starting in the early 1950s, the company did invaluable work, not least of which was the development of Asiatic hybrid lilies. Wet weather in spring and fall contributed to the nursery's eventual relocation of some production fields to the drier Yakima Valley of eastern Washington. Tender geophytes are somewhat more variable in suitability. In Oregon and Washington, dahlias are an important agricultural crop, grown and shipped across the United States. Caladium, however, fail to thrive, since they do not receive the summer heat this tropical tuber demands.

Geophytes for Subtropical Florida

Subtropical means that winter in Florida is different than conditions in regions with snow and consistent cold temperatures. November is often shorts and T-shirt weather rather than the long pants and a good jacket over a long-sleeved shirt type. In southern and central Florida, the most noticeable signals are shorter days and sun that doesn't rise as high in the sky, changing the angle of sunlight and shadow patterns. There's more of a seasonal differentiation in northern Florida, but that is still in comparison to elsewhere in the state than it is to parts outside Florida. For example, tender geophytes such as gladiolus, caladium, and dahlias would be planted in March when conditions are frost-free in the northern portions of Florida, in February in central Florida, and as early as December or January in southern Florida. Lycoris are winter-planted, from November to January, and remain in the ground year-round throughout the state. Hippeastrum are planted from November to February in central and southern Florida, February or March in the northern region, and are also permanent additions to the garden, though they should be protected with a thick, airy mulch in the northern region. Crinums may be planted in February or March in northern Florida, in November and December elsewhere in the state, and are also perennial members of gardens throughout Florida. Geophytes such as agapanthus, crinum, crocosmia, gladiolus, hymenocallis, and rain lilies, that in cold winter regions would require digging and winter storage in protected quarters, often do just fine state-wide when left in the ground. Tender geophytes such as achimenes and dahlias need to be dug and stored over the winter state-wide. Calla and eucharis need to be dug and stored only in the northern portion of Florida. Remember that good drainage often improves survival for winter-dormant geophytes.

Index